MEDIEVAL CLASSICS

GENERAL EDITORS

V. H. Galbraith and R. A. B. Mynors

DECRETA LANFRANCI

LANFRANC'S

MONASTIC CONSTITUTIONS

and the anonymous

INSTRUCTIO NOVICIORUM

THE INSTRUCTION OF NOVICES

Decreta Lanfranci

Monachis Cantuariensibus Transmissa

Thomas Nelson and Sons Ltd
London Edinburgh Paris Melbourne Toronto and New York

The Monastic Constitutions
of Lanfranc

Translated from the Latin with Introduction
and Notes by
David Knowles LITT.D. F.B.A.
Professor of Medieval History, University of Cambridge

Thomas Nelson and Sons Ltd
London Edinburgh Paris Melbourne Toronto and New York

THOMAS NELSON AND SONS LTD
Parkside Works Edinburgh 9
3 Henrietta Street London WC2
312 Flinders Street Melbourne C1
5 Parker's Buildings Burg Street Cape Town

THOMAS NELSON AND SONS (CANADA) LTD
91–93 Wellington Street West   Toronto 1

THOMAS NELSON AND SONS
385 Madison Avenue New York 17

SOCIÉTÉ FRANÇAISE D'ÉDITIONS NELSON
25 rue Henri Barbusse Paris Ve

———

First published in this series January 1951

CONTENTS

▾

ACKNOWLEDGMENTS

I wish to thank the following who have helped me during the preparation of this book : Dr Rose Graham ; Professor R. A. B. Mynors, who read both typescript and proofs, and had a number of corrections and suggestions to make ; Dom Thomas Symons, who also read the proofs and gave help ; and Mr J. B. L. Tolhurst, who never failed to answer the numerous queries addressed to him. In addition, my thanks are due to Canon S. L. Greenslade, then Librarian to the Chapter, and to the Dean (The Very Rev. C. A. Alington) and Chapter of Durham, for kindly allowing one of their most precious volumes to be temporarily transferred to the University Library, Cambridge, and to the Chapter Clerk, Mr C. F. Battiscombe, who conveyed it thither.

INTRODUCTION

THE document printed and translated in this volume is the directory drawn up by Lanfranc, William the Conqueror's great Archbishop of Canterbury, for the monastic community of his cathedral of Christ Church. It is of interest as giving the fullest and most methodical account known to exist of the life lived by English monks in the period immediately following the Norman Conquest.

The monachism introduced into England in different but ultimately coalescing forms by Augustine of Canterbury, by Irish and Welsh monks, and by Aidan of Iona, had enjoyed a period of wide expansion and fervour in the century (650–750) covered by the lives of Cuthbert, Wilfrid, Benet Biscop, Aldhelm, Bede the Venerable and Boniface. In the ninth century it had vanished, owing to the Scandinavian invasions in the north and east, and the general decline in fervour in the south and west. In the tenth century there was a great revival, associated with the names of Dunstan, Ethelwold and Oswald ; some forty monasteries were founded, among them some of the most celebrated in the Middle Ages, and monks were chosen from them to fill almost all the sees of England, while the cultural and artistic life of the monks was the highest in the country. This monasticism was strictly and traditionally Benedictine— that is to say, the basis of the life was the Rule, kept exactly in all essentials, and interpreted and expanded by customs derived from abroad, from Ghent and from the great Cluniac reform as reflected in the customs of the abbey of Fleury-sur-Loire. We are fortunate in possessing in the *Regularis Concordia* the directory drawn up for England by St Ethelwold with the consent of St Dunstan, and promulgated by King Edgar *c.* 970. Though for the most part based on Continental practice, it is

by no means a slavish imitation, and contains several features, liturgical, devotional and practical, not found in any Continental code.[1]

The new foundations suffered in their turn from Danish invasions and the dynastic struggles of the early eleventh century, and though recent historians have passed a far less severe judgment on the English monks in the days of Edward the Confessor than that commonly expressed by writers of the last few generations, who echoed the strictures of the Anglo-Norman chronicler, yet in many respects a considerable decline in fervour and numbers had taken place.

Meanwhile, there had been a remarkable new birth in the young duchy of Normandy. Here, from the early years of the eleventh century onwards a series of foundations had been made, resulting in the existence by 1066 of some twenty-five flourishing abbeys. These, like the English monasteries, had adopted the liturgical and other practices of Cluny ; in their case the conveying agency was William, Abbot of Dijon and later of Fécamp. The Norman monasticism had its own specific differences, rising out of racial and cultural peculiarities : the abbey churches and cloisters were designed on a scale hitherto unknown, with a consequent expansion of ceremonial and domestic life, while the intellectual activity radiating from north Italy and central France soon affected the Norman monasteries, some of which, and above all Bec and its daughter, Caen, became celebrated as centres of theological as well as of literary activity. Moreover, the leading monks had their full share of the energy and organising ability of their race, and they were fortunate in receiving notable recruits from the south, among whom were two of outstanding distinction of mind and religious virtue, Lanfranc and Anselm, both monks of Bec.

When, therefore, the conquest of England had been effected

---

[1] An edition of the *Regularis Concordia* is included in the series to which the present volume belongs.

and William, himself the founder or patron of several abbeys, turned his attention to ecclesiastical affairs, it was natural that he and his counsellors, among whom Lanfranc, now Archbishop of Canterbury, was the chief, should look critically upon the old English monasteries and should resolve upon reforming them after the Norman model and strengthening them with Norman superiors.

(Lanfranc, the lawyer of Pavia who had sought a career and found a vocation north of the Alps, was at this time the most celebrated teacher and the ablest administrator in the transalpine Church.) Though already advanced in years (he was born in the first decade of the century) he was at the height of his powers, and was to live without diminution of activity till 1089. This is not the place to rehearse the story of his life and writings ; (it has been told more than once in the recent past, and historians to-day are unanimous in ranking him very high, not only as an organiser and statesman, but as a wise and devoted monk and bishop.) Here it need only be remarked that Lanfranc, though a late-comer to the cloister, never ceased to regard his monastic profession as the determining event of his life ; when archbishop, he remained a monk both at heart and in the practice of his daily religious duties, and he looked to monks to form the spearhead of the reform of the Church. To his contemporaries wisdom—the gift, that is, of judging events and problems as seen as it were from above, in their deepest causes—together with a warmth of kindliness and affection, which his public activities as agent of the Conqueror have somewhat obscured for historians, were the qualities which most distinguished him.[1] He was, besides, in the judgment of one of the keenest observers of the generation that followed, a most skilled director of souls.[2]

[1] The author of the ' Life of Lanfranc,' by J. A. Giles in vol. i of his *Opera Lanfranci*, says of him (p. 291) that he was ' *homo . . . sapientia omni aevo mirabilis.*'

[2] William of Malmesbury, *Gesta Pontificum* (Rolls Series), 70–1 : ' *artis artium, id est regiminis animarum, peritissimus . . . manet nec in aevo abolebitur . . . illius caritas* '

Among the old English monasteries four of the cathedral churches—Canterbury, Winchester, Worcester and Sherborne —formed a group apart and unique.[1] In the reform of the tenth century the secular canons at Winchester and Worcester, who fell below the standards demanded by the great monastic bishops, were replaced by monks, and the metropolitan church of Canterbury, where a succession of monks ruled as archbishops after Dunstan, undoubtedly received a monastic community late in the eleventh century, whatever may have been its character in the remote past.[2] In such cases the monks conducted the services of the cathedral under the bishop, who stood in place of the abbot ; as the sees concerned were, with very few exceptions, occupied by monks during the period between Dunstan and the Conquest, this arrangement caused no difficulty. At Canterbury, however, the community, exposed to a number of disturbing agencies, appear to have lost much of their monastic character, and latterly they had had in Stigand a superior who, whatever may be said in his defence, was not a monastic reformer. Lanfranc was unfamiliar with the institution of monastic cathedrals, and at first proposed to remove the monks from Winchester, Canterbury and the other sees where they were established ; he was, however, a monk himself, and it is not surprising that he finally decided to retain the monastic character of his church, and make it an example to the whole of England. He therefore brought over from Normandy Henry, a monk of Bec and Caen like himself, and with him, probably, a certain number of other monks, as soon as his new buildings at Canterbury were able to receive them. He himself, as standing in the place of abbot, discharged his responsibility as superior by composing for their guidance the directory which is here printed.

Lanfranc, though a reformer, was no innovator. It was

[1] For these monasteries as a group, see D. Knowles, *The Monastic Order in England*, 619–31

[2] cf. J. Armitage Robinson, ' The Early Community at Christ Church, Canterbury,' in *Journal of Theological Studies*, xxvii (1926), 225–40

no part of his policy to give his monks a new form of life, such as was to appear within a few years at Cîteaux. Norman monasticism was flourishing and observant, and he wished the English houses to reflect all th... ...t across the Channel. Cons... he did what so many refo... ning abbots had done before him; he assembled the custom... ies of several of the most notable and fervent houses, and conflated from them a... and disciplinary scheme. Dr... stic though he could be to action, he was conservative in te... per; he made no attempt to... down his traditions, so... to say, in order to construct from the material a s... ...e of his own. The book of customs or uses was by tradition a liturgical directory which gave the various usages in s... s and ceremonial throughout the year; details of social and domestic life and discipline were only incidental, and little or nothing was said of the extra-liturgical occupations of the monks or of the higher organization of the monastery. Lanfranc followed, or rather because to follow, such an arrangement ...d for almost half of his work followed the course of the litu... ical year from 1 October, making several diress... ...sc... be such domestic institutions as bathing, and giving with ...ally exuberant detail the ceremonial of Lent and Holy W... . Then, when he had passed through the year and grouped the various feasts, he turned to the organisation of the community, its discipline, and the many rites connected with the last illness, death and burial of a monk. In this part his arrangement is more logical and original than that of his predecessors. So far as can be known it is his own arrangement, and this, together with its fulness and clarity, makes of it a valuable and interesting historical document.

Lanfranc himself tells us that he has compiled his directory from the customs of the monasteries most in repute in his day. The words necessarily imply at least two or three different sources, perhaps more, and we are fortunately able to identify some, at least, of his originals. A considerable number of

customaries exist from the tenth and eleventh centuries, and the resemblances between some of these and Lanfranc are so close that we can be certain that the archbishop had before him either these particular documents or documents deriving from exactly the same tradition.[1]

Had we no further information than Lanfranc's words we could be reasonably certain that Bec, Lanfranc's own mother, would be one of the celebrated abbeys he refers to, and the Constitutions of Lanfranc have often been considered as those of Bec pure and simple. The writer directly responsible for this opinion is the composer of the *Apostolatus*,[2] but the ultimate source of the misconception is medieval, going back to the chroniclers Ralph de Diceto [3] and Robert of Torigni.[4] The inaccuracy of such a description and its origin have been convincingly demonstrated by Dr Rose Graham ; it does indeed contradict the clear statement of Lanfranc himself as well as the corroborative assertion of Matthew Paris. Nevertheless, there is a *prima facie* likelihood that the Bec customs would have been freely drawn upon by Lanfranc. No manuscript exists of the original or early Bec uses ; the sole surviving document containing a customary of the house from the medieval centuries dates from between 1290 and 1310, and it is known that the customs had been revised previously by Abbot Roger II (1188–94).[5] Nevertheless, there are a few striking similarities, even on points of detail, which seem to show direct copying [6] ; it has indeed been suggested with great probability that the author of the earliest liturgical customs of Bec had been Lanfranc himself, who was prior there during

[1] For a brief review of Lanfranc's sources, see R. Graham, ' The Relations of Cluny to some other Movements of Monastic Reform,' in *Journal of Theological Studies*, xv (1914), 179 foll., reprinted in *English Ecclesiastical Studies*, 1–29

[2] *Apostolatus*, tractatus II, sect. vi, p. 117. For this book see below, p. xxviii

[3] Radulphi de Diceto, *Opera Historica* (Rolls Series), I 215

[4] In *Chronicles of the reign of Stephen, etc.* (Rolls Series), IV 49

[5] See A. A. Porée, *Histoire de l'Abbaye du Bec*, I 476

[6] e.g. the commemoration of St Anastasia at the second Mass on Christmas Day, which does not occur in the Cluniac rite ; see below p. 13

the formative years following 1045. Whoever may have been responsible, the Bec use is of the family of Cluny.

The Bec customs, however, are not the only, or even the principal source. Very clear resemblances appear between Lanfranc and the older Cluny customs, and also those composed at Cluny between 1030 and 1048, under abbot Odilo.[1] More important than any of these, however, are the customs of Cluny composed by the monk Bernard in 1067.[2] Bernard, whose fame has been somewhat eclipsed by that of his younger contemporary, Ulrich, departed from the traditional form of customary, which gave short directions keeping very close to the seasons of the liturgical year, and provided, in a series of chapters, an account of every aspect of life at Cluny. A glance at the footnotes to the pages that follow will show how carefully Lanfranc had read Bernard, though they will show also that he was far from following Bernard's order of treatment at all slavishly. Besides these sources, a few resemblances can be seen to some Flemish customs, which perhaps came by way of St Wandrille. Of one possible source there is no trace. Lanfranc must have heard of the *Regularis Concordia*, and it is most probable that a copy existed at Canterbury, but no trace of resemblance to it appears in Lanfranc's constitutions ; the most characteristic passages of the *Concordia*, such as those prescribing frequent communion, prayers for the royal house and the description of the embryo drama on Easter morning, find no echo here.

---

[1] Several sets of Cluny customs have been printed by Dom Bruno Albers in *Consuetudines Monasticae*, I–IV. Those printed in vol. i and attributed to the Italian Cluniac house of Farfa have been shown to come from Cluny itself, between 1030 and 1048 ; cf. *Revue Bénédictine*, xvii 164 ; xxiv 374–85.

[2] Printed by Dom M. Herrgott in *Vetus Disciplina Monastica* (Paris, 1726). Lanfranc may have made acquaintance with Bernard's customs when arranging for the foundation of Battle Abbey in 1077.

THE MONASTIC LIFE IN THE ELEVENTH CENTURY

Between the Rule of St Benedict and the life at Bec or Canterbury in the days of Lanfranc lay five centuries of development. The isolated, self-contained and self-sufficient community of Monte Cassino, made up of a few priests and clerics, lay monks of every degree of social standing and literacy, and children of all ages, who divided their day between common prayer, meditative reading and physical work, had gradually been transformed into one composed chiefly of priests, or those proceeding to the priesthood, with only a few late vocations who remained without orders. The children were still there, though they were shortly to disappear, but in addition there was a small army of servants who manned the extensive offices. Physical work had disappeared entirely as a normal occupation, and had been replaced by the sedentary occupations of copying and painting manuscripts, and by private study and composition. Meditative reading had lost its purely spiritual character, and had become merged with the intellectual work. Above all, the common prayer and simple psalmody and chant in the oratory had become a lengthy and elaborate round of Hours, Masses, ceremonials and extra-liturgical psalmody and prayers. The monastery was now an integral part of the social life of the country and was often situated at the heart of a town.

All these external changes reflected (and had also in part effected) a subtle but none the less notable change in the conception of the monastic life. In the monastery of the Rule every detail of the horarium and discipline is calculated to advance the individual monk in his journey towards perfection of life ; even the abbot, though he enjoyed patriarchal powers over those vowed to obedience, existed solely to serve and guide them. By Lanfranc's day the emphasis has shifted, and although the personal sanctification of the individual is not forgotten, the monk is now primarily one who devotes his

life to the liturgical service of God and to intercession for the
world ; he is one of the class of those who pray for society
while others fight for it or till the soil for its support. Whereas
the life of the Rule, like that of the desert, is an ascesis in
which the individual goes from strength to strength, from light
to light, in the Anglo-Norman monasticism he undertakes a life
of prayer and penance that shall earn for him after death
a special reward.

THE LITURGICAL HORARIUM

The reader who is neither a specialist in monastic history
nor acquainted with the routine of a modern monastery will
find it hard to extract from Lanfranc's pages a clear conception
of the day's time-table, the more so as there are no references
to clock-time, while he alludes to (though he does not always
explicitly mention) no less than four different arrangements
of the day which took effect at different times of the year and
on days of varying liturgical solemnity—to say nothing of a
number of different combinations which might occur within
this framework. Thus the ordinary day in winter (1 November
to the end of Lent) differed from the ordinary day in summer
(Easter to 14 September), while this twofold arrangement
was cut across by the varying régime by which a single meal
was taken on ordinary days from 14 September to Easter, and
on fast days throughout the year, whereas on Sundays and
certain feasts throughout the year (outside Lent) two meals
were taken and certain other small changes made. In Lent
and on ecclesiastical fasts, again, the horarium itself was
different from that of an ordinary day in the season concerned.
Even this does not exhaust the factors governing the changes,
for October on one hand, and the period from Septuagesima
to Ash Wednesday on the other had certain peculiarities of
their own. For the benefit of those who would wish to see
at a glance how the day was arranged, the typical winter and

summer horaria are set out below (p. xxxv), but the precise
arrangement is in certain cases little more than conjectural,
and the reader who wishes for an exercise in the interpretation
of liturgical directions cannot do better than compile for himself a horarium to correct or supplement the one here given.
Before setting out the order of the various duties, however, it
may be well to give a brief explanation of their content.[1]

The core of the service in choir was the Divine Office, the
Opus Dei of St Benedict. Of this the first and by far the longest
portion was that known to St Benedict and Lanfranc as
nocturns, but to modern monasticism as *matins*. This, beginning
with an invitatory and hymn, consisted of two (or, on Sundays
and greater feasts three) divisions or *nocturns*, each made up of six
psalms (or, in the case of the third nocturn, of three canticles)
and three (or, on Sundays and feasts, four) lessons, each followed
by a responsory. To the third nocturn were added the *Te Deum*
and the Gospel of the day. In all this there were numerous
grades of solemnity, implying more frequent or more elaborate
chant, repetitions, incensing, etc. ; these differences applied to
all the parts of the Office in varying measure.

Next came the office known to St Benedict and Lanfranc
as *matutinae*, and to modern monks as *Lauds* (from the three
last *Laudate* psalms which always occur in it) ; this consisted
of four psalms, a canticle, the *Laudate* psalms, a chapter, response,
hymn, *Benedictus* and prayers. *Prime* followed, with a hymn,
three psalms and prayers ; then the so-called Little Hours of
Terce, *Sext* and *None*, consisting each of a hymn, three psalms
and prayers ; then *Vespers*, with four psalms, chapter, response,
hymn, *Magnificat* and prayers, and finally *Compline*, with the
confession, three psalms, hymn, chapter and prayers. In St
Benedict's time this had been all, save for a simple Mass on
Sundays and feasts. By the eleventh century, however, much
had been added : first of all a daily meeting for discipline and

---

[1] For a fuller account, see vol. vi of *The Monastic Breviary of Hyde Abbey*,
ed. J. B. L. Tolhurst (see below, p. xxxii)

business, the Chapter, so-called from the portion of the Rule read therein, with its accompaniment of prayers; then the solemn High Mass; then a second earlier Mass (the 'Morrow,' 'Morning' or 'chapter' Mass), and then a whole series of extra psalms, prayers and minor offices; these will now be described in brief.

(1) The threefold devotion (*Trina Oratio*) recited before Matins, before Terce or Prime and after Compline; consisted of seven (or five) psalms (i.e. nineteen in all), with prayers for various persons and intentions.

(2) The Gradual Psalms (Ps. 119–33 inclusive), to which were added in winter the remaining seventeen (Ps. 134–50), were said after the *Trina Oratio* before Matins.

(3) The seven Penitential Psalms (Ps. 6, 31, 37, 50, 101, 129, 142 in Vulgate) were said after Prime before the Litany.

(4) The Litany of the Saints with versicles and collects was said after Prime; it was said again on certain days before High Mass.

(5) The psalm *Verba mea* (5) together with Ps. 6, 114, 115 and 129 were recited for the dead after Chapter, and at night for thirty days after the death of a monk and in November, the month of All Souls.

(6) The psalms for relations and benefactors (*Psalmi Familiares*) consisting of two or four psalms said after each hour of the Office, with certain prayers of very great variety at different houses and periods.

(7) The 'prostrate psalms,' i.e. two psalms recited by the monks while prostrate after each Hour during Lent, with certain collects.

(8) The Suffrages, or anthems and prayers of various saints said after Lauds and Vespers.

(9) The Office of the Dead, a short office consisting of Vespers, Matins (usually one short nocturn only) and Lauds, was

said daily save on Sundays and feasts, and during octaves
and Paschal time.

(10) The Office of All Saints, consisting of Vespers and Lauds
only, was recited daily save on greater feasts and during
octaves.

All these additional devotions, besides taking up a very considerable amount of time, imposed a mental and physical
strain which must have seriously lessened the monk's capacity
for intellectual or artistic work, as also his disposition for private
mental prayer of an affective or contemplative kind. It is
noteworthy that in the reforms of the end of the eleventh
century much of this extra-liturgical psalmody was cut off,
to be replaced either by work (as with the Cistercians) or by
solitary prayer (as with the Carthusians and others).

CHARACTERISTICS OF THIS MONASTICISM

While much that is in Lanfranc might be taken for an
account of a strict black monk observance in any age, a few
points have been found repellent by modern sensibility. One
such is the system of child oblation. That children should be
brought up from infancy in the cloister, without home life, or
the free society of other boys and girls, and without entry into
many wide areas of innocent experience of life, appears to
many as an abuse. Even granted that they were free to depart
when adolescent there must, we cannot help thinking, have been
many barriers of custom and sentiment against such a departure (and in fact it is not easy to name a recorded case),
and many disabilities in one so nurtured for life in the medieval
world. For the monastery, too, the system must have entailed
the presence of many ill-fitted for the life, while even those whose
vocation was genuine must, we would think, have lost something
from lack of contact with all outside the walls. In point of

fact, as is noted elsewhere, it is easy to compile a long list of children of the cloister who developed virile and many-sided characters, and if two such men as St Benedict and Lanfranc, both eminent for strength and wisdom, and living five centuries apart, did their best to perpetuate the system, there must have been much in it that was apt to the social and educational conditions of the time.) When we recall also that, fifty years after Lanfranc's death, the age-old institution was everywhere on the decline, we shall probably not be wrong in seeking its justification in the lack of domestic and social amenities and the absence of lay education between A.D. 600 and 1100.

Another feature of the constitutions which some perhaps will find distasteful is the combination of delation and corporal punishment that takes so large a place in Lanfranc's penal code. Delation, it may be remarked, is no part of St Benedict's scheme, but in its form of chapter-accusation it was universal in all monastic bodies throughout the Middle Ages. Granted that all wished, at least as a matter of principle, to keep the Rule and customs in their fullness, it might be assumed that they would be grateful for all charitable criticism and correction. As for corporal punishment, it is as prominent—perhaps even more so—in the Rule of St Benedict, though we have no means of knowing how frequent its application was in practice either at Monte Cassino or at Canterbury. It was no doubt one of the ' things harsh and hard,' the *dura et aspera*, of which the novice had due warning before taking his vows, and it was therefore, at least in prospect and intention, a penalty for moral failure duly foreseen and accepted with a good will. *Autres temps, autres moeurs.* A humanitarian society shrinks from inflicting physical pain, even if there be good reason, whatever the age of the culprit ; the retributive or satisfactory value of pain or punishment is no longer an acceptable basis for argument, and the Wise Man's advocacy of the rod for fools and children is of no force against a prevailing sentiment. Yet that fashion has much to do with the matter will easily

be acknowledged by those whose schooldays were passed in cloisters, and those not least in renown, where summary expiation followed faults unknown to moral theologians with an inevitability and a frequency which even a child of Lanfranc's Canterbury, though perhaps not the old monk Osbern,[1] might have considered draconic.

There is much that neither Lanfranc's constitutions nor any other monastic customaries can tell us. Who would suppose, for example, that at the Bec from which so many of these uses were taken the great Anselm was even at that moment writing one of his luminous treatises, or talking to a circle of eager listeners on a level high enough to escape our grasp after nine hundred years of philosophy, or that he was giving to others the spiritual direction which still serves our need to-day—the same Anselm who was soon to be doing the like at Canterbury, happy with his monks like an owl with her brood in the dim spaces of a barn, too soon to be blinded by the sun's glare and mobbed by lesser birds without.[2] Or who would know from Lanfrancs' pages that among his readers were some, perhaps, of the older English who were illustrating a book's margin with figures copied, half from life and half from the Utrecht psalter? These, indeed, are spaces that we must fill for ourselves from other sources. Yet surely no reader can travel through Lanfranc's regulations without gaining the impression that they were composed for a flourishing and self-confident monasticism. There is no sense of strain, no hint that the writer is fighting a losing battle against relaxation or decay, or that he is preoccupied with the restraint of abuses. Lanfranc is clearly writing for those who accept a life of strict claustral exercises as a desirable way of devoting their lives to God and who, whatever their frailties and lapses may be,

[1] cf. his recollections of childhood in *Memorials of St Dunstan* (Rolls Series), 140–2
[2] cf. Anselm's words in chapter, quoted by Eadmer, *Vita Anselmi* (Rolls Series), 364 : ' *Sicut bubo dum in caverna cum pullis suis est laetatur et suo sibi modo bene est . . . ita et mihi* '

hope to fulfil the spirit, and not only the letter, of their profession.)

The reader whose interest lies in monastic or general history rather than in liturgy may well find the latter half (from p. 72 onwards) of Lanfranc's work more to his purpose than the liturgical directions of the earlier pages. There are, however, a number of digressions or pauses on the way through the liturgical year which will repay attention. Such, for example, are the careful description of the monastic bath (p. 10), the account of the distribution of books at the beginning of Lent (p. 19), the long account of the Palm Sunday procession (p. 23), the account of the two Maundy ceremonies (pp. 31–8), and the account of the procession on the Rogation days. The modern reader looks in all documents for a personal touch. There are few in Lanfranc's directory, but those acquainted with many customaries and uses will not fail to see, often in small details, a humanity and consideration which sit well upon one who is interpreting the most humane of monastic legislators to his own generation. The care shown for the sick (p. 119), the sympathy for those undergoing punishment or rigorous confinement (p. 101) and the courtesy expressed in the elaborate ceremonial of the Maundy (p. 37) may be taken as examples; they are not the only instances that might be quoted.

The Scope of the Constitutions

There has been some discussion in recent years as to the scope of Lanfranc's reform.[1] It is true that the covering letter is addressed to Prior Henry alone, and that in it Lanfranc explains his use of the term ' abbot ' when writing to a

---

[1] See J. Armitage Robinson, ' Lanfranc's Monastic Constitutions,' in *Journal of Theological Studies*, X (1909), 375–88 ; and additions and corrections in R. Graham, ' The Relations of Cluny to some other Movements of Monastic Reform,' ibid., XV (1914), 179 foll., reprinted in *English Ecclesiastical Studies* (London, 1929), 1–29 ; cf. also D. Knowles, *The Monastic Order in England*, 123–4. To the houses mentioned in the last named as accepting Lanfranc's Constitutions should be added Battle, Evesham and Eynsham.

community of which the archbishop was head. Nevertheless, there is scarcely a single detail in the body of the work which is applicable to Canterbury alone, whereas many touches give an impression that the writer expects that others besides Prior Henry will be applying his directions. In the sequel, we know them to have been applied, at least in great part, at a dozen or so of the principal cathedrals and abbeys of England. Their reception, however, in these houses was due either to the personal influence of Lanfranc (as at St Albans and Rochester) or to their intrinsic excellence, not to an act of external authority. The statement, sometimes made in the past, that they were intended by Lanfranc for imposition upon all the monasteries of England, is based partly upon the title which they bear in most printed editions, and partly upon a misconception of the bond of union which joined the various monasteries to each other, and of the authority which an Archbishop of Canterbury could *ex officio* wield over those who were not directly his subjects.

The Title of Lanfranc's Work

None of the existing manuscripts bears a medieval title; all begin with the first words of the letter to Prior Henry without any heading. In the medieval catalogues this work is often described as constitutions (*constitutiones*) or statutes (*statuta*); Reyner's heading of decrees (*decreta*) is without any apparent manuscript authority.[1] They have been referred to in this introduction and elsewhere as ' constitutions.'

---

[1] The title *Decreta Lanfranci pro ordine S. Benedicti* is given by Reyner, and on p. 117 of *Tractatus* II of the *Apostolatus* he states : ' *in illo libro* [i.e. the manuscript he was following] *hic est titulus.*' Nevertheless, as Armitage Robinson showed (art. cit.), the title is not given by the Cotton or any other manuscript and must therefore be considered an explanatory or tendentious heading added to the transcript used by Reyner. No manuscript has a medieval title ; the heading to the Durham manuscript, *Constitutiones Lanfranci Archiepiscopi Cantuariensis*, is in a late (? xvii cent.) hand, and is presumably taken from the entry in a medieval catalogue.

THE MANUSCRIPTS

Six manuscripts of this work of Lanfranc are known to exist. They are :

(1) Durham Cathedral Chapter Library MS B IV 24. This volume is made up of a number of documents and notes of great antiquity and interest, including the Anglo-Saxon version of the Rule. It is described in full by R. A. B. Mynors, who includes it among the books of Bishop William of St Carilef, the refounder of the cathedral priory, who was consecrated bishop on 3 January 1081 and died on 1 January 1096. The text of Lanfranc's constitutions, according to Professor Mynors, is ' written in a late eleventh century Christ Church, Canterbury, hand,' and probably formed part of the gift of books from Canterbury to the bishop.[1] At the latest therefore, it was sent as a code from Canterbury within a few years after Lanfranc's death, and may even date from very shortly after the composition of the original by the archbishop.

(2) British Museum MS Cotton Claudius C vi, f. 174b–f. 202. This is part of a volume from Christ Church, Canterbury, the other half being Brit. Mus. Royal MS 7 E vi. The text of Lanfranc is in a hand of the twelfth century, and in the opinion of the late Sir G. F. Warner [2] could be dated as from the second quarter of the century.

(3) Corpus Christi College, Cambridge, MS 462. The text of Lanfranc (f. 87–f. 134) comes, with the rest of the book, from Dover Priory, a dependency of Christ Church, and is of the twelfth century, possibly c. 1150–70.

(4) Hereford Cathedral Chapter Library MS P V 1. This text is of the early twelfth century, and may, in the opinion of Professor R. A. B. Mynors, be a Canterbury hand. There

[1] *Durham Cathedral Manuscripts* (Oxford, 1939), p. 45
[2] Quoted by Armitage Robinson, art. cit., 386

is nothing in the book to indicate its provenance ; there was no black monk house large enough to observe Lanfranc's constitutions at or near Hereford ; the nearest abbey was at Gloucester.

(5) Cambridge University Library MS Mm 1 19 no. 4. The text here is in a small late twelfth century hand of a charter type. There is no indication of provenance, but some miscellaneous notes referring to places in Worcestershire occur at the beginning of the volume ; it is possible, therefore, that the book came from Worcester Cathedral priory.

(6) Corpus Christi College, Cambridge, MS 63. The text of Lanfranc (f. 179–f. 188) is in a hand of the early fourteenth century, and the book is from Canterbury, Christ Church. Alone of the manuscripts, it contains an abbreviated text. The introductory letter is given, then all is omitted down to the section on the abbot (below, p. 72). No doubt the omitted liturgical section was considered as wholly out of date, whereas the more general details of discipline, etc., still had an interest.

Other manuscripts, of which there is medieval record, are not now known to exist. Pre-eminent among them must be reckoned the copy which, according to Matthew Paris, was written by Lanfranc with his own hand for his nephew Paul, Abbot of St Albans, and was available when Paris wrote.[1] Durham possessed a second copy,[2] and Boston of Bury records one at Battle[3] ; in addition, copies must also have been kept in houses which are known to have accepted the constitutions.

For the purposes of this edition all the existing manuscripts

---

[1] *Gesta Abbatum S. Albani* (Rolls Series), I 61 : ' *consuetudines, quas trans-misit scriptas Lanfrancus abbati Paulo . . . quas qui videre desiderat, in consuetu-dinario . . . scriptas poterit invenire : et est libellus ille idem quem Lanfrancus scripsit et Anselmus legit et approbavit* '
[2] Mynors, op. cit., 45 *note*
[3] Cited by Robinson, art. cit., 383

have been collated save for the Hereford book (no. 4 above).
When all the others had been examined it seemed clear that
no serious divergences existed between the manuscripts, that
there was no question of versions or recensions, and that there
was not even any evidence to justify the classification of the
manuscripts into families. A full collation of the Hereford MS
therefore appeared unnecessary, especially as Professor Mynors,
who kindly looked at the book and examined a few selected
passages, found it to resemble very closely the Durham MS in
text. Lanfranc's constitutions, in fact, had great immediate
and practical value, but no literary or doctrinal importance.
When once the liturgical customs had been changed, as they
were within a century at the latest, they would cease to be
copied, save by a monk working privately with an antiquarian
interest, such as was apparently possessed by the writer of the
Canterbury MS (no. 6 above).

For the text which follows, the Durham manuscript has been
taken as the authority, partly as being the earliest in date, and
partly because its provenance, taken together with its date,
suggest that it may well have been a text sent down from
Canterbury, possibly by Lanfranc himself, to serve as a norm
for the newly-organised Durham community. It is therefore
to be presumed that it preserves the original form of the text
more exactly than a copy made at Canterbury a few decades
later, when constant copying and perhaps, also, small modifi-
cations in daily practice might have led to minute changes.

The Durham text has been followed exactly, save in one
or two places only, where an obvious scribal error has resulted
in a fault of spelling or grammar ; in such cases the reading
of the Durham manuscript is given in a footnote, and their
rarity is an indication of the uniform excellence of the text.[1]
I have given all the significant variants of A (Cott. Claudius
C vi) as this is the manuscript used for Reyner's edition,
reprinted by d'Achéry & Giles. All remaining variations

[1] See below, pp. 37, 46, 69

between the present text and that of the *Apostolatus* are therefore either misprints or scribal errors or readings introduced from another (unknown) manuscript. As for the other manuscripts, since each has numerous small variants peculiar to itself, almost all of which appear to be due to error or idiosyncracy on the part of the scribe, it seemed useless to set these out—perhaps some five hundred in all—and consequently only a few selected readings are given beneath the text.[1] These are chosen either because the agreement of two or more manuscripts makes it possible that they preserve an alternative reading of early date, or because a particular manuscript has a reading of intrinsic verbal or liturgical interest. No attempt has been made to show where the printed texts depart from the unanimous manuscript reading save where, in one or two places, this is clearly due, not to error in transcription or printing, but to the adoption of a conjecture in a supposedly corrupt passage.[2]

The spelling of the Durham manuscript has been reproduced exactly, and even its few inconsistencies have been retained. Its arrangement of the sections has also been followed, but paragraphs have occasionally been inserted (as by all other editors) to relieve the reader and indicate important changes of topic.

EDITIONS

Lanfranc's constitutions have been printed several times :

(1) The *editio princeps* was one of the *pièces justificatives* accompanying the three treatises published in 1626 at Douai by Dom Clement Reyner with the title *Apostolatus Benedicti-*

---

[1] Almost every manuscript shows small divergences of reading in several of the liturgical ' cues ' (e.g. in the number of words given in the *incipit* of a psalm) ; no doubt the scribe was consciously or unconsciously reproducing the formula familiar to his daily life. The other variants are mostly of the *et-ac, deinde-tunc, aut-vel* type, together with inversions of two or more words.

[2] e.g. below, pp. 45, 82

norum in Anglia.[1] This learned work, which had a complicated history behind its composition, was primarily
controversial in design ; it was planned by a small group
of the newly refounded English Benedictine Congregation
as a reply to allegations that neither St Gregory the
Great nor St Augustine of Canterbury were Benedictine
monks, and that the black monk monasteries of England
before the Dissolution were all Cluniac, and controlled by
French Cluniac authorities. The former opinion was an
aberration of the great Baronius ; the latter had been
propounded by a certain Dom J. Barnes († 1661), a whilom
monk of the English congregation who had transferred to
Cluny in France.[2] To rebut the contention of Barnes, a
number of medieval disciplinary codes and chapter decrees
were printed ; among these were Lanfranc's constitutions,[3]
understood as having been authoritatively issued for
general observance, and therefore supplying a proof that
English monks did not take their orders from abroad.
Reyner, as he expressly states in his dedication, did no
more than give his name to the title-page ; the body of
the treatises were probably the joint work of Dom Leander
(Jones) of St Martin [4] and Dom Augustine Baker. The
latter, who, in addition to being a lawyer and antiquary

[1] The best account of this book is that by Dom Stephen Marron in the
Douai Magazine (a publication of the repatriated English Benedictines of
Douai Abbey, Woolhampton, Berks.), III 3 (Jan., 1925), pp. 205–8. cf.
also *The Life of Father Baker*, by Salvin and Cressy, ed. Dom J. McCann
(London, 1933), p. 202. For Reyner himself, the best source of information
is *Memorials of Father Baker*, ed. J. McCann and R. H. Connolly (Catholic
Record Society, vol. xxxiii, 1933), pp. 236–7. He should not be confused
with his brother, whose baptismal (not religious) name was Clement ; both
the *Dict. Nat. Biography* and N. Birt, *Obit Book of the English Benedictines*, are
treacherous.
[2] Barnes's views were set out in his *Examen Trophaeorum*, a very rare book
of which only one copy (in the Bibliothèque Nationale, noted by Dom
J. McCann) is known to exist.
[3] In *Apostolatus*, tractatus III, pp. 211 foll.
[4] This was the name in religion of John Jones, a convert of some note
who had shared rooms at Oxford with Laud and was later used as papal
emissary to the archbishop. He became President of the English Benedictine Congregation ; cf. *Dict. Nat. Biography* under John Jones.

of repute, was also a celebrated writer on mystical theology, spent some years of the third decade of the seventeenth century in collecting in London and elsewhere materials for the *Apostolatus*, and also for a work on English monastic antiquities which would have anticipated Dugdale's *Monasticon*. As the friend or acquaintance of Sir Robert Cotton, Sir Henry Spelman, John Selden, Archbishop Ussher and others, he had access to all the principal collections of documents ; he was in the habit of taking about with him a scribe to copy such materials as he desired, and often visited Cotton's library for this purpose.[1] No doubt it was this copyist, working at Baker's command, who was responsible for the text printed by Reyner.

In the *Apostolatus* itself two inconsistent accounts are given of the manuscript used for Lanfranc's constitutions.[2] At the head of the text a note states that it was derived from a Canterbury manuscript in the palace of the Bishop of Durham, i.e. Durham House in the Strand, where Laud for a time resided as Prebendary of Westminster, and which had been returned to the Bishop of Durham early in the reign of James I.[3] On a later page, however, the manuscript used is described as a Durham register.

The late Dean Armitage Robinson took considerable pains to investigate the matter, and came to the conclusion that the manuscript used for the *Apostolatus* was the Cotton manuscript listed above. His proof was detailed and thorough, and although a serious *prima facie* difficulty stands

[1] The fullest account of this and of Baker's historical projects is in the life by his younger contemporary, Prichard, in *Memorials of Father Baker*, 109–13. Two of the four volumes of Baker's transcripts ultimately found their way to Jesus College, Oxford, their present owner (MSS 75–8) ; in recent years they have lain in deposit in Bodley's Library.

[2] At the head of the text (p. 211) it is said to come ' *ex antiquo manuscripto ecclesiae Christi Cantuariae, quod habetur in palatio Dunelmensi Londini.*' But in Tractatus II, 117 there is reference to a ' *manuscriptum registrum coenobii Dunelmensis, ex quo describi curavimus totam observantiam Lanfrancianam . . . quarum in illo libro hic est titulus, Decreta D. Lanfranci pro ordine S. Benedicti.*'

[3] cf. A. W. Clapham and W. H. Godfrey, *Some Famous Buildings and their Story*, p. 154, and Robinson, art. cit., 386 *note* 2

in the way of this identification, a re-examination of Armitage Robinson's arguments, conducted with the manuscript in question available for reference, has convinced the present writer that they are adequate, and that one, at least, if not both the notes in the *Apostolatus* are erroneous. The circumstances of the publication of the *Apostolatus* were such as to make an error of this kind very probable, for the transcripts made by a hired copyist for Dom Baker, who was always in at least remote danger of arrest in England, were sent abroad, probably after passing for comment through the hands of Dom Leander Jones, and were then printed without possibility of correction, and a note or query on the copy might easily have appeared to Reyner or to the printer as a firm statement.

When Armitage Robinson was making his investigations he did not take what for some would have been the first step : he did not, that is to say, collate the text of the *Apostolatus* with the manuscript from which he maintained it to be derived. Had he done so, he might well have gone no further, for the differences between the text as printed by Reyner and as given by MS Cotton Claudius C vi are so numerous (amounting to more than two hundred, excluding normalisations of spelling) that it might seem at first sight that the one could not represent a transcript of the other. The difficulty is a real one, but not insurmountable. Many of the variants are certainly, and almost all may probably be, mere copyist's errors ; nowhere does Reyner's text give a reading which indicates a clearly different manuscript tradition, whereas on a number of small points, where the Cotton manuscript differs from all or some of the others, Reyner has this peculiar reading.

Besides involuntary differences, Reyner's presentation of the text departs considerably from the manuscript used —and from all other manuscripts—in giving divisions into

chapters and sections, with appropriate titles and numeration. This subdivision is of great convenience to the reader, and for purposes of reference, and is on the whole satisfactorily accomplished, but as it has no manuscript authority it has been abandoned in the text that follows ; as a partial substitute, a synopsis of the work has been given below (pp. xxxviii–ix), which follows, while slightly elaborating, the scheme of the *Apostolatus*.

(2) Reyner's text was reprinted at Paris in 1648 by the Maurist, Dom Luc d'Achéry.[1] After paying tribute to the learning of the editor of the *Apostolatus* (who was in fact a man of straw), d'Achéry animadverted somewhat sharply on the scribal corruptions which he had noticed or suspected. He had, however, no access to any manuscript, and therefore reprinted Reyner with a very few corrections.[2]

(3) In 1737 David Wilkins printed the work in the first volume of his *Concilia*.[3] He followed the Durham manuscript, and as his transcript was a fairly accurate one, and as he made no arbitrary subdivisions, his is the most satisfactory edition that has hitherto appeared. Although he does not mention it, he clearly had before him one of the existing printed texts, for in a passage where the manuscript seems at first sight to give a false reading, he prints in his text the conjecture which d'Achéry had taken over from Reyner.[4]

(4) J. A. Giles, in 1844, reprinted d'Achéry's text, making no reference to Wilkins.[5] His choice is not surprising, since he was following d'Achéry for the other works of Lanfranc,

---

[1] *Beati Lanfranci Cantuariensis archiepiscopi Opera Omnia*
[2] In his preface *ad Lectorem* (without pagination) he refers to Reyner's text as ' *characteribus obliteratis mendisque librarii oscitantis passim referta quae, prout facultas suppetiit (nullus enim codex manuscriptus occurrit) correximus.*' D'Achéry went on to criticise many passages where he suspected interpolation.
[3] *Concilia Magnae Britanniae et Hiberniae* (1727), I 328 foll.
[4] Below, p. 82
[5] *Lanfranci Opera* (2 vols., Oxford, 1844), vol. i, pp. 85–191

but it is remarkable that he omits all mention of Reyner, of whose edition (together with that of Wilkins) he was apparently either unaware or forgetful.[1] Giles did not examine the Cotton manuscript, nor did he collate those at Corpus Christi College and Durham ; he did, however, consult the Cambridge University manuscript, though the changes he introduced from it were scarely as significant as his words imply.[2]

(5) Finally, Giles's text was reprinted by Migne in his *Patrologia Latina*, vol. cl, coll. 443–513 (1854).

As will be seen, therefore, four of the five printed editions are based upon Dom Baker's transcript of Cotton Claudius C vi. The fifth (that of Wilkins) follows the Durham manscript. No critical edition has hitherto been attempted.

---

[1] ibid., i. 406 : ' *Eas* [*sc.* constitutiones] *edidit D'Acherius ex antiquo Msto. ecclesiae Cantuariensis* ' ; cf. also his preface, p. v.

[2] ibid. : ' *Textum cum Msto. Cant. Mm L 19 accurate contulimus ; inde paucas quasdam, quae multum ad textum emendandum profecere, lectiones excerpsimus* '

SUGGESTED BOOKS FOR FURTHER REFERENCE

A READER unfamiliar with the monastic offices and with the ceremonies of the Roman rite may find himself at sea in the earlier pages of Lanfranc. The historian or antiquary will turn naturally for help to the official service books : the monastic breviary, the Roman missal, the gradual and anti-phoner, the *Ceremoniale Episcoporum* and the *Rituale Romanum*. With these, even in their modern versions, he will have little difficulty in following Lanfranc's general directions. For the benefit of those who have the use of a good working library references have been given in the footnotes to three modern editions of medieval service books, two of which were in use in houses that followed Lanfranc's directory, and all of which present very fully the observance he describes. All three are publications of the Henry Bradshaw Society.

Missale ad usum ecclesiae Westmonasteriensis, ed. J. Wickham Legg (3 vols., nos. I, V and XII, published in 1891, 1893, 1896).

Officium ecclesiasticum abbatum secundum usum Eveshamensis monasterii, ed. H. W. Wilson (no. VI, in 1893).

The monastic breviary of Hyde Abbey, ed. J. B. L. Tolhurst (6 vols., LIX, LXX, LXXI, LXXVI, LXXVIII, LXXX, 1930–1942).

The last volume of the last-named is an elaborate and learned introduction, describing in detail the daily offices, regular and supernumerary. It is by far the fullest and most accurate treatment of the subject. To these may be added :

Antiphonaire monastique de Worcester, being vol. xii of *Paléographie musicale* (Tournai, 1922).

All these are books not easily come by save at a few great libraries. Those who have neither time nor opportunity to consult them will find considerable help from two or three very accessible books, such as e.g. *The New Missal* (Latin and English), ed. H. P. R. Finberg, and *The Holy Week Book* (Latin and English), both published and sold by Messrs Burns, Oates & Washbourne. The modern monastic breviary is available only in Latin.

Among other books may be noted :

CONTEMPORARY MONASTIC LIFE

Dom U. BERLIERE, *L'Ordre monastique* (Paris, 3rd ed., 1924).

Dom U. BERLIERE, *L'Ascèse bénédictine* (Paris, 1927).

Dom DAVID KNOWLES, *The Monastic Order in England* (Cambridge, 1940).

Dom C. BUTLER, *Benedictine Monachism* (London, 2nd ed. 1927).

LANFRANC

A. J. MACDONALD, *Lanfranc* (Oxford, 1926).

'Lanfranc,' article in *Dictionnaire de Théologie Catholique.*

LANFRANC'S CONSTITUTIONS

J. ARMITAGE ROBINSON in *Journal of Theological Studies* (quoted above).

R. GRAHAM, *ibid.* (quoted above).

D. KNOWLES, *The Monastic Order in England*, pp. 123–4.

HISTORY OF CHRIST CHURCH

J. ARMITAGE ROBINSON, 'The Early Community at Christ Church, Canterbury,' in *Journal of Theological Studies*, xxvii (1926), 225–40.

Dom THOMAS SYMONS, 'The Introduction of Monks at Christ Church, Canterbury,' *ibid.*, xxvii (1926), 409–11.

R. A. L. SMITH, *Canterbury Cathedral Priory* (Cambridge, 1943).

BUILDINGS OF CHRIST CHURCH

R. WILLIS, *History of the Conventual Buildings of Christ Church, Canterbury* (1869).

C. E. WOODRUFF and W. DANKS, *Memorials of Canterbury Cathedral* (London, 1912).

Article ' Cantorbéry ' in *Dictionnaire d'Archéologie chrétienne et de Liturgie* (Cabrol and Leclercq).

THE MONASTIC HORARIUM AS INDICATED BY LANFRANC [1]

WINTER [2]	SUMMER [3]
Rise in night habit and shoes	Rise in night habit and shoes
Prayers	Prayers
Trina Oratio : I	*Trina Oratio : I*
Last 32 psalms of psalter, *cum precibus et collectis*	The fifteen (Gradual) psalms, *cum precibus et collectis*
MATINS	MATINS
psalmi familiares	*psalmi familiares*
Matins of the dead (till 2 Feb.)	
Lauds of the dead	
Sit in choir or pray elsewhere	
Oratio [4]	
LAUDS	LAUDS
psalmi familiares	*psalmi familiares*
Suffrages	Suffrages
	Lauds of All Saints
(October only) Bed	Lauds of the dead
	Verba mea, etc. (when said)
Oratio	
	Bed
	Oratio
	Trina oratio : II
PRIME	PRIME
psalmi familiares	*psalmi familiares*
Miserere, etc.	*Miserere,* etc.
Seven penitential psalms [5]	Seven penitential psalms
Litany of the saints	Litany of the saints
Sit in cloister (reading)	Sit in cloister (reading)
Put on day shoes and wash	Put on day shoes and wash
Oratio	
Trina oratio : II	
TERCE	
psalmi familiares	
MORNING MASS [6]	MORNING MASS

CHAPTER
Verba mea, etc.

Talk in cloister (tasks, work, etc.)
Children's breakfast

Oratio
SEXT
psalmi familiares

Talk in cloister (tasks, etc.)
Procession (Wednesdays and Fridays)

Oratio
Litany of the saints
HIGH MASS
Oratio

Sit in choir
Servers' breakfast

NONE
psalmi familiares

DINNER

Sit in cloister (reading)

Oratio
VESPERS
psalmi familiares
Suffrages
Vespers of All Saints

CHAPTER
Verba mea, etc.

Talk in cloister (tasks, etc.)

Oratio
TERCE
psalmi familiares
Litany of the saints

Sit in cloister (reading ? or tasks)

HIGH MASS

Sit in cloister (reading)
Children's and servers' breakfast

Oratio
SEXT
psalmi familiares

DINNER
Siesta

Dress and wash

Sit in cloister (reading)

Oratio
NONE
psalmi familiares
Drink in refectory
Talk in cloister (tasks)

Oratio
VESPERS
psalmi familiares
Suffrages
Vespers of All Saints

Vespers of dead	Vespers of dead
Sit in cloister	
Matins of dead (3 Feb. to Easter)	SUPPER
Change to night shoes	Matins of dead
Sit in cloister (if light) ; in chapter-house (if dark)	Change to night shoes
Drink in refectory (when no *caritas*)	
Collatio in chapter-house	Collatio in chapter-house
Caritas in refectory (when taken)	*Caritas* in refectory (when taken)
COMPLINE	COMPLINE
Trina oratio : III	*Trina oratio : III*
Retire to dormitory	Retire to dormitory

[1] Lanfranc gives scattered indications only, leaving several arrangements in doubt. One or two gaps and doubtful points have been completed from similar contemporary schemes. Lanfranc does not give a single indication of clock time. Lauds were intended to be the daybreak office, and Prime was not said till daylight was full. In the pre-Conquest English monasteries dinner in summer was at noon, and None was said at 2.30 p.m.

[2] i.e. ferial days in winter. The winter routine ran in its main outline from 1 October (or 15 Sept.) to Holy Week, but Lent had numerous peculiarities.

[3] i.e. ferial days in summer ; from Low Sunday to 14 Sept. (or 1 Oct.). In its main outline (two meals, etc.) this was similar to the routine on Sundays and feasts throughout the year.

[4] The *oratio* before or after an Hour was either a few vocal prayers, or a short space for silent prayer, or both.

[5] In the darkest winter months the penitential psalms and litany were said before Prime, and the monks then sat in choir till daylight.

[6] Lanfranc makes no allowance of time for private Masses ; these were celebrated according to devotion during any space between conventual duties in the morning.

SYNOPSIS OF THE MONASTIC CONSTITUTIONS

SECOND PART—THE ADMINISTRATION AND
DISCIPLINE OF THE HOUSE

ABBREVIATIONS

The manuscripts of Lanfranc's Constitutions are denoted in footnotes by the following letters :

A   Brit. Mus. MS Cotton Claudius C vi—this is the manuscript followed by Reyner (D'Achéry, Giles and Migne)

B   Corpus Christi College, Cambridge, MS 462

C   Cambridge University Library MS, Mm 1. 19

D   Durham Cathedral Chapter Library, B iv. 24—this was followed by Wilkins and is used in this edition

E   Corpus Christi College, Cambridge, MS 63

The following abbreviations are also used :

Albers   *Consuetudines Monasticae*, ed. Dom Bruno Albers, 5 vols. (I, Stuttgart and Vienna, 1900 ; II, III, IV and V, Monte Cassino, 1905, 1907, 1911, 1912)

HB   *The Monastic Breviary of Hyde Abbey*, ed. J. B. L. Tolhurst. Vols. I–V are the text of the book ; Vol. VI is the editor's liturgical introduction

LATIN TEXT
and
ENGLISH TRANSLATION

DECRETA LANFRANCI MONACHIS
CANTUARIENSIBUS TRANSMISSA

LANFRANCUS, indignus sanctae Dorobernensis [1] aecclesiae antistes, dilectissimis fratribus suis Henrico [2] priori et caeteris salutem et benedictionem. Mittimus uobis nostri ordinis consuetudines scriptas, quas excerpsimus ex consuetudinibus eorum cenobiorum, quae nostro tempore maioris auctoritatis sunt in ordine monachorum.[3] Addidimus quoque perpauca, et mutauimus nonnulla, et maxime in celebrandis quibusdam festis, excellentius in nostra aecclesia oportere ea agi censentes propter primatem sedem. In quibus nec nobis qui praesentes sumus, nec iis qui post nos uenturi sunt, in aliquo praeiudicamus, ut non uel eis addere, uel ab eis tollere, uel in eis permutare aliqua ualeamus, si aliter ea commodius posse fieri uel magistra ratione [4] uel doctiorum auctoritate intelligamus. Quantumlibet enim quisquam proficiat, maximus ei defectus est existimare se ultra non posse proficere ; nam numerus fratrum auctus uel diminutus, facultates locorum, varietates rerum quae saepe eueniunt, diuersitates sensuum, quod alii quidem sic, et alii sic intelligunt, pleraque diu seruata plerumque aliter ordinari compellunt ; hinc est quod nulla fere aecclesia imitari aliam per omnia potest. Illud tamen cautissime attendendum est, ut ea sine quibus anima saluari non potest omnibus modis inuiolata seruentur, fidem dico,

---

[1] The Roman name for Canterbury was Durovernum (medieval Dorobernum) Cantiacorum.

[2] Henry, a monk of Bec, is described by the writer of the Life of Herluin (in *Lanfranci Opera*, ed. Giles, p. 273) as a ' tall and fruitful tree ' of Herluin's planting. He was summoned to Canterbury by Lanfranc at a date unknown, perhaps between 1070 and 1075, and remained prior till he was elected abbot of Battle in 1096 ; he died there in 1102 (*Chronicon monasterii de Bello*, ed. J. S. Brewer, p. 44).

THE MONASTIC
CONSTITUTIONS OF LANFRANC

LANFRANC, unworthy bishop of the holy church of Canterbury,[1] to his dearly beloved brethren, prior Henry [2] and the other monks, health and benediction.

We send you the customs of our monastic life which we have compiled from the customs of those monasteries which in our day have the greatest prestige in the monastic order.[3] We have added a few details, and have made certain changes, particularly in the ceremonies of certain feasts, considering that they should be kept with greater solemnity in our church by reason of the primatial see which is there. In this we do no prejudice to our own freedom or that of those who come after us ; we are all free to add or to take away or to make changes if we think alteration to be an advantage, following right reason [4] or the judgment of those better informed ; for however far a man advance, it is the worst of failings for him to suppose that he can go no further. An increase or decrease in the number of monks, conditions in different places and the inevitable changes of circumstance, added to diversity of opinion shown in this or that way of thinking—all these often make for changes in matters which have long been unaltered. Hence it is that no one church can exactly imitate the practices of another. What we have to consider with the greatest care is that what is necessary for the soul's salvation should be safeguarded in every way : faith, that is, and

---

[3] For a discussion of these sources v. introduction, pp. xi–xiii; some of the clearest examples of derivation are indicated in the footnotes below.

[4] cf. *Regula* I 16 : *experientia magistra*, itself a quotation from Cassian, *Collationes* XIX 7.

contemptum mundi, caritatem, castitatem, humilitatem,
patientiam, obedientiam, de perpetratis culpis paeni-
86 tudi/nem earumque humilem confessionem, frequentes
orationes, competens silentium, multaque in hunc
modum ; haec ubi seruantur, rectissime potest dici
regulam sancti Benedicti et monachorum ibi ordinem
custodiri, quoquo modo uarientur caetera, quae pro
arbitrio diuersorum in diuersis sunt cenobiis instituta.
Cuiusmodi sunt quod in praecipuis solennitatibus alibi
in tunicis [1] tantum, quos * frocos vocant, et alibi in albis
et cappis cantores ad uesperas responsorium canunt,
quod in eisdem festiuitatibus in aliis locis albis solummodo, et in aliis cappis etiam induti procedunt ; quod
in quibusdam cenobiis uiceni uel triceni, aut plus aut
minus simul in alueis, et in quibusdam singuli in singulis
catinis pedes in claustro ante mandatum abluunt ; quod
pleraque monasteria mense Februario, transacta beatae
Mariae festiuitate,[2] officium mortuorum post uesperas
dicere incipiunt, et pleraque usque ad Septuagesimam
praestolantur.   Huius generis alia plurima existunt,
quae pro sua prolixitate breuiter enumerari non possunt.
Haec tamen ipsa, postquam seruanda subiectis a pastori-
bus ordinantur, ab iis, quorum tota uita in obedientia
sita est, sine culpa minime uiolantur.   Inde uero nemo
turbetur, quod in tractatu earum consuetudinum nomen
abbatis tantum, non episcopi uel archiepiscopi, ponitur.
Ordo quippe monachorum describitur, quorum per
abbates frequentius quam per antistites uita disponitur.
Quamuis et ipsi antistites, si paternam curam uice Christi

---

* quas A   *man. pr.* C E
    [1] The tunic or frock, a garment similar in shape to the modern cassock
and reaching to the calves or ankles, was the workaday dress of the monk.
The cowl (*cuculla*) an ampler garment with very wide sleeves, was worn
on full-dress occasions.

contempt of the world, together with charity, chastity, humility, patience, obedience ; penance for faults committed and a humble confession of them ; frequent prayers ; silence in fitting measure ; and many other things of this kind. Where these are preserved it may truly be said that the Rule of St Benedict and the monastic life are kept, whatever variety there be in matters which have been differently ordered in different monasteries. Such matters are : that in one house the cantors at Vespers sing the responsory on principal feasts in tunics [1] only, or ' frocks ' as they are called, while elsewhere they wear albs and copes ; that on the same festivals they go in procession at some houses in albs only, and at others wearing copes as well ; that in some monasteries twenty or thirty, more or less, wash their feet together in troughs in the cloister before the maundy, while elsewhere each washes alone in a bowl ; that many monasteries begin in February to say the office of the dead after Vespers when once the feast of Our Lady [2] is past, whereas others wait till Septuagesima. There are many other matters of this kind, too complex for a brief review. All such arrangements, once they have been settled for their subjects by superiors, cannot without blame be violated by those whose whole life is one of obedicnce.

Let no-one be surprised that in the course of these customs the title of abbot, and not that of bishop or archbishop, is used. We are describing a monastic way of life, and monks are more often ruled by an abbot than by a bishop—though indeed bishops, if being in Christ's place they take a father's care of their subjects,

---

[2] i.e. the Purification of Our Lady, 2 February. Both Cluny and the *Regularis Concordia* differ here from Lanfranc's arrangement ; cf. Tolhurst, *Hyde Breviary* VI 112, 139.

subiectis suis impendant, non absurde abbates, id est patres, congruo suis actibus uocabulo appellari queant.

Deus pacis et dilectionis uobiscum maneat, et ipse pace et dilectione sua uos repleat, et ab omnibus peccatis clementer absoluat. Amen, AMEN.

KALENDIS OCTOBRIS remaneat meridiana quam facere 87 solent monachi in / aestate [1] ; a dominica prima huius mensis cantetur et legatur de libris machabeorum usque ad festiuitatem omnium sanctorum. Canantur ymni dominicis diebus usque ad aduentum Domini ; ad nocturna Primo dierum omnium, ad laudes Aeterne rerum conditor. Privatis diebus post matutina usque ad festiuitatem omnium sanctorum reuertantur ad lectos suos [2] ; illucescente autem die pulsetur a custode aecclesiae paruulum signum modice. Surgentes fratres in nocturnalibus suis, et infantes et iuuenes [3] cum luminaribus suis, ueniant in aecclesiam, et facta oratione [4] cantent primam, et psalmos familiares [5] cum collectis suis et septem psalmos, [6] et letaniam. [7] Inde exeuntes sedeant in claustro. Pueri uero primitus alte legant, et postea si opus fuerit cantent. [8] Omni tempore antequam legant infantes nullus in claustro legat aut cantet, nisi in silentio, nec ad confessionem pergat. Antequam sonet signum ad apparatum terciae nullus calciet se diurnalibus

---

[1] October, in the monastic horarium, was a transition period ; although the winter arrangement of a single meal began on 14 September, the long lessons from Scripture in the night office began only on 1st November. Lanfranc follows the usual custom in discontinuing the siesta during October ; cf. Albers II 31 (ancient Cluny customs) : ' dimittitur meridiana.'

[2] Albers II 31

[3] Bernard of Cluny II xxxi 351. The *infantes* or *pueri,* offered to the monastery by their parents, were the ' children of the cloister ' till the age of fifteen ; the *juvenes* were the elder boys, now fully monks, but still under supervision.

[4] A phrase often recurring, but difficult to translate adequately. Often, as here, it refers to the unspecified and perhaps not always formally regulated prayers said in silence before the office. At St Mary's, York, the psalm

may not improperly be called abbots, that is, fathers, for the name suits the act.

May the God of peace and love abide with you ; may He fill you with His peace and love and mercifully free you from all your sins. Amen, AMEN.

ON THE FIRST OF OCTOBER the monks shall discontinue the siesta which they are wont to take in the summer.[1] From the first Sunday of the month the books of the Macchabees shall be chanted and read until the feast of All Saints. On Sundays till Advent the hymn at Matins shall be *Primo dierum omnium,* and at Lauds *Aeterne rerum conditor.* On ferial days until the feast of All Saints they shall return to bed after Lauds[2] ; when day is breaking the small bell shall be sounded lightly by the warden of the church. Then the brethren, rising in their night shoes, and the children and young monks[3] with lanterns shall enter the church, and when a prayer has been said[4] they shall sing Prime, and the psalms for relatives[5] with their collects, and the seven penitential psalms,[6] and the litany.[7] After this they shall retire and sit in the cloister. The children shall begin by reading aloud, and afterwards, if need be, practise the chant.[8] No-one shall ever read or rehearse the chant in the cloister, save in silence, until the children begin to read, nor shall he go to confession. Before the bell rings for preparation for Terce no-one shall put on his day shoes

---

Miserere (50 ; A.V. 51) was prescribed. At the present day a short preparatory prayer is followed by the *Pater, Ave* and *Credo.*

[5] For the 'familiar' psalms, offered for benefactors and friends, *v.* Introduction, p. xvii.

[6] i.e. Ps. 6, 31, 37, 50 (51), 101 (102), 129 (130), 142 (143).

[7] Here a shorter form of the modern Litany of the Saints.

[8] Bernard of Cluny I xxvii 201

suis, exceptis iis quibus extra claustrum cura oboedien-
tiae iniuncta est, et hi priusquam exeant aliquantulum
in claustro sedere debent, et expectare ut prius infantes
in scolis suis legant. Cum appropinquauerit tempus
horae terciae, pulsetur a secretario modice signum
minimum quam skillam uocant, et statim pergant in
dormitorium et calcient se diurnalibus[1] et cultellos
accipiant ; deinde ad lauatorium uadant,* et prius
lauent se, et postea pectinent. Dehinc ad aecclesiam
ueniant, aquam benedictam sumant, in chorum uadant,
et incumbentes terrae infantes expectent. Cum uero
infantes loti fuerint, et se pectinare inceperint, pulsetur
maius signum ad horam. Accedentes et ipsi ad aquam
benedictam in chorum ueniant, et dimisso signo omnes
simul tres orationes[2] faciant. Quibus factis pulsetur
minus signum et canatur tercia. Inchoato psalmo
Miserere mei Deus,[3] surgentes missam matutinalem[4]
celebranturante et retro[5] facient, et se induere pergant.
Celebrata missa sedeant omnes in choro praeter aliquos
88 conuersos,[6] qui sacerdotem et eos qui ad / missam seruierunt adiuuare debent. Quod cum expleuerint redeant
et ipsi in chorum. Tunc iubente abbate prior sonet
signum minimum. Deinde eant omnes in capitulum

---

* ueniant C B
[1] This implied putting on stockings or gaiters as well as shoes. The
visit to the dormitory, here as elsewhere, permitted also of one to the rere-
dorter, which Lanfranc seldom mentions by name.
[2] These are one of the three groups known as the *Trina Oratio*, consisting
of five or seven psalms with prayers and occurring before Matins, before
Terce (usually), and after Compline. For the devotion *v.* Dom T. Symons,
A Note on the Trina Oratio, in *Downside Review* XLII (January 1924), 67ff.,
and Tolhurst, *HB* VI 57ff.   cf. also Introduction, *supra* p. xvii.
[3] Ps. 50 (51)
[4] This, the Morrow, Morning or Chapter Mass was celebrated at the
altare minus at the east end of the monastic choir.
[5] The solemn bow from the centre of the choir to those on the left and
right, which was made by the individual on arrival at, or departure from,
a conventual duty ; it was performed by making first a low obeisance and
then, while still bending low, a half-circular turn. cf. Ducange, *s.v.*

save those who have been given a task to do for the monastery outside the cloister ; even these should sit for a time in the cloister before they go out, and wait for the children to begin to read in their school.

When the third hour approaches, the sacristan shall sound lightly the smallest bell which is called the *squilla*, and all shall at once go to the dormitory,[1] put on their day shoes and take their knives. Then they shall go to the wash-place and wash themselves and comb their hair. Then they shall go to the church, take holy water, enter the choir and wait on their knees for the children. When these have washed and begun to comb their hair the large bell shall ring for the Hour. Then the children shall take holy water and enter the choir, and when the bell ceases all shall say the Three Prayers[2] together. After this the small bell is rung and Terce is sung. When the psalm *Miserere*[3] is begun those who are to celebrate the Morrow Mass[4] shall rise, make their full bow[5] and go to vest. When Mass has been celebrated all shall sit in choir save for the converses[6] who have to assist the priest and those who have ministered at the Mass. When they have done this let them return to choir. Then at the abbot's word the prior shall sound the smallest bell and straightway all shall go to chapter, walking in order of seniority two by two, monks first and then the children. After chapter the board shall be

---

[6] These were monks who, while fully members of the community, were technically illiterate owing to their entry as adults from the world, and who therefore did not proceed to Orders. Though performing many of the duties and tasks, in church and monastery, later entrusted to lay-brothers, they were essentially different from the *conversi* of the Cistercians and other later orders, who lived in separate quarters, and had no seat or voice in the monastic choir and chapter. As the term ' lay-brother ' has been appropriated to religious of the latter kind, the archaic word ' converse ' (*v.* O.E.D. *s.v.*) has been used above.

duo et duo sicut sunt priores, maiores prius, postea
infantes. Peracto capitulo, pulsata tabula,[1] dicto ab
abbate uel priore Benedicite, loquantur in claustro.
Infantes capitulum suum teneant, et postea in refectorium pergant.[2] Post sextam nullus in claustro loquatur
donec infantes de monasterio exeant, et minimus eorum
alta uoce Benedicite dicat. Facto intervallo, pulsata
ad apparatum missae skilla, pulsato ad missam signo,
oratione facta dicatur ab infante letania,[3] induantur qui
celebraturi sunt missam et seruituri sunt ad missam.
Quarta et sexta feria si post sextam et ante missam per
claustrum processuri sunt, non pulsetur skilla ad apparatum missae, sed cum tempus processionis secretarius
instare prospexerit, sonet unum de mediocribus signis ;
quo audito, statim silentium fit in claustro. Discalcient
se, manus abluant, in aecclesiam uadant, factaque
oratione, et pulsatis duobus signis, dictis quae dici
solent, processionem faciant sicut in eisdem diebus in
quadragesima et in aestate, de qua posterius dicendum
est. Post missam pulsato signo agatur oratio.[4] Post
orationem uadant in refectorium accipere mixtum [5]
ebdomadarii coquinae et mensae lector. Si uero alii
sint qui pro utilitate aecclesiae maiori missae non
possint interesse, in potestate abbatis uel prioris sit
utrum et ipsi mixtum accipere, et statutam ebdomadariis

---

[1] The word *tabula* has two distinct technical uses in monastic customs :
(1) a board struck or rapped by a small mallet (as here), and (2) the notice-
board on which the weekly officials were inscribed.
[2] i.e. to take the *mixtum* ; *v. infra*, note 5
[3] This term is ambiguous, signifying sometimes the Litany of the Saints,
sometimes the *Kyrie*, etc., with or without versicles. Here it probably
stands for the Litany of the Saints, which was recited for the second time
in this place on ferial days in some houses ; cf. *HB* VI 69–70.
[4] Albers II 33. *Oratio* here was probably a space of time for private
or mental prayer ; cf. *Regula* XX 10.
[5] This was the name originally given to the ' bread and bever ' (' panem
et biberes,' *Regula* XXXV 22), allowed by St Benedict to the cooks and

rapped,[1] and when the abbot or prior has said 'Bless ye the Lord' there shall be speech in the cloister. The children shall hold a chapter of their own, and afterwards go to the refectory.[2] After Sext no-one shall talk in the cloister till the children come out of church and the youngest says 'Bless ye the Lord.' After a certain time the lesser bell is sounded for preparation for Mass ; after the great bell for Mass has rung and a prayer has been said one of the children shall say the litany,[3] and those who are to celebrate and serve the Mass shall vest.

If there is a procession in the cloister after Sext and before Mass on Wednesdays and Fridays, the lesser bell is not rung for preparation for Mass, but when the sacristan perceives that the time of the procession is at hand, he shall ring one of the small bells, and when this is heard silence shall at once fall in the cloister. The brethren shall take off their shoes, wash their hands and enter the church ; after the prayer two bells shall ring, the customary prayers shall be said and they shall go in procession as on the same days of the week in Lent and in the summer, as will be described later.

After Mass a bell is rung and there is a space for prayer [4] ; after prayer the weekly kitchen servers and the reader at table go to the refectory for their *mixtum*.[5] If there are others who cannot be present at High Mass owing to affairs of the house, the abbot or prior shall have power to decide whether they too shall receive the *mixtum* and the measure of bread and drink allotted to

---

servers an hour before the community meal. Later, it came to be applied to the refreshment allowed to the children and sick as a kind of breakfast. In some houses it came to include cheese and milk (cf. *Monastic Order* 457) and possibly porridge or soup. In the later middle ages a soup, often including eggs, was common ; cf. L. Gougaud, *Anciennes Coûtumes Claustrales* 62 *n.* 8, and *Revue Bénédictine* XXV (1923) 192.

debeant quantitatem panis et potus habcrc.[1] Alii uero
fratres interim in choro sedeant, et qui uoluerint legant.
Seruitoribus in chorum redeuntibus pulsetur signum,
cantetur nona. Cantata nona exeat prior ad percu-
tiendum cimbalum,[2] ebdomadarii coquinae, et caeteri qui
seruituri sunt, ad iniuncta sibi officia.

KALENDAE NOVEMBRIS si die dominica euenerint,
festiuitas omnium sanctorum solenniter agatur ; sequentibus uero priuatis diebus responsoria dicantur Vidi
89 Dominum, / et lectiones longae ex prophetis. Si vero
dies kalendarum feria secunda aut tercia aut quarta
euenerit, praecedente dominica inchoetur hystoria [3] Vidi
Dominum, sed tamen interualla non nisi post kalendas
incipiant. Si uero quinta uel sexta feria uel sabbato
kalendae extiterint, sequente dominica inchoetur hystoria
et lectiones ex prophetis ; lectiones uero grandes et
interualla mox post festiuitatem inchoentur.[4] Ab hac
festiuitate usque ad quintam feriam ante pasca, nisi
duodecim lectiones aut octauae fuerint, canantur priuatis
diebus post orationes ante nocturna officia triginta psalmi [5]
ab Ad Dominum cum tribularer usque Omnis spiritus
laudet Dominum. Primi decem pro defunctis sine Gloria,

---

[1] The weekly servers (and reader) were the original beneficiaries of
St Benedict's ordinance.
[2] The bell or gong hanging in the cloister near the refectory, and sounded
some minutes before the hour of meals.
[3] Historia—a liturgical technical term, with several meanings. Originally used for the lessons of the second nocturn on feasts, usually narrating
the life of a saint, it came to be used also of the lessons of the first nocturn
(always from Scripture) and (as here) of the responsory following the first
lesson, which was often sung to chant of special elaboration. V. Ducange,
s.v., and, for the Vidi Dominum HB II 149v–50.
[4] The single short lesson of summer continued (as at the present day)
until the first Sunday of November, when the book of Ezechiel was begun ;
henceforward till Easter three lessons from Scripture (or a homily on the
Gospel) were read nightly at Matins on ferial days. The first Sunday
of each month in the liturgy is that nearest to the first day of the month,
not the first to occur within the month. The horarium, however, with the

the weekly servers.[1] Meanwhile the other brethren shall sit in choir, and those who wish may read. When the servers return to choir a bell shall be rung and None chanted ; when this is done the prior shall go out to beat the gong,[2] and the weekly kitchen servers and other waiters shall go to their tasks.

IF THE FIRST OF NOVEMBER fall on a Sunday, the feast of All Saints shall be kept with solemnity, and on the ferial days that follow the responses *Vidi Dominum* and the rest, and the long lessons from the Prophets shall be read. If the first of November is on a Monday, Tuesday or Wednesday, the response *Vidi Dominum* [3] is begun on the previous Sunday, but the interval after Matins shall begin only after the first of the month. If the first is on a Thursday, Friday or Saturday, the response and the lessons from the Prophets shall begin on the following Sunday, but the long lessons and the interval after Matins begin immediately after the feast.[4] From this feast till Maundy Thursday, save when there are twelve lessons or during an octave, on ferial days after the prayers before Matins the Thirty Psalms shall be recited [5] from *Ad Dominum cum tribularer* to *Omnis spiritus laudet Dominum*. The first ten without doxology are for the dead, the next ten for the community, with two

---

variation of interval between the early morning offices, changed only with the calendar month.

In summer Lauds (sung when day was beginning to break) followed immediately after Matins and its supplementary offices. In winter there was an interval, originally used for reading or prayer, during which a return to bed was later sanctioned. The second interval was that occurring at times between Lauds and Prime, *v. infra*, p. 7 (foot of page)

[5] Albers II 33

sequentes decem pro congregatione bini cum una Gloria,
extremi decem pro familiaribus et benefactoribus, et hi
bini cum una Gloria, singuli cum precibus et collectis
suis.[1] Et post nocturna et familiares psalmos officium
mortuorum,[2] et matutinae laudes de omnibus sanctis, et
Verba mea si tricenarium habent. Post haec descen-
dentes a dormitorio sedeant in choro ; infantes in capitulo
cum luminaribus diligenter a magistris custodiantur,
canentes quod necessarium erit,[3] aut si nimis profunda
nocte surrexerint, pausent iacentes ad sedilia sua. Isto
interuallo debet prior cum absconsa accensa per chorum
ire ac uidere quam regulariter sedeant [4] ; deinde per
altaria et membra monasterii, ne forte aliquis ibi dormiat.
Si uero aliquem orantem inuenerit silenter pertranseat.
Quod si aliquem dormientem reppererit, euigilato in
chorum, signo facto, reuerti praecipiat. Deinde debet
per claustrum et in capitulum ire, ac uidere qualiter se
habeant magistri et infantes, et per loca alia ubi necessarium esse perspexerit. Cum tempus fuerit pulsato
signo, uenientibus pueris, facta oratione canantur matutinae laudes, commemoratio sanctorum.[5] Prima cum
psalmis familiaribus et precibus et collectis suis cum
septem psalmis et letania.[6] Post haec ita omnia agenda
90 sunt, ut supra / dictum est in mense Octobri. Secretario
autem sollicite providendum est, ut tali hora matutinas
laudes faciat incipere, quatenus omnia luce clarescente
finiantur. Si autem aliqua dubietate deluditur, et
aliquid noctis post letaniam fuerit, sicut supra in primo

---

[1] For the Gradual Psalms (Ps. 119 (120)–150) v. Tolhurst, *HB* VI 64ff.
[2] Albers II 34. For the Office of the Dead and its arrangement, v.
Tolhurst, *HB* VI 107ff.
[3] i.e. rehearsing the day's chant
[4] V. *infra*, p. 77
[5] For the Commemoration of All Saints and the ' familiar ' psalms v.
HB VI 81–93 ; 101–7.
[6] i.e. the Litany of the Saints

psalms to each doxology, the last ten for relations and
benefactors, two psalms to each doxology, each with
their prayers and collects.[1] After Matins and the psalms
for relatives, the office of the dead is recited,[2] and Lauds
of All Saints and the psalm *Verba mea* if a month's
commemoration is being kept.

After this, when the brethren come down from the dormitory they shall sit in choir, and the children shall be
carefully looked after by their masters in the chapter-house
with lights burning, practising such chant as may be necessary.[3] If they have risen very early in the night they
may rest lying by their seats. During this interval the
prior should go round the choir with a dark lantern to
see that the monks are sitting in an orderly manner[4];
then he should go round the chapels and other parts of
the church, lest perchance someone may have fallen
asleep there. If he come across one praying he shall
pass by in silence, but if he find a sleeper he shall wake
him and give him a sign to return to choir. Then he
should go through the cloister and chapter-house to see
how the children and their masters do, and whithersoever else he may judge necessary. When it is time
and the bell has rung and the children have arrived in
choir, a prayer is said and Lauds are sung, with a
commemoration of the saints.[5] Prime is sung with the
psalms for relatives and the *preces* and collects, with the
seven penitential psalms and litany.[6] After this, all is
done as has been said above for October. The sacristan
shôuld however see to it carefully that Lauds begin so
that full daylight has come when the whole is over. If
he makes a mistake and it is still night when the litany
ends, the brethren shall do as above in the first interval,

interuallo ita se habeant fratres, uidelicet ut praeter
sanguine minutos nullus reuertatur ad stratum. Clarescente uero die exeant in claustrum sedere. Ad
completorium ymnus Christe qui lux es et dies.[1]

DOMINICA ante adventum Domini canatur hystoria
de sancta Trinitate.[2] Ymnus Primo dierum. Psalmi
Domine in virtute tua, et reliqui. In tercio nocturno
pronuncietur euangelium Cum subleuasset, et idem
legatur a sacerdote reuestito cum collecta Excita Domine.
Ad laudes psalmi Dominus regnauit. Antiphonae de
Trinitate, et similiter super horas usque ad uesperas,
cum capitulis et uersibus et collectis. Ad Benedictus
antiphona et collecta de Trinitate. Post collectam
dicatur antiphona ex euangelio Cum subleuasset,[3] cum
Gloria Patri ; uersus Dominus regnauit ; collecta
Excita, Domine.[4] Sermo in capitulo, et missa matutinalis
de dominica, maior de sancta Trinitate. Si festiuitas
duodecim lectionum ipsa die euenerit, non mutetur ipsa
duodecim lectionum festiuitas.

SABBATO praecedente dominicam de aduentu Domini
dimittatur ad uesperas oratio de cruce usque post octauas
Epyphaniae. Si festiuitas sancti Andreae in hac die
euenerit, agantur pleniter uesperae de apostolo.[5] Finitis
uesperis, incipiatur antiphona Ecce nomen Domini,[6] cum
Gloria Patri. Dicta antiphona sequatur uersus et collecta
de aduentu Domini. In crastino ad inuitatorium duo
fratres in albis,[1] in sede episcopali in cappis. Et ubicun-

---

[1] Albers II 34. For a text of this hymn, the work of an unknown
author of the early sixth (?) century, v. HB V 452v, and Oxford Book of Medieval
Latin Verse, no. 13. It was used at Compline in the Mozarabic and Ambros-
ian rites, and in some French uses, and in the early Middle Ages in the
monastic use in the winter from Advent to Easter, but was ultimately
superseded entirely by the Te lucis.

that is to say, none shall return to bed save such as have been bled ; when full daylight comes they shall leave the church and sit in the cloister. At Compline the hymn shall be *Christe qui lux es et dies*.[1]

ON THE LAST SUNDAY BEFORE ADVENT the lessons of the Trinity are sung[2]. The hymn is *Primo dierum* and the psalms *Domine in virtute tua* with the rest. In the third nocturn the gospel *Cum subleuasset* is read by a priest vested, with the collect *Excita, Domine*. At Lauds the psalms are *Dominus regnauit*, etc. ; the antiphons are of the Trinity, as also at the hours till Vespers, with chapters, verses, collects ; the antiphon at the *Benedictus* and collect are of the Trinity. After the collect the antiphon from the gospel *Cum subleuasset* [3] is said, with doxology, the versicle *Dominus regnauit* and the collect *Excita Domine*.[4] The sermon in chapter and the Morrow Mass shall be of the Sunday ; the High Mass of the holy Trinity. If a feast of twelve lessons occurs on that day, it is not transferred.

ON THE SATURDAY preceding the first Sunday in Advent the prayer of the Cross is discontinued at Vespers until after the octave of the Epiphany. If the feast of St Andrew falls on this day, Vespers in their entirety are of the apostle.[5] After Vespers the antiphon *Ecce nomen Domini* [6] is begun, with doxology. After the antiphon the versicle and collect of Advent follow. Next day two brethren in albs shall sing the invitatory[7]; in copes, if

---

[2] Bernard of Cluny II i 283–4. The commemoration of the Trinity on this Sunday was presumably abandoned when the feast of the Trinity was introduced on the octave of Pentecost.

[3] Jo. VI 5. This is not the gospel of this Sunday in the Roman missal.
[4] *HB* II 168   [5] Albers I 131
[6] This is the Magnificat antiphon of the Vespers of Saturday before the First Sunday of Advent.   [7] Albers II 35

que ordo monachorum, qui hic describitur, ad inuitatorium et ad Benedictus et ad Magnificat praecipitur
91 esse in albis, / in sede episcopali institutum est esse in
cappis. Lectiones de Isaia propheta usque ad natiuitatem Domini.¹ In matutinis laudibus psalmi Miserere
mei Deus, et reliqua. Ad Benedictus sacerdos in alba
incenset altaria. Ad primam capitulum Domine miserere
nostri omnibus dominicis et festis ad natiuitatem Domini.
Gloria in excelsis Deo minime dicatur ; ad maiorem
missam diaconus et subdiaconus casulis ² sint induti.
Dominicis et aliis festis quibus duodecim lectiones
faciunt, adipem comedant.³ Si festiuitas sancti Andreae
in hac die euenerit, praecedente sabbato sicut in uigilia
ieiunetur, et missa de uigilia dicatur. Commemoratio
ad uesperas, et in crastino ad matutinas laudes, et missa
matutinalis de apostolo agatur. Festiuitas uero in
crastinum differatur. Ad uesperas ipsius diei capitulum
et caetera quae sequuntur de apostolo dicantur ; dehinc
commemoratio de aduentu. Privatis diebus preces
Oremus pro omni gradu ecclesiae.⁴ Feria quarta, sexta
et sabbato quatuor temporum pronuncientur euangelia
ipsorum dierum. Uigilia Thomae apostoli, si dies
dominica non fuerit, radantur fratres et sic balneentur,
qui uolunt balneari, ut duobus diebus ante dominicam
nativitatem sint omnes balneati.⁵ Si necesse sit ipso
apostolicae festiuitatis die balneari possunt. Ipsa autem

---

¹ Albers II 35
² In penitential seasons chasubles (in modern usage shortened in front
by folding, hence the name *planetae plicatae*) are worn instead of the customary
dalmatic and tunicle.
³ Albers I 5. *Adeps*, the modern suet and lard, which were not allowed
in seasons of fasting.
⁴ Albers II 35. The *preces* for every degree of the Church were said at
Canterbury on ferias of Advent and Lent ; cf. Tolhurst, *HB* VI 157.
⁵ Monastic legislators were influenced by the words of the Rule (XXXVI
14) : ' The use of baths is to be offered to the sick whenever expedient ;
to those in health, and in particular to the young, it is to be allowed less

it be a cathedral. And whenever it is prescribed in this directory that monks should wear albs at invitatory, *Benedictus* or *Magnificat*, it is ordained that copes should be worn in a cathedral. The lessons until Christmas shall be taken from the prophet Isaias.[1] At Lauds the psalms are *Miserere mei Deus* and the rest. At the *Benedictus* a priest in an alb shall incense the altars. At Prime the chapter *Domine miserere nostri* shall be said on all Sundays and feasts until Christmas. The *Gloria in excelsis* shall not be said at Mass ; at High Mass the deacon and subdeacon shall wear chasubles.[2] On Sundays and feasts of twelve lessons lard may be eaten.[3] If the feast of St Andrew fall on this day, the preceding Saturday shall be the vigil-fast, and Mass shall be of the vigil. There shall be a commemoration of St Andrew at Vespers and next day at Lauds, and the Morrow Mass shall be of the apostle. The feast itself, however, shall be transferred to the following day. At Vespers on Sunday the chapter and what follows shall be of the apostle, with a commemoration of Advent.

On ferial days the *preces* ' Let us pray for every degree of the Church ' shall be said.[4] On Wednesday, Friday and Saturday of Ember week the proper gospel of the day shall be read.

On the vigil of Thomas the apostle, if it be not a Sunday, the brethren shall be shaved and let those who will take a bath, in such wise that all shall have taken it two days before Christmas Day.[5] If need be, they may take their bath even on the feast of the apostle. Let the

---

often.' Baths were usually prescribed at the three festal seasons of Christmas, Easter and Pentecost, but in many customaries the liberty of those unwilling to take them is carefully safeguarded. cf. Albers V 122, 124 (Verdun) and IV 166 (Fructuaria). Lanfranc was probably familiar with the three occasions, though he mentions Christmas alone explicitly and Easter in passing (*v. infra*, p. 26).

balnea hoc ordine disponantur.[1] Praecedente die debet
abbas, aut qui ordinem tenet, prouidere unum seniorem
religiosum atque prudentem, cui praecipiat curam
habere de ipsis, qui commoneat fratres qua hora ire
debeant, et uidere quam ordinate ibi se contineant.
Qui senior illuc pergens uideat qualiter sint praeparata,
et quales famuli ibi sint deputati, scilicet non infantes,
nec iuuenes, sed aetate prouectiores. Quod si aliquid
incongruum uiderit, indicet camerario, et ille statim
emendet, reuersusque senior in claustrum, commoneat
fratres quot opus esse cognouerit. Sed hoc caueat, ne
adolescentes et nouitii simul eant, sed cum senioribus.
Illi uero fratres, quos commonuerit, postquam rasi
92 fuerint, / accipientes uestimenta, quae mutare debent,
pergant ad locum in quo balnea praeparantur, ibique
exuentes uestimenta sua sic ordinate, ut in dormitorio
facere consueuerunt, intrent unusquisque ubi ei fuit
demonstratum, et deposito uelo quod ante eos pendet,
sedeat cum silentio. Si quid uero ei necessarium fuerit,
modeste signo aliquo petat, famulus uero eleuato uelo
deferat illi celeriter quod petit, et statim reuertatur.
Postquam satis ablutus fuerit, non delectetur ibi diutius
demorari. Surgens uero calceatus atque uestitus, sicut
in dormitorio consueuit, ablutis manibus reuertatur in
claustrum. Adolescentes qui sunt in custodia cum
custodibus suis eant et reuertantur. A prima usque ad
completorium omnibus horis possunt ire fratres ad
balnea, set nullus praesumat ire absque licentia fratris,
cui hoc commissum est.

SI UIGILIA dominicae natiuitatis in dominica die
euenerit, duo fratres inuitatorium de dominica in albis

---

[1] Attempts to trace the derivation of the long account which follows
have not been successful ; possibly it is Lanfranc's own, based on current
practice at Bec.

bathing be ordered as follows.[1] On the previous day the abbot or superior should appoint a devout and prudent senior and order him to take charge of the matter, to warn the brethren when to bathe, and to see that they conduct themselves there in an orderly way. This senior shall see that all is ready, and that the right attendants are provided—mature men, neither children nor youths. If he see anything unfitting, let him tell the chamberlain, who shall at once remedy it. Then the senior shall return to the cloister and give notice to as many of the brethren as can be accommodated. Let him take care that the youths and novices go not all together, but with their elders. The brethren whom he has notified shall, when shaved, take their change of clothes and go to the place where the baths are prepared, and there, taking off their clothes in due order as they are wont to do in the dormitory, they shall enter the bathing place as directed, and letting down the curtain that hangs before them they shall sit in silence in the bath. If anyone needs anything let him signal for it quietly, and a servant lifting the veil shall quickly take him what he wants and return at once. When he has finished washing himself, he shall not stay longer for pleasure but shall rise and dress and put on his shoes as he does in the dormitory, and having washed his hands shall return to the cloister. The young monks in ward shall go and return with their masters. The brethren may go to the baths at any hour from Prime to Compline, but none shall presume to go without the permission of the brother in charge.

IF THE VIGIL OF CHRISTMAS fall on a Sunday, two brethren in albs shall sing the invitatory of the Sunday,

dicant, primum et secundum nocturnum de ipsa dominica fiant, tercium et matutinae laudes de uigilia. Post
primam collectam commemoratio de dominica. Missa
matutinalis de dominica, maior de uigilia.[1] Alia uero die
sicut priuatis diebus signa pulsentur, et triginta psalmi
dicantur.[2] Inuitatorium duo canant, sed non in albis.
Euangelium pronuncietur. Capitulum ad nocturnum et
oratio et uersus de uigilia. Caetera sicut retroactis
diebus,[3] scilicet officium mortuorum, matutinae de omnibus sanctis, infantes in dormitorium uadant et in capitulum reuertantur. Ad laudes sicut aliis diebus pulsetur
unum signum, factaque oratione supra formas pulsentur
omnia signa, quibus cessantibus incipiant matutinas
laudes.[4] Psalmi Dominus regnauit et reliqui. Primam
antiphonam ebdomadarius incipiat. Capitulum Paulus
seruus Christi Iesu.[5] Sacerdos indutus alba incenset
altaria. Preces Ego dixi, Domine.[6] Psalmum unum
Miserere mei Deus. Commemoratio sanctorum, prima,
93 psalmi, letania. Dicta tercia et / missa matutinali,
signum capituli diutius solito [7] est pulsandum, ut cunctis
occupationibus praetermissis ad initium capituli omnes
conueniant, ut cum Christi Domini nostri natiuitas
pronunciatur prosternant se cuncti in terram, lector etiam

---

[1] Bernard of Cluny II iii 285
[2] Bernard of Cluny II iv 286 ; cf. Porée, *Histoire de l'Abbaye du Bec* II
297.   For the thirty (Gradual) psalms, see above, p. 7.
[3] cf. Albers II 36
[4] Albers II 36. ' Debet . . . secretarius . . . Laudes significare prius
uno signo sicut privatis diebus. Facta autem oratione super genua, non
super formas, sonet totum classicum.' Bernard of Cluny II iv 286 :
' Ad Laudes pulsatur signum, sed quod aliis privatis diebus pulsari solet
. . . qua [oratione] facta pulsantur omnia signa . . . hebdomadarius
incipit primam antiphonam.' The *formae* were portable desks or benches
placed in the middle of the choir between the two rows of stalls. Later
they were replaced by permanent choir furniture.
[5] Romans I 1 ; cf. *HB* I 17
[6] For these *v.* Tolhurst, *HB* VI 40, 157
[7] Bernard of Cluny II iv 287 : ' Ad ipsum Capitulum prolixius scilla
pulsatur . . . et cum Dominica Nativitas . . . pronunciatur, cuncti in
faciem cadunt.' The solemn chanting of the Christmas martyrology on

and the first and second nocturns shall be of the Sunday ; the third nocturn and Lauds shall be of the vigil. After the first collect there shall be a commemoration of the Sunday ; the Morrow Mass shall be of the Sunday, the High Mass of the vigil.[1] On any other day save Sunday the bells shall be rung as on ferial days, and the Thirty Psalms shall be said.[2] Two brethren, not in albs, shall sing the invitatory. The gospel of the vigil shall be read, together with the chapter of the second nocturn, the prayer and versicle. All else shall be as on previous days,[3] that is, the office of the dead, and Lauds of All Saints, and the children shall go to the dormitory and return to the chapter-house. For Lauds as on other days one bell shall be rung, and when the prayer has been said by the monks kneeling at their benches all the bells shall be rung, and when they cease Lauds shall begin.[4] The psalms are *Dominus regnauit* and the rest. The hebdomadary shall begin the first antiphon ; the chapter is *Paulus, seruus Christi Jesu*.[5] A priest in an alb shall incense the altars. The *preces Ego dixi, Domine*[6] and the psalm *Miserere mei Deus* shall be said, with a commemoration of the Saints, Prime, the psalms and the litany. When Terce has been said, and the Morrow Mass, the bell for chapter is to be rung for longer than usual,[7] that all may be present at the beginning of chapter abandoning all other occupations, so that when the birth of Christ our Lord is announced all may prostrate themselves on the ground ; the reader also prostrates before the lectern and all pray until, his prayer ended, the

---

Christmas Eve is still customary wherever the Office is celebrated in choir. The entry read daily is always that referring to the following day ; on Christmas Eve, after the date of Our Lord's birth, by Hebrew, Greek and Roman computation, has been given, with the name of the reigning emperor etc., and the statement that all the world was then at peace, the Nativity at Bethlehem is announced in a loud tone, while all kneel.

ante analogium, pariter orantes usque dum qui ordinem
tenet, oratione facta, erigat se. Pronuncietur euangelium, et ex eo sermo agatur.[1] Post sextam facto
interuallo pulsetur signum ; conueniant fratres in aecclesiam ; orationem communiter faciant ; letania minime
dicatur ; induantur missam celebraturi, sacerdos honorifice,[2] leuita dalmatica, duo subdiaconi tunicis, unus ad
prophetiam[3] et alter ad epistolam ; duo albis ad repon-
sorium ; cantor ebdomadarius cappa ad chorum ; tres
conuersi, unus ad thuribulum, duo ad candelabra ;
pulsetur classicum[4] ; ad canonem supra formas prosternantur[5] ; tabulae refectorii coopertae.[6]

IN NOCTE dominicae natiuitatis omnia signa primum
pulsentur. Ad inuitatorium quatuor fratres in cappis.
In unoquoque nocturno ad terciam lectionem duo
sacerdotes cappis induti duo thuribula circumferant,
primo duobus altaribus maiori et matutinali, dehinc
fratribus in choro sedentibus. In tercio nocturno pronuncientur euangelia haec : Liber generationis, Exiit
edictum, Pastores, In principio.[7] Quibus expletis cum
responsoriis suis incipiat dominus abbas Te Deum laudamus. Quo dicto, legat euangelium Liber generationis.
Dicta oratione incipiat cantor antiphonam O beata infantia. Quam canentes eant ad altare sanctae Mariae,[8] et

---

[1] Albers II 37. On ferial days the discourse in chapter was based
upon the section of the Rule just read ; on feast days the gospel of the
day gave a text.
[2] In Bernard's Cluniac uses the particular type of vestment is specified ;
for this Lanfranc sometimes substitutes a general term as here, while sometimes it would appear that he deleted an inappropriate word without
substituting another (cf. *infra*, p. 13 *n.* 3).
[3] This lesson, from Isaias lxii.1 (cf. *Missale Westmon.* I 32) does not
occur in the Roman Missal.
[4] The *classicum* was the peal of all the bells.
[5] Albers IV 9
[6] Albers II 37

superior rises. The gospel of the day shall be read, and a sermon made upon it.[1] After Sext, and an interval, the bell shall ring and the brethren shall gather in church ; prayer shall be made in common ; no litany shall be said ; the celebrants shall vest as follows : the priest in a rich vestment,[2] the deacon in a dalmatic, two subdeacons in tunicles, one for the prophecy[3] and the other for the epistle ; two others in albs shall sing the responsory ; the cantor of the week with a cope to lead the choir ; three converses, one with the thurible and two with candles. A peal of bells[4] shall be rung, and at the canon they shall prostrate themselves at their benches ;[5] the refectory tables shall be draped.[6]

ON CHRISTMAS NIGHT all the bells shall ring before the Office. There shall be four brothers in copes for the invitatory. In each nocturn at the third lesson two priests in copes shall bear two thuribles and incense first the high altar and Morrow Mass altar, and then the brethren seated in choir. In the third nocturn the following gospels shall be read : *Liber generationis ; Exiit edictum ; Pastores ; In principio.*[7] When these are finished with their responsories the lord abbot shall begin the *Te Deum.* When this has been said, he shall read the gospel *Liber generationis.* When the prayer has been said the cantor shall begin the antiphon *O beata infantia.* While they sing this they shall proceed to the Lady altar,[8]

---

[7] Matt. i.1 ; Luke ii.1 ; Luke ii.15 ; John i.1. The three last are the gospels read in the three Christmas Masses.

[8] Bernard of Cluny II v 288 ; Bec customs (Porée II 298). At Cluny the procession went to the altar of Our Lady ; there is no procession in the old Cluny customs in Albers II, but in those of Farfa (ibid. I 10) the antiphon *O magnum mysterium* or *Sancta et immaculata virginitas* is sung. The Hyde breviary (I 20v) has the antiphon *O mundi domina.*

ibi dictis matutinis de omnibus sanctis uadant in dormitorium. Deinde pulsetur unum de maioribus signis,
sicut pulsari solet skilla in duodecim lectionibus post
capitulum ante matutinalem missam. Tunc fratres qui
ad missam induendi sunt uadant ad locum constitutum,
ubi sit optimus ignis a famulis camerarii praepara-
tus [1]; baccilia quoque et manutergia et aqua calida ad
94 abluendas manus. Hac sola uice antequam lauent / pec-
tunt capita sua.[2] Alio enim tempore prius lauant, postea
pectinant. Post haec pergant in aecclesiam, et facta
oratione induant se ad celebrandam missam, sacerdos,
leuita dalmatica, duo subdiaconi tunicis,[3] unus ad
prophetiam et alter ad epistolam; ad responsorium et
alleluia quot cantor praeceperit, et hi in cappis; tres
conuersi, tres cantores in choro, ante quos duo candelabra
cum cereis accensis; infantes omnes.[4] Pulsetur classicum,
et post inchoetur missa,[5] Gloria in excelsis Deo et sequen-
tia [6] canantur. Celebrata missa exeat sacerdos, et qui ad
missam seruierunt, et qui in choro albis uel cappis induti
fuerunt; quibus disuestitis, et pulsatis omnibus signis,
cantent matutinas laudes. His ita expletis, factaque
commemoratione de sancta Anastasia,[7] et dictis familiaribus psalmis, reuertantur ad strata. Apparente autem
luce, pulsetur ut supra unum de maioribus signis. Quo
audito expedite surgentes omnes, et abluti manus et

[1] Bernard of Cluny II v 288 : 'introducuntur famuli a Camerario
cum bacilibus et manutergiis ut faciant optimum ignem.'
[2] Presumably to ensure absolute cleanliness when beginning Mass ; on
other days the ministers, having recently made their toilet, would have no
need to comb their hair.
[3] Albers II 38 : 'sacerdos induatur alba cum auro, diaconus dalmatica,
duo subdiaconi tunicis.' Bernard of Cluny II v 288 : 'sacerdos rubea
casula et aurata.'
[4] 'In albs' seems to be Lanfranc's meaning, but the words are missing in
the text. See Bernard of Cluny II v 288 : 'etiam albis revestiuntur.'
[5] Albers II 38
[6] There is no sequence in the Roman missal. The *Missale Westmon.*
I 35, gives one beginning *Nato canunt omnia.*

and having said Lauds of All Saints there they go to the dormitory. Then one of the larger bells shall be rung, as the little bell is wont to be rung on feast of twelve lessons after chapter before the Morrow Mass. Then the brethren who are to vest for Mass shall go to the appointed place, where there shall be a good fire prepared by the chamberlain's servants,[1] with basins and towels and warm water for washing the hands. On this occasion alone they comb their hair before washing[2]; at all other times they wash first and then comb their hair. After this they shall proceed into the church and, after praying, the celebrant and ministers vest for Mass[3]; the deacon in a dalmatic, two subdeacons in tunicles, one for the prophecy and the other for the epistle ; for the responsory and the *alleluia* there shall be as many as the cantor orders, and these shall be in copes. There shall be three converses and three cantors in choir, and in front of them two candlesticks with lighted tapers ; all the children shall be in albs.[4] The peal of bells shall ring, and then Mass shall begin.[5] The *Gloria in excelsis* shall be sung, and the sequence.[6] When Mass is done the priest and ministers shall retire, together with those in choir who were in albs or copes ; when they have unvested, and all the bells have been rung, they shall sing Lauds. When these have been done, and a commemoration has been made of St Anastasia,[7] and the psalms for relatives have been said, they shall return to bed. When day breaks, one of the large bells shall be rung as before. When it is heard all shall rise speedily, and those who are to vest for Mass shall wash their

---

[7] The second Mass *in aurora* of Christmas Day still retains a commemoration of St Anastasia, at whose church under the Palatine the *statio* for that Mass was held ; cf. *Dict. Archéol. chrét.* (Cabrol et Leclercq), *s.v.*

facies qui ad missam induendi sunt, ueniant in oratorium,
factaque oratione induantur sicut ad priorem missam.
Ad quam missam, antequam incipiatur, pulsetur classicum. Expleta autem missa, uadant in dormitorium
calciare se ; postea solito more loti et pexi, faciant in
oratorio orationes tres solitas. Dicta tercia omnes induti
cappis faciant processionem.[1] Ad quam terciam dicatur
antiphona Hodie intacta virgo.[2] Cum autem venitur ad
locum ubi dicitur Ipsum adoremus, ab omnibus flexis
ad terram genibus supplicetur, et hoc seruetur quoties-
cunque praedicta antiphona in monasterio cantatur.

TRES SEQUENTES festiuitates, id est, beati Stephani,
Ioannis apostoli, sanctorum Innocentium, uno et eodem
modo celebrentur. Ecclesia his tribus diebus, sicut in
die dominicae natiuitatis, ornata permaneat. Pulsentur
signa, accendantur luminaria, agantur caetera omnia
sicut in aliis duplicibus, et secundae dignitatis festiui-
95 tatibus, de quibus poste/rius dicendum est. Ad vesperas
super psalmos imponant antiphonas de ipsis festiuitatibus, quibus et quas cantor praeceperit. Transactis
primis diebus de ipsis festiuitatibus nulla commemoratio
fiat, nisi in extremis ipsarum festiuitatum diebus ; et
tunc tantum tres lectiones fiant. Per totam ebdomadam
missa matutinalis Puer natus [3] ; maior in quinta die
Dominus dixit ; in crastino introitus Puer natus, et quod
sequitur de Lux fulgebit.[4] Hi duo dies agantur sicut
in priuatis duodecim lectionibus, nisi quod tres lectiones
fiant. Pronuncientur uicissim in eis euangelia dominicae
natiuitatis. Festiuitas sancti Sylvestri agatur sicut

----

[1] Bernard of Cluny II v 289
[2] *HB* I 21
[3] Bernard of Cluny II vi 291. *Puer natus est* is the introit of the Third
Mass of Christmas Day.
[4] The fifth day, i.e. 29 December, when the office is of the octave

hands and faces ; they shall go into the oratory and having prayed shall vest as at the earlier Mass. At this Mass, before it begins, a peal of great bells is rung. When Mass is done they shall go to the dormitory to put on their shoes ; then, having washed and combed themselves in the usual way, they shall say the Three Prayers in church as usual, and when Terce has been said all shall make a procession in copes.[1] At Terce the antiphon *Hodie intacta virgo* [2] shall be said. When they come to the words *Ipsum adoremus* all shall kneel down in worship, and this shall be done as often as the aforesaid antiphon is sung in church.

The THREE FOLLOWING FEASTS, that is, of blessed Stephen, John the apostle and the Holy Innocents, shall all be kept in one and the same way. The church shall remain decorated for these three days as on Christmas Day. The bells are rung, lights are burnt and all else is done as on other doubles and feasts of the second rank, as shall be described later. At Vespers the cantor shall appoint those who are to intone the antiphons of the feasts, and shall decide which are to be said. When the feast days have passed there shall be no commemoration of them save on the last day of their octaves, and then only three lessons shall be read. Throughout the week the Morrow Mass shall be *Puer natus* [3] ; the High Mass on the fifth day *Dominus dixit* [4] ; on the next day the introit shall be *Puer natus*, and the rest shall be taken from *Lux fulgebit*. These two days shall be kept as ordinary days of twelve lessons, save that only three lessons shall be read. The gospels of Christmas shall be read on them in turn. The feast of St Sylvester shall be kept as an

---

of Christmas. *Dominus dixit*—the introit of the Midnight Mass ; *Lux fulgebit*—the introit of the Aurora Mass.

priuata festiuitas duodecim lectionum. Tercium nocturnum et laudes de dominica natiuitate : officium Dum medium silentium¹ ante epyphaniam dicatur. Circumcisio Domini celebretur sicut una de tribus superioribus festiuitatibus, excepto quod aula monasterii non ornatur, quae quinta dominicae natiuitatis die disparari debet.

In crastino post circumcisionem Domini incipiant legere epistolas sancti Pauli.² Post nocturnas agant officia mortuorum, postea pulsetur signum, cantent matutinas laudes, et matutinas de omnibus sanctis. Postea reuertantur ad lectos. Hoc modo agatur usque ad octauas epyphaniae, nisi fuerit festiuitas duodecim lectionum.

In uigilia epyphaniae non ieiunetur.³ Officium ad missam Lux fulgebit. Ad uesperas super psalmos una antiphona Stella ista.⁴ In crastino ad inuitatorium tres in cappis.⁵ Processio non agatur ipsa die, nisi dies dominica sit. Tunc enim fit in albis ante terciam per claustrum, sacerdote eunte per officinas, sicut mos est dominicis diebus.⁶ Ad uesperas dicantur antiphonae et psalmi usque ad capitulum sicut in die natiuitatis. Ultima octauarum die agatur totum seruitium noctis de ipsis octauis, commemoratio tantum de sancto Hilario, et missa matutinalis ; uesperae usque ad capitulum sicut in die epyphaniae.

Post octauam diem epyphaniae inchoentur respon-
96 soria de / psalmis.⁷ Psalmodia uero, et caeteraom nia, agantur nocte ac die sicut ante natiuitatem.

¹ Now the introit of the Mass of the Sunday within the octave of Christmas. cf. Bernard of Cluny II vi 292, where, after discussing various uses he adds : 'hoc providendum est, ut ante Epiphaniam officium *Dum medium silentium* dicatur.'
² Albers II 8, xii   ³ Albers II 39
⁴ Now the fourth antiphon of Vespers and the fifth of Lauds in the monastic breviary. In the Hyde Breviary (I 41v) it occurs as a Magnificat antiphon.   ⁵ Albers II 39 (four in copes)

ordinary feast of twelve lessons. The third nocturn and Lauds shall be of Christmas ; the Mass *Dum medium silentium* [1] shall be said until the Epiphany. The Circumcision of the Lord shall be celebrated as one of the three feasts mentioned above, save that the nave of the church is not decorated ; the decorations should be removed on the fifth day after Christmas.

ON THE DAY AFTER THE CIRCUMCISION they shall begin to read the epistles of St Paul.[2] After the night office the office of the dead shall be said, then a bell shall ring and they shall sing Lauds and Lauds of All Saints. Afterwards they shall return to bed. Thus shall it be done until the octave of the Epiphany, unless a feast of twelve lessons occurs.

THE VIGIL OF THE EPIPHANY is not kept as a fast.[3] The Mass is *Lux fulgebit*. At Vespers the psalms are sung under a single antiphon *Stella ista*.[4] On the following day there shall be three in copes at the invitatory.[5] There shall be no procession on the feast, unless it fall on a Sunday. Then it is made through the cloister before Terce, with the brethren in albs, a priest going through the monastery buildings, as is customary on Sundays.[6] At Vespers the antiphons and psalms before the chapter shall be sung as on Christmas Day. On the last day of the octave the whole night office is of the octave, with only a commemoration of St Hilary, as is also the Morrow Mass ; Vespers till the chapter are as on the Epiphany.

After the octave of the Epiphany the responsories from the psalms shall be begun.[7] The psalmody and all else by night and day shall be as before Christmas.

---

[6] i.e. with holy water   [7] *HB* I 49v

UIGILIA purificationis sanctae Mariae dicantur ad
uesperas antiphonae O admirabile, et reliquae [1] ; psalmi
de ipsa feria Dixit Dominus cum caeteris, capitulum
Ecce ego mitto angelum ; in crastino cantica Populus
qui ambulabat.[2] Ad terciam sint omnes albis induti.
Dicta tercia ponatur ante altare tapetum, ubi supra
ponantur candelae, quas benedicat sacerdos ; aqua
benedicta aspergat et incenset, alba et stola indutus.[3]
Postea custos diuidat eas singulis singulas tribuens. Cum
autem ceperint accendi cantor incipiat antiphonam
Lumen ad reuelationem.[4] Qua dicta, et cum uersibus
cantici Nunc dimittis, quantum cantor satis esse perspexerit,[5] repetita, exeant ad processionem, cantore incipiente antiphonam Aue gratia, et alias si necesse
fuerit ; per maiores monasterii portas introeant, ante
crucifixum stationem faciant.[6] Finito cantu, quem inceperant, cantore statim incipiente antiphonam Cum
inducerent, canentes chorum intrent, pulsentur signa,
et missam celebrent. Post refectionem in claustro sedeant
donec seruitores de refectorio exeant.[7] Qui cum exierint,
et monasterium ingressi fuerint, pulsentur duo maiora
signa, et canatur nona. Qua cantata exeat prior et
sonet cimbalum, et postea uadant in refectorium.[8] Hanc
consuetudinem habeant usque ad dominicam palmarum,
exceptis ieiuniorum diebus. Hac die inchoandus est
psalmus Ad Dominum cum tribularer,[9] qui pro uigilia
mortuorum dicendus est usque ad kalendas Novembris.
Ad uesperas antiphonam Tecum principium, psalmum

---

[1] HB III 209v
[2] Then, as now, the Christmas canticle (Isaias IX 2ff.).
[3] Albers II 40–1   [4] Missale Westmon. II 761
[5] Bernard of Cluny II ix 297
[6] i.e. the crucifix at the entrance to the choir.
[7] Albers II 41
[8] For the drink in common, roughly the equivalent of afternoon tea.
[9] Ps. 119 (120). cf. Albers II 32. At Cluny the Gradual psalms
were not recited before Septuagesima ; cf. Lanfranc's preface, supra, p. 2.

ON THE VIGIL OF THE PURIFICATION of our Lady the antiphons at Vespers shall be *O admirabile* with the rest [1] ; the psalms of the feria *Dixit Dominus* with the rest ; the chapter *Ecce ego mitto angelum*. On the following day, the canticle is *Populus qui ambulabat*.[2] At Terce all shall wear albs ; when Terce is done a carpet shall be spread before the altar, on which the candles to be blessed by the priest shall be placed ; he shall sprinkle them with holy water, and incense them, vested in alb and stole.[3] Afterwards the warden of the church shall distribute them to all. When they begin to be lighted the cantor shall begin the antiphon *Lumen ad reuelationem* [4] ; when this is finished, and repeated with as many verses of the canticle *Nunc dimittis* as the cantor sees to be needful,[5] they shall go out in procession, the cantor beginning the antiphon *Ave gratia*, and such others as may be necessary. They shall enter the church by the great door and halt before the crucifix [6] ; when the piece that they have begun is finished, the cantor shall immediately begin the antiphon *Cum inducerent*, and they shall enter the choir singing. The bells shall ring, and Mass be celebrated. After their meal they shall sit in the cloister until the servers leave the refectory.[7] When they have come out and entered the church two great bells shall ring, and None be sung. When None is done the prior shall go out and sound the gong, and then they shall go into the refectory.[8] They shall follow this manner until Palm Sunday, save for fast days.

On this day (Feb. 2) the psalm *Ad Dominum cum tribularer clamaui* is begun [9] for Matins of the dead, and is continued till the first of November. At Vespers the first antiphon is *Tecum principium* and psalm *Dixit Dominus* ; the second antiphon *Redemptionem* and the psalm *Confitebor* ; the third antiphon *Exortum est* and

Dixit Dominus ; antiphonam Redemptionem, psalmum
Confitebor ; antiphonam Exortum est, psalmum Beatus
uir ; antiphonam De fructu, psalmum Memento.¹ Priuatis diebus post uesperas agant uigiliam mortuorum, nisi
in crastino sit festiuitas duodecim lectionum. Post
nocturna usque ad quintam feriam ante pascha, priuatis
97 diebus dicant solitos duos / psalmos,² cum precibus et
collecta ; postea Exultabunt Domino.³ Dehinc matutinas
de omnibus sanctis, reliqua omnia sicut ante natiuitatem
Domini.

DOMINICA prima septuagesimae alleluia ex toto
dimittatur ; loco alleluia per singulas horas Laus tibi,
Domine, rex aeternae gloriae, usque ad pascalis uigiliae
uesperas dicatur.⁴ Hystoria In principio fecit Deus ⁵
canatur ; quinque libri Moysi et Iosue et iudicum et
Ruth ad legendum ponantur dominicis diebus, et
caeteris duodecim lectionibus usque ad pascha. Capitulum ad primam Domine, miserere nostri ⁶ dicatur ;
Gloria in excelsis Deo et Ite missa est usque ad pascale
sabbatum minime dicatur ; dalmatica et tunica ad
missam usque ad coenam Domini minime induantur ; ⁷
loco earum casulis ministri uestiantur.⁸ Ipso die adipem
comedant ; deinceps usque ad pascha abstineant.⁹

FERIA QUARTA in capite ieiunii capitula Conuertimini
ad me ¹⁰ et caetera quae sequuntur. Post sextam reuertantur in claustrum locuturi ; cum tempus fuerit pulsetur unum de mediocribus signis, quo pulsato statim
silentium fiat in claustro. Discalcient se,¹¹ et pergant

¹ Ps. 109 (120), 110 (111), 111 (112), 131 (132) ; cf. *HB* III 212v
² i.e. *Ad Dominum*, 119 (120) and *Voce mea*, 142 ; cf. *HB* VI 110
³ The first antiphon of Lauds of the Dead.
⁴ Albers II 41. The *Alleluia* was probably sung for the last time (as
now) at Vespers on the preceding Saturday, but the exact moment varied
at different houses, cf. Tolhurst, *HB* VI 232–3.

psalm *Beatus vir*, the fourth *De fructu* and the psalm *Memento*.[1] On ferial days after Vespers they shall sing Vigils of the dead, unless a feast of twelve lessons fall on the morrow. After the night office until Maundy Thursday on ferial days they shall say the usual two psalms [2] with *preces* and collect. After this the versicle *Exultabunt Domino* [3]; then Lauds of All Saints and the rest as before Christmas.

ON SEPTUAGESIMA SUNDAY *alleluia* shall be wholly discontinued ; in its place at each hour shall be said *Laus tibi, Domine, rex aeternae gloriae*, until Vespers on Holy Saturday.[4] The lesson *In principio fecit Deus* [5] shall be sung ; the Pentateuch, and the books of Josue, Judges and Ruth shall be set to be read on Sundays and other days of twelve lessons until Easter. The chapter at Prime shall be *Domine miserere nostri*.[6] The *Gloria in excelsis* and *Ite missa est* shall never be said till Holy Saturday. The dalmatic and tunicle shall never be worn at Mass until Maundy Thursday [7] ; in their place the ministers shall wear chasubles.[8] On Septuagesima itself they shall eat lard ; thenceforward they shall abstain from it till Easter.[9]

ON ASH WEDNESDAY the chapter *Conuertimini ad me* [10] and the rest shall be said. After Sext they shall return to the cloister for speech ; when the hour is come one of the small bells shall be rung, and silence fall at once in the cloister. They shall take off their shoes [11] and go to

---

[5] Genesis I 1
[6] Albers I 27 ; Isaias xxxiii.2 ; cf. *HB* V 452
[7] Albers II 42
[8] The 'folded chasubles' ; cf. *supra*, p. 9 *n*. 2
[9] Bernard of Cluny II xii 300 ; where 'ad Ps. dimittitur' in Migne is clearly a misprint for *adeps*.
[10] Joel II 12 ; cf. Tolhurst, *HB* I 67
[11] So as to be barefoot when receiving the ashes

abluere manus, et sic uadant in aecclesiam sine ulla mora, faciantque orationem unam communiter. Qua facta, pulsentur duo signa inchoante infante Exurge Domine [1] ; psalmus Deus, auribus nostris [2] ; his expletis dicat sacerdos Ostende nobis Domine ; sequatur Kyrieleison, Pater noster, Et ne nos ; psalmus Deus misereatur nostri [3] ; capitulum Et ueniat super nos ; collecta pro peccatis, Exaudi quaesumus, Domine, supplicum preces. Post haec benedicat sacerdos cineres stolam tantum habens, et sparsa desuper aqua benedicta mittat cineres super capita fratrum dicendo : Memento quia cinis [4] es, et in cinerem reuerteris. Interim cantetur antiphona Immutemus,[5] cum uersibus psalmi Deus misereatur nostri uno aut pluribus si opus fuerit. Hoc facto exeant ad 98 processionem, cantantes has / antiphonas Exaudi nos ; Iuxta uestibulum.[6] Quae duae antiphonae, id est, Exaudi nos, et Iuxta uestibulum, ad omnes processiones quadragesimae quae quarta et sexta feria fiunt eodem ordine cantentur. Percantatis antiphonis, incipiant duo infantes letaniam ; hoc ordine agatur processio sexta feria, quae sequitur caput ieiunii, et quarta et sexta feria per totam quadragesimam, usque ad quartam feriam ante pascalem festiuitatem, nisi festiuitas duodecim lectionum in ipsis feriis euenerit. Notandum quia si in capite ieiunii festiuitas duodecim lectionum euenerit, non celebratur ipsa die, set differtur in crastinum.

---

[1] Porée, *Histoire du Bec* II 592, where in an extract from MS Bibl. Nat. lat., 1208, 56v and 57, a *puer* intones the *Exsurge*.
[2] Ps. 43 (44). For this and what follows *v. Missale Westmon.* II 549ff.
[3] Ps. 66 (67)

wash their hands, and then go into the church without delay and make prayer together. When this is done two bells shall ring and a child intone *Exurge, Domine* [1] with the psalm *Deus, auribus nostris audiuimus* [2]; then the priest shall say *Ostende nobis, Domine*, and there shall follow *Kyrie eleison, Pater noster, Et ne nos*, and the psalm *Deus misereatur nostri*, [3] with the chapter *Et ueniat super nos*, with the prayer for remission of sins, *Exaudi quaesumus, Domine, supplicum preces*. After this the priest shall bless the ashes vested only in a stole, and when he has sprinkled holy water he shall put ashes on the heads of the brethren, saying ' Remember that thou art ashes, [4] and to ashes thou shalt return.' Meanwhile the antiphon shall be chanted, *Immutemur*, [5] with one or more verses of the psalm *Deus misereatur nostri* as may be needed. After this they shall go out in procession, singing the antiphons *Exaudi nos* and *Iuxta uestibulum*, [6] and these two antiphons shall be sung in this order at all Wednesday and Friday processions in Lent. When the antiphons have been sung two of the children shall begin the litany. In this manner shall a procession be made on the Friday after Ash Wednesday and Wednesdays and Fridays throughout Lent until Wednesday in Holy Week, unless a feast of twelve lessons come on one of these ferias. Note also that if a feast of twelve lessons fall on Ash Wednesday, it is not celebrated then but on the following day.

---

[4] The Westminster Missal and the Roman Missal have *pulvis* (cf. Genesis III 19).

[5] Albers II 42. Lanfranc reads (with others) *immutemus habitum*. Other liturgical books read *immutemur habitu* with the modern Gradual.

[6] Bernard of Cluny II xiii 302

Dominica prima quadragesimae inuitatorium duo in albis.[1] Post completorium suspendatur cortina inter chorum et altare.[2] Feria secunda ante terciam debent esse coopertae crux, coronae, capsae, textus qui imagines deforis habent.[3] Priusquam fratres intrent capitulum, custos librorum debet habere congregatos libros in capitulo super tapetum extensum,[4] praeter eos, qui praeterito anno ad legendum dati sunt ; illos enim intrantes capitulum ferre debent, quisque suum in manu sua. De qua re praemoniti esse debent a praedicto librorum custode in capitulo praecedentis diei. Legatur sententia regulae sancti Benedicti de obseruantia quadragesimae.[5] Facto igitur ex ea sermone praedictus librorum custos legat breue, qualiter praeterito anno fratres habuerunt libros. Cum uero audierit unusquisque nomen suum pronunciari, reddat librum, qui ad legendum sibi alio anno fuerat commendatus. Et qui cognouerit se non perlegisse librum quem recepit, prostratus culpam dicat, et indulgentiam petat. Iterum praedictus librorum custos unicuique fratri alium librum tribuat ad legendum ; distributis per ordinem libris, praefatus librorum custos in eodem capitulo inbreuiet nomina librorum et eos recipientium. Si hac die festiuitas duodecim lectionum euenerit, legantur duae lectiones in capitulo, una de euangelio, et altera de obseruantia quadragesimae ;[6] altera statim legatur post alteram ; lecta poste/riore lectione tunc primum dicat lector : Tu autem, Domine. Ipsa die incipiant preces Oremus pro omni gradu

---

[1] Albers II 43
[2] Albers I 33 ; Bernard of Cluny I lxiii 257
[3] Albers II 44. This is now done on the Saturday before Passion Sunday.
[4] See Appendix A, p. 150
[5] *Regula* XLIX. The direction as to the issue of books occurs in ch. xlviii 35ff. ' In this season of Lent all shall receive a book from the

On the first Sunday of Lent the invitatory shall be sung by two in albs.[1] After Compline a curtain shall be hung between the choir and the altar.[2] On Monday before Terce the crucifix, hanging circlets and reliquaries, and gospel books with images upon them, shall be covered.[3] Before the brethren go in to chapter, the librarian should have all the books save those that were given out for reading the previous year collected on a carpet in the chapter-house[4]; last year's books should be carried in by those who have had them, and they are to be warned by the librarian in chapter the previous day of this. The passage from the Rule of St Benedict concerning the observance of Lent shall be read,[5] and when a sermon has been made on this the librarian shall read out a list of the books which the brethren had the previous year. When each hears his name read out he shall return the book which was given to him to read, and anyone who is conscious that he has not read in full the book he received shall confess his fault prostrate and ask for pardon. Then the aforesaid librarian shall give to each of the brethren another book to read, and when the books have been distributed in order he shall at that same chapter write a list of the books and those who have received them. If a feast of twelve lessons falls on this day two lessons shall be read in chapter, one from the gospel and the other on the observance of Lent[6]; the one shall be read directly after the other, and not till the second has been read shall the reader say *Tu autem, Domine.* On this day shall the prayers begin ' for every degree of the Church,' the prostrate psalms,

---

library (*bibliotheca* = book-press), which they shall read from beginning to end ; these books are to be given out at the beginning of Lent.'
[6] Bernard of Cluny II xiii 304

aecclesiae ; psalmos prostratos, id est, septem poeni-
tentiales, et septem primos graduum,[1] binos quidem,
unum hinc, et alterum inde per singulas horas usque ad
uesperas ; ad uesperas uero quatuor cum capitulis et
collectis pro peccatis, adiungentes in fine, Et ad beneficia
recolenda, quibus nos instaurare dignatus es, tribue
uenire gaudentes.[2] Hac die incipiant absconsam portare
ad secundam tantum lectionem. Tribus diebus, id est,
secunda feria, quarta, et sexta usque ad pasca,[3] nec
pulsetur tabula post capitulum, nec loquantur in claustro.
Quarta et sexta feria post sextam, antequam de choro
exeant, dicant Deus, auribus nostris.[4] In his duabus
feriis post nonam sedeant in claustro, factoque paruo
interuallo, pulset secretarius unum de mediocribus signis ;
tunc discalcient se omnes, et lauent manus, ueniantque
in chorum, et facta oratione inchoet infans antiphonam
Exurge, Domine, adiuua nos. Pulsentur duo signa ;
dicat sacerdos Ostende nobis, Domine ; subsequantur
Kyrieleison, Pater noster. Psalmus quarta feria Deus
misereatur nostri ; sexta feria, Deus in adiutorium meum.[5]
Item sacerdos Et ueniat super nos ; oratio pro peccatis.
Postea inchoet cantor antiphonam, et eant ad processionem. Letania ut supra.[6] Ad hanc processionem
nullus uadat calciatus, nisi sacerdos et leuita. Si quis
pro aliqua infirmitate nudis pedibus ire nequiuerit, de
processione remaneat. Redeuntes de processione nullus
praesumat se calciare sine licentia. Expleta missa et
facta oratione, ad uesperas lauent pedes et manus, et
canant uesperas.

---

[1] Bernard of Cluny II iii 303. The Penitential Psalms are Ps. 6,
31 (32), 37 (38), 50 (51), 101 (102), 129 (130), 142 (143).
[2] cf. Tolhurst, *HB* VI 100–101
[3] Albers II 44
[4] Ps. 43 (44). Albers I 35, has : 'et alia que restant ad ipsum
servitium pertinentia.'

that is, the seven penitential psalms and the first seven gradual psalms.[1] Two are said, one from each group, at every hour till Vespers ; at Vespers four are said with their chapters and collects for the remission of sins, with the addition ' and grant that we may come in joy to the commemoration of the blessings with which thou hast deigned to renew us.' [2] On this day they shall begin to bear the lantern at the second lesson only. On three days of the week, that is, Monday, Wednesday and Friday,[3] until Easter, the board is not rapped after chapter, nor is there talking in the cloister. On Wednesday and Friday after Sext before they leave the choir they shall recite *Deus, auribus nostris*.[4] On these two days they shall sit in the cloister after None, and after a short interval the sacristan shall ring one of the small bells ; then all shall take off their shoes, wash their hands and go to choir, and after prayer a child shall begin the antiphon *Exurge, Domine, adjuua nos*. Two bells shall be rung and the priest shall say *Ostende nobis, Domine*, followed by *Kyrie eleison* and *Pater noster*. The psalm on Wednesday shall be *Deus misereatur nostri*, and on Friday *Deus in adiutorium meum*,[5] and the priest shall say *Et veniat super nos* and the prayer for remission of sins. After this the cantor shall begin the antiphon, and they shall go in procession. The litany shall be said as above.[6] No-one shall walk shod in this procession save priest and deacon. If anyone by reason of some infirmity cannot go barefoot he shall stay away from the procession. On the return no-one shall presume to put on his shoes without permission. When Mass is done and they have prayed, let them wash their feet and hands for Vespers, and say Vespers.

---

[5] Ps. 66 (67), 69 (70)   [6] *supra*, p. 5

SI FESTIUITATEM celebrari in quadragesima contigerit,
praecedente * die dum canitur Agnus Dei ad maiorem
missam colligatur cortina,[1] et auferantur de choroformae,
quae auferri solent in duodecim lectionibus.   Missa
finita agatur oratio uespertina sicut sabbato.   Post
100 collectam de festiui/tate dicatur antiphona de feria, cum
Gloria Patri ; psalmi prostrati minime dicantur ; post
uesperas de omnibus sanctis canantur uesperae mortuorum ;   uigilia mortuorum minime agatur [2] ;   in die
festiuitatis post matutina de omnibus sanctis dicantur
matutina mortuorum.   Postea reuertantur ad lectos.
Post primam, dictis consuetis psalmis familiaribus cum
capitulis et collectis suis, dicantur septem psalmi cum
letania.   Per singulas horas usque ad uesperas, a prima
incipientes, dicant psalmum Inclina, Domine, pro his
quos prostrati dicturi erant.[3]   Post capitulum sedeant in
claustro cum silentio usque dum pulsetur signum ad
terciam ;   infantes quoque post capitulum suum des-
cendentes de dormitorio, hoc interuallo in scola sua
sedeant et legant.   Totam diem solenniter agant ;
utraeque missae ad maius altare celebrentur.   Ad
missam ieiunii nec letania praemittatur, nec ad canonem
supra formas curuentur.   Ad uesperas, nisi in crastino
sit festiuitas duodecim lectionum, inter signa dicant
Deus, auribus nostris [4] ;   post collectam festiuitatis, collectam de feria cum Gloria Patri ; post uesperas de
omnibus sanctis, uesperas pro defunctis.   Uigilia mortuorum ipsa die minime agatur.   Post completorium
cortina extendatur, et formae in chorum referantur.

---

* praecedenti A B
[1] Bernard of Cluny II xiii 305 ; I lxiii (during the *Pax Domini*)
[2] Albers I. 38
[3] Ps. 85 (86) ; cf. Tolhurst, *HB* VI 168
[4] Ps. 43 (44)

IF IT HAPPEN that a feast occur in Lent, on the previous day when *Agnus Dei* is sung at the High Mass, the curtain is pulled back [1] and the desks taken away which are wont to be taken away from choir on feasts of twelve lessons. When Mass is done the evening prayer is made as on Saturdays. After the collect of the feast the antiphon of the feria shall be said with the doxology ; the prostrate psalms shall not be said ; after Vespers of All Saints the Vespers of the dead shall be said, but not Matins of the dead. [2] On the feast day after Lauds of All Saints, Lauds of the dead shall be said. After this they shall return to bed. After Prime, when the usual psalms for relatives have been said, with their chapters and collects, the seven penitential psalms and litany shall be said. At every hour to Vespers, beginning with Prime, they shall say the psalm *Inclina, Domine* for those for whom the prostrate psalms are said. [3] After chapter they shall sit in silence in the cloister until the bell rings for Terce ; the children likewise, coming down from the dormitory after their chapter, shall sit during this interval in their school and read. The whole day shall be kept with solemnity and both Masses shall be celebrated at the high altar. At the Mass of the feria the litany shall not be said beforehand, and they shall not bow over the desks at the canon. At Vespers, unless the following day is a feast of twelve lessons, they shall say the psalm *Deus, auribus nostris* [4] while the bells are ringing ; after the collect of the feast that of the feria shall be said, with the doxology. After Vespers of All Saints, Vespers for the dead shall be said. Matins for the dead shall not be recited. After Compline the curtain shall be pulled across, and the desks replaced in the choir.

SABBATO ad uesperas ante passionem Domini dimittatur oratio de cruce,[1] nec ad responsoria, nec ad inuitatoria, nec ad missas dicatur Gloria usque ad pasca,[2]
nisi missa familiaris sit in conuentu, uel extra conuentum,[3] et nisi festiuitatem alicuius sancti hoc tempore
celebrari contingat ; quae si euenerit, et ad responsoria
et ad missam dicatur Gloria Patri, sicut alio tempore.
Hoc tempore legatur Ieremias usque ad pasca.

DOMINICA in palmis ad inuitatorium duo in albis.[4]
Euangelium pronuncietur Cum appropinquasset,[5] de quo
et lectio, et sermo in capitulo. In quo capitulo ordinet
abbas uel prior processionem, et quid quisque portare
debeat, et / qualiter ordinate eant ac redeant fratres.
Sacerdotes ad priuatas missas unam tantum collectam
dicant[6] ; euangelium Cum appropinquasset ; passionem
nullus legat nisi frater qui infirmis cantat[7] ; missa matutinalis cum una collecta. Post matutinalem missam
benedicatur aqua, ad quam sint omnes albis induti.
Fiat processio per claustrum ut mos est omnibus dominicis diebus[8] ; intrantibus aecclesiam pulsentur signa, et
finito responsorio, et dictis quae dici solent dominicis
diebus, canatur tercia. Cantata tercia legatur euangelium Turba multa.[9] Postea accedens abbas, aut sacerdos, benedicat palmas, et flores, et frondes ante maius

---

[1] Bernard of Cluny II xiii 306
[2] ibid., where the *Gloria Patri*, not the *Gloria in excelsis*, is in question ;
cf. Albers I 42.
[3] A *missa familiaris* is usually a ' private ' Mass ; here it would seem
to have the meaning, also found (*v.* Ducange) of a Mass *pro familiaribus*,
i.e. relations and benefactors.
[4] Albers II 45. For all that follows consult the Roman Office of Holy
Week ; only the principal differences are noted. In Lanfranc's day the
monastic uses contained a core of the Roman rite overlaid with monastic
and local variants. Later, the Roman rite prevailed entirely for the
Triduum Sacrum, though the monastic use reasserted itself for Easter Sunday.

AT VESPERS ON SATURDAY BEFORE PASSION SUNDAY the prayer of the Cross ceases,[1] and the doxology is omitted at responsories, invitatories and Masses until Easter,[2] unless a votive Mass be said in the presence of the community, or apart from them,[3] or a feast of a saint occur during this time. If this happens, the doxology is said at responsories and Mass as at other times. During this season Jeremias shall be read until Easter.

ON PALM SUNDAY, at the invitatory, there shall be two in albs.[4] The gospel *Cum appropinquasset*[5] shall be recited, and there shall be a lesson and a sermon from it in chapter. At this chapter the abbot or prior shall arrange for the procession, as to what each one shall carry and how the brethren shall go and return in due order. The priests at private Masses shall say only one collect[6] and the gospel *Cum appropinquasset*. No-one shall read the Passion save the brother who says Mass for the sick.[7] The Morrow Mass shall be said with a single collect. After the Morrow Mass the water shall be blessed, with all present in albs. There shall be a procession through the cloister as usual on Sundays[8]; when they enter the church the bells shall be rung, and when the responsory is done, and the rest as is customary on Sundays, Terce shall be sung. When Terce is done the gospel *Turba multa*[9] shall be read. Then the abbot or priest shall approach and bless the palms and flowers

---

[5] Matt. xxi. 1. This is the Gospel read at the Blessing of Palms; in the Mass the Passion according to St Matthew is read.

[6] Bernard of Cluny II xiv 307. This is the rubric also of the modern Roman missal. Commemorations would further lengthen a long office.

[7] In the Roman rite the Passion is read at private Masses.

[8] Bernard of Cluny II xiv 307. This is the ordinary Sunday procession; that following the Blessing of the Palms is described below.

[9] Matt. xxi. 8

altare supra tapetum posita [1] ; aqua benedicta aspergat,
et incenset. Accedentes secretarii distribuant ea ; palmas
abbati et prioribus et personis honestioribus ; flores et
frondes caeteris. Interim cantore incipiente canatur
antiphona Pueri ebreorum, et alia Pueri ebreorum. His
ita expletis proficiscatur processio, cantore incipiente
quae ad hanc processionem cantari oportet. Qua de
choro exeunte, pulsentur omnia signa. Praecedant
famuli cum vexillis, [2] sequatur conuersus ferens situlam
cum aqua benedicta ; alii duo portantes duas cruces ;
item duo cum duobus candelabris, accensis desuper
cereis ; alii duo ferentes duo thuribula igne et thure
referta. Quod thus in thuribulo debet ponere uel
abbas, si in choro est, conuersis thuribula, et acerram
cum thure deferente * cantore ; uel ipse cantor, si abbas
deest. Ipse enim distribuit quae portanda sunt, et processionem ordinat. Hos sequantur duo subdiaconi
portantes duos textus euangeliorum ; post quos laici
monachi, deinde infantes cum magistris ; post quos
caeteri fratres praecedentes abbatem, qui ultimus pro-
cedit, duo et duo, sicut sunt priores. Haec sunt quae
ad hanc processionem cantanda sunt, uel omnia, uel
quantum permiserit spatium loci, quo ituri sunt [3] : Ante
sex dies ; Cum appropinquaret ; Prima autem azimo-
102 rum ; Dominus Iesus ; Cogitauerunt ; Cum audisset /
populus ; Omnes collaudant. Cum autem peruentum
fuerit ad ipsum locum fiat statio a toto conuentu. Cantore autem incipiente antiphonam Occurrunt turbae,
exeant duo sacerdotes albis induti, qui portent feretrum,

* deferentibus A *supra rasuram.* deferente cantore A *man. pr.*
 [1] Bernard of Cluny II xiv 307 : ' cum frondibus et palmis ante magnum
altare sacratis.' For a version of the Blessing *v. Missale Westmon.* II 563ff.
 [2] The *vexilla* were banners, such as appear in the Bayeux tapestry ;
cf. Martène, *De antiquis mon. ritibus* III xii 363 : ' Praeeunt vexilla et
draco,' and Tennyson's ' the Dragon of the great Pendragonship.' For
the order of the procession *v.* Albers I 44 and Porée *Bec* II 595.

and boughs placed on a carpet before the high altar.[1] He shall sprinkle them with holy water and incense them. The sacristans shall then come and distribute them, giving palms to the abbot and the priors and distinguished persons, and flowers and boughs to the others. Meanwhile the cantor shall begin the two antiphons *Pueri Hebraeorum*. When these are done the procession sets out, the cantor intoning whatever is to be sung. As they leave the choir all the bells are rung. The servants go first with banners [2]; a converse follows with a bucket of holy water ; two others bear two crosses ; yet another two bear two candlesticks with lighted tapers ; and two more carry thuribles filled with fire and incense. This incense is to be put in the thurible in choir by the abbot if present, the converses bringing to him the thuribles and the cantor the incense-boat ; if the abbot is away the cantor shall put it in, for it is he who gives out to each what is to be carried, and arranges the procession. The converses are followed by two subdeacons carrying two gospel books ; after them come the lay monks, then the children with their masters ; after them the rest of the brethren two and two in conventual order before the abbot, who walks last.

The following are the antiphons to be sung in the procession, either all, or as many as the length of the journey allows [3] : *Ante sex dies* ; *Cum appropinquaret* ; *Prima autem azymorum* ; *Dominus Jesus* ; *Cogitauerunt* ; *Cum audisset populus* ; *Omnes laudant*. When they reach the starting-point of the procession all the community halts in position ; when the cantor begins the antiphon *Occurrunt turbae* two priests shall come forward, vested in albs, to carry the shrine, which shall have been brought

---

[3] See Appendix B, p. 150

quod parum ante diem ab eisdem sacerdotibus illuc esse
debet delatum, in quo et corpus Christi esse debet re-
conditum. Ad quod feretrum praecedant statim qui
uexilla portant, et cruces, et caetera quae superius dicta
sunt. Et stantibus iis qui feretrum portant, stabunt et
ipsi a dextera et a sinistra ipsius feretri ordinate sicut
uenerunt. Pueri uero accedentes stabunt uersis uultibus
ad ipsas reliquias [1] cum magistris suis, et quibusdam
cantoribus, qui auxilio eis esse possint.* Maiores uero
uersi erunt ad inuicem, eo modo quo in choro stare
solent. Sic autem ordinetur haec statio, ut modicum
interuallum sit inter pueros et maiorem conuentum.
Finita antiphona Occurrunt turbae, incipiant pueri, et
qui cum eis sunt, antiphonam Osanna filio Dauid,
flectentes genua et in principio et in fine antiphonae,
quia in utroque Osanna dicitur ; quam antiphonam
chorus repetat, et similiter genua flectat. Deinde a
pueris cantetur antiphona Cum angelis, in fine tantum
antiphonae genua flectentibus. Quae antiphona a
conuentu repetatur et similiter uenia accipiatur. [2]

Taliter his peractis, abbate uel cantore incipiente
antiphonam Aue rex noster, transeant portitores feretri
per medium stationis, praecedentibus his qui uexilla
portant, et caeteris superius dictis portitoribus, seruato
ab omnibus ordine in redeundo, quem habuerunt in
eundo. Quibus transeuntibus flectant genua, non simul
omnes, sed singuli hinc et inde, sicut feretrum transibit
ante eos. Percantata hac antiphona, cantent et alia, si
spatium loci plura poposcerit. Cum uenerint ad portas
ciuitatis stationem faciant, separatis ab inuicem prout
locus patietur utrisque lateribus, feretrum uero ante

* + pueris C
[1] This may either refer to the relics contained in the shrine with the
Blessed Sacrament, or be a remnant of the earlier rite, when relics alone
were carried.

thither by these same priests a little before daybreak ; in it the Body of Christ shall have been laid. Those who carry the banners and cross and the rest as above shall go straight to this shrine, and when those who carry it halt they too shall halt on the left and right of it in the same order as they have been walking. The children shall draw near and stand facing towards the relics [1] with their masters and some cantors who are to help them in singing. The *statio* shall so be arranged that there is a fair interval between the children and the community. When the antiphon *Occurrunt turbae* is done, the children and those with them shall begin the antiphon *Hosanna filio David*, genuflecting both at the beginning and end of the antiphon, because in each place ' hosanna ' occurs. The choir shall repeat the antiphon, and genuflect in like manner. Then the children shall sing the antiphon *Cum angelis*, genuflecting only at the end of it ; this antiphon shall be repeated by the choir with a similar genuflection. [2]

When this is done the abbot or cantor shall intone the antiphon *Ave, rex noster*, and those who bear the shrine shall pass down between the ranks of the *statio*, preceded by those who carry the banners and by the other servers before mentioned, all keeping the same order in returning that they had in going. As they pass all shall genuflect, not all together but in turn on the right and left as the shrine passes them. When this antiphon is finished they shall sing another, if the time taken demands this. When they come to the gates of the city they shall halt, forming two ranks with such space between as the place may provide ; the shrine

---

[2] The phrase *veniam petere, accipere*, etc., originally used of the act of ' doing penance,' came to bear the entirely neutral sense of ' genuflect.'

introitum portarum sic ponatur super mensam pallio
103 coopertam, ut praedicti / portitores ex utroque latere
stantes, habeant ad feretrum in medio eorum positum
uersas facies suas. Locus uero super introitum portarum
honeste debet esse paratus cortinis et dorsalibus.

Taliter ordinata statione, canant pueri de loco apto,
et qui praecepto cantoris cum eis erunt, Gloria, laus ;
et similiter chorus respondeat. Pueri, Israel es tu rex ;
et chorus, Cui puerile. Item pueri, Plebs ebrea tibi ;
et chorus, Cui puerile. Item pueri, Coetus in excelsis ;
et chorus, Gloria, laus.[1] His dictis, inchoet cantor
responsorium Ingrediente Domino,[2] et ingrediente civi-
tatem processione duo maiora signa pulsentur, donec
caetera signa, processione intrante in chorum, pulsentur
ad missam. Sic ordinata processio ueniens usque ante
portas monasterii faciat stationem seruantibus pueris
ordinem suum inter utrumque chorum. Deponatur
iterum feretrum super mensam pallio coopertam. Cantor
uero sic antea incoeptum habeat responsorium Collegerunt ut tunc prope cantatum sit ; quo cantato tres aut
quatuor fratres induti cappis, quas secretarius ibi paratas
habeat, canant uersum, Unus autem, stantes inter
chorum et reliquias. Quo finito cum regressu intrent
aecclesiam, cantore inchoante antiphonam Principes
sacerdotum, et aliam Appropinquabat. Et ingressi
aecclesiam faciant iterum stationem per omnia similem
ante crucifixum prius detectum. Atque ibi a tribus
uel a quatuor fratribus cantetur in cappis responsorium Circumdederunt me. Quo cantato incipiat abbas

---

[1] For the liturgical history of the *Gloria, laus, v. Dictionnaire Archéol. chrét.*
The text of the early portion is in the *Oxford Book of Medieval Latin Verse*,
no. 27 ; the author was St Theodulph of Orléans (ob. 821). There is no
explicit direction in Lanfranc (as in the Roman missal) that the singers
of the hymn are to be within the doors, nor that the crossbearer shall give
a ceremonial knock for admission.

[2] *HB* I 92

shall be set upon a table covered with a cloth before the gates in such manner that the bearers standing on either side shall face the shrine in their midst. There shall be fair hangings and curtains prepared above the gateway. When the procession is thus halted, the children and others with them in a suitable place at the direction of the cantor shall sing *Gloria, laus*,[1] and the choir shall answer in turn, the children singing *Israel es tu rex* and the choir *Cui puerile decus* ; the children *Plebs Hebraea tibi* and the choir *Cui puerile* ; the children *Coetus in excelsis* and the choir *Gloria, laus*. When this is done the cantor shall intone the responsory *Ingrediente Domino*,[2] and as the procession enters the city the two great bells shall ring and continue till the others begin when the procession enters the choir and the bells ring for Mass. The procession therefore following the same order shall come to the doors of the church and halt, with the children drawn up between the two rows of the choir. Here again the shrine shall be set down upon a table covered with a rich cloth. The cantor shall have so arranged the beginning of the responsory *Collegerunt* that it shall then be almost finished ; when it is done three or four of the brethren, vested in copes which the sacristan shall have ready there, shall sing the versicle *Unus antem*, standing between the choir and the relics. When it is done with its repeat they return to the church, the cantor intoning the antiphon *Principes sacerdotum* and the other *Appropinquabat*. And entering the church they make another halt in the same way before the crucifix which shall have been previously uncovered. There three or four brethren in copes shall sing the responsory *Circumdederunt me* ; when it is done the abbot shall begin the responsory

responsorium Synagogae, et intrent chorum sonantibus
ad missam signis. Missam celebrent, palmas et frondes
in manibus habeant, easque post oblationem panis et
uini, diacono incipiente, cuncti per ordinem offerant.[1]

Tabulae refectorii coopertae sint. Post mensam
meridiana hora in lectis suis quiescant. Appropinquante
hora nona pulset secretarius signum minus modice ;
104 tunc surgant om/nes, et lauent manus et facies, et pectant,
se, et pergant in aecclesiam, sedeantque in choro.[2] Cum
infantes loti fuerint, et ad tersoria ire coeperint, pulsante
maius signum secretario, surgant omnes de sedilibus suis,
et ingressis chorum infantibus faciant prius orationem,
postea cantent nonam. Qua cantata pulsato cimbalo
a priore pergant omnes in refectorium.[3] Talis ordo de
meridiana seruetur tota aestate, exceptis ieiuniorum
diebus, usque kalendas Octobris.

FERIA TERTIA radendi sunt fratres in claustro simul.
Ipsa die et in crastino debent esse balnea praeparata.
Quae quo ordine fiant, et quomodo illuc fratres ire, et
qualiter ibi se habere debeant, superius dictum est, cum
sermo esset de balneis ante Christi natiuitatem prae-
parandis.

FERIA QUARTA non agatur processio,[4] caetera agantur
more solito usque ad uesperas. Ante uesperas non
dicantur psalmi Deus auribus nostris [5] ; pulsentur signa
sicut in festis diebus, responsorium Circumdederunt me.
Ebdomadarius canat preces, Ego dixi Domine ; psalmus

---

[1] It will be noted that there is no suggestion here (or in Bernard of
Cluny) that on Sunday or on the other days the Passion is sung solemnly
and dramatically, as later in the medieval centuries.
[2] Albers II 46 ; this is followed very closely by Lanfranc.

Synagogae and they shall enter the church with the bells ringing for Mass. They shall celebrate Mass and hold the palms and leaves in their hands [1] ; and after the offering of bread and wine all in order, beginning with the deacon, shall offer them at the altar.

In the refectory the tables shall be draped. After the meal they shall rest on their beds for the noonday siesta ; when the ninth hour draws nigh the sacristan shall ring the small bell gently and all shall rise and wash their hands and faces and comb their hair ; they shall go to church and sit in choir. [2] When the children have washed and begin to go to the towels, the sacristan shall ring the big bell and all shall rise from their seats, and when the children have entered the choir they shall pray first and then sing None. After this the gong shall be rung by the prior and all shall go into the refectory. [3] This shall be the afternoon arrangement for the whole summer till the first of October, save for fast days.

ON TUESDAY OF HOLY WEEK the brethren shall be shaved in the cloister together, and on that day and on the following the baths should be made ready. The order of these, and the manner of going to them, and the behaviour there, have been described above when the bathing before Christmas was described.

ON WEDNESDAY there shall be no procession, [4] but all else shall be done as usual until Vespers. Before Vespers the psalms *Deus auribus nostris* etc. [5] shall not be said ; the bells shall be rung as on a feast day and the responsory shall be *Circumdederunt me*. The hebdomadary shall chant

---

[3] i.e. for the drink in common, *v. supra*, p. 16

[4] cf. Bernard of Cluny II xiv 308, and Porée, *Bec* II 597 : ' non fit processio.'

[5] Ps. 43 (44)

ad preces solummodo Miserere mei, Deus¹ ; psalmi
prostrati non dicantur. Post uesperas de omnibus sanctis
dicantur uesperae pro defunctis ; officium mortuorum,
quod post mensam dici solet, non dicatur ; ymnus ad
completorium Te lucis ante terminum, qui similiter
dicendus est omnibus diebus usque ad kalendas Novem-
bris.² Post completorium cortina deponatur.

FERIA QUINTA tot candelae accendantur ante altare,
quot antiphonas, et quot responsoria cantari oportet.³
Finitis tribus orationibus sedentes psallant singuli silenter
quindecim psalmos, absque Gloria Patri, cum capitulis
et collectis consuetis⁴ ; ad Pater noster prosternant se
super formas, at abbate signum faciente surgant. Inter
psallendum, et ante nocturnam pulsentur signa sicut in
duodecim lectionibus. Pulsatis omnibus signis inchoet
ebdomadarius antiphonam Zelus domus tuae.⁵ Cum
105 incipiunt psalmum, / petant ueniam super formas, et ad
matutinas laudes similiter. Per singulas antiphonas, et
singula responsoria, extinguantur singulae candelae.
Lectiones sine Iube domne uel Tu autem legantur.
Primae tres de lamentationibus Ieremiae sine cantu et
alfabetis praescriptis⁶ ; in secundo nocturno, de exposi-
tione psalmi Exaudi, Deus, orationem meam cum
deprecor⁷ ; in tertio, de epistola Pauli : Conuenientibus
uobis ; antiphonae omnes et uersiculi absque finis

¹ Ps. 50 (51)
² At Bec (Porée II 597) the *Christe* is used on Wednesday, and thenceforward the *Te lucis*.
³ Elsewhere (Albers I 46) it was the practice to have as many candles
as there are psalms and canticles, i.e. fifteen. Bernard of Cluny is silent
on the point.
⁴ Porée, *Bec* II 598
⁵ The first antiphon of Thursday Matins ; *v. HB* I 95
⁶ cf. Bernard of Cluny II xv 309 : ' quae sine cantu et praescriptis
alphabetis leguntur.' These ' Lamentations,' together with the prefixed

the *preces*, *Ego dixi Domine* ; the psalm *Miserere mei, Deus* [1] shall alone be said at the *preces*, and the prostrate psalms shall not be said. After Vespers of All Saints, Vespers of the dead shall be said, but the office of the dead, which is wont to be said after the meal, is not said. The hymn at Compline is *Te lucis ante terminum*, which is to be said on all days until November.[2] After Compline the curtain shall be removed.

For THE NIGHT OFFICE OF THURSDAY candles shall be lighted before the altar according to the number of antiphons and responsories to be sung.[3] When the Three Prayers have been said they shall say to themselves the fifteen psalms, seated, without doxology, with the usual chapters and collects.[4] At the *Pater noster* they shall prostrate themselves over the desks and rise when the abbot gives a signal. While they are reciting the psalms and before the night office the bells shall ring as in feasts of twelve lessons. When all the bells have done ringing the hebdomadary shall begin the antiphon *Zelus domus tuae*.[5] When they begin the psalm they shall bow over their desks, and at Lauds likewise. At every antiphon and every responsory a candle shall be put out. The lessons shall be read without *Jube domne* and *Tu autem*. The first three shall be from the Lamentations of Jeremias, without chant and omitting the letters of the Hebrew alphabet [6] ; in the second nocturn they shall be from the exposition of the psalm *Exaudi, Deus, orationem meam cum deprecor* [7] ; in the third, from the epistle of St Paul, *Conuenientibus uobis*. All the antiphons and versicles shall be without the final modulation. At

---

letters of the Hebrew alphabet—Aleph, Beth, etc.—were later sung to elaborate melodies.

    [7] Ps. 63 (64). The lessons are from the exposition by St Augustine.

melodia. In matutinis laudibus, cum incipiunt psalmum
Laudate Dominum, uadant magistri inter infantes, qui
et uersi sint ad priores, sicut et ipsi infantes ; iuuenes
uero, qui in custodia sunt, mixtim sint in ordine seniorum.
Candelae extinguantur in toto monasterio, praeter unam,
quae in choro ardeat [1] ; quae et ipsa, cantore incipiente
antiphonam Traditor autem, extinguatur. Finita antiphona curuentur super formas sub silentio dicentes
Kyrieleison ; Pater noster ; preces : Ego dixi, Domine ;
psalmum Miserere mei, Deus, solum sine Gloria Patri ;
collectam: Respice, quaesumus, Domine ; signoque facto
ab abbate, uel priore,[2] surgentes inclinent sicut solent,
ante et retro, et stet unusquisque in loco suo usquequo
magister infantum laternas accensas in chorum deferat,
et ipsis infantibus tribuat [3] ; secretarius quoque accendat
lumen ante altare, unde iuuenes laternas suas accendant.
His ita peractis, reuertantur omnes ad lectos suos.

Lucescente die, ita ut pueri et iuuenes sine laternis
possint exire, pulsetur a secretario paruulum signum
modice. Statim surgentes fratres calcient se nocturnalibus suis, et sic ueniant in chorum curuantes se super
formas in ordine suo quousque infantes ueniant.[4] Qui
dum uenerint, peracta oratione, factoque signo ab
abbate surgentes statim incipiant ymnum Iam lucis orto
sidere, absque Deo Patri sit gloria. Et inchoata antiphona, dicantur regulares psalmi, et Quicunque uult,
sine Gloria Patri. Finita antiphona curuati super formas
106 dicat unusquisque / apud se in silentio Kyrieleison ;
Pater noster ; Credo in Deum ; preces usque ad confessionem ; factoque signo ab abbate dicatur confessio.

---

[1] This (taken as symbolising Christ) is now the middle candle of the
fifteen on a single stand, and is hidden during the *Benedictus*, to be brought
forth and extinguished at the end of the office.
[2] Bernard of Cluny II xv 309. There is no mention of the noise
(*strepitus*) now made at the end of this silent pause.

Lauds, when the psalm *Laudate Dominum* is begun, the masters shall join the children and face the seniors with them ; the young monks under ward shall be mingled with the seniors. The candles shall be put out in the whole church save one, which burns in the choir [1] ; it too, when the cantor begins the antiphon *Traditor autem*, shall be put out. When the antiphon is done they shall bow themselves over the desks, saying in silence *Kyrie eleison* and *Pater noster*, together with the *preces Ego dixi, Domine*, the psalm *Miserere mei* without doxology and the collect *Respice, quaesumus, Domine*. When a signal has been given by the abbot or prior [2] they shall rise and bow as usual, and everyone shall stand in his place until the master of the children brings lighted lanterns into choir and gives them to the children [3] ; the sacristan shall light a lamp before the high altar, and the young monks shall light their lanterns therefrom. When this is done all shall return to bed.

When day breaks, so that the children and young monks can go about without lanterns, the sacristan shall ring the small bell gently. Rising at once the brethren shall put on their night shoes, and coming to choir bow over their desks in order till the children come. [4] When they arrive, and prayer has been made, at a signal from the abbot all shall rise and at once begin the hymn *Jam lucis orto sidere*, without the doxology. After the antiphon the usual psalms follow and the Athanasian creed without doxology. When the antiphon is finished each, bowing over his desk, shall say to himself in silence *Kyrie eleison* ; *Pater noster* ; *Credo*, with the *preces* up to

---

[3] The children and young monks were always required to carry lanterns when going about after dark ; *v. infra*, p. 116

[4] Probably a Bec observance ; cf. Porée, *Bec* II 599

Deinde silenter quae sequuntur dicant Conuerte nos, et caetera ; Miserere mei, Deus, sine Gloria ; collectam : Domine Deus, qui ad principium.[1] Post haec dicantur in alto septem psalmi absque Gloria, cum solita letania ; deinde sedeant in claustro usque terciam. Cum tempus terciae fuerit, sonet secretarius minimum signum sicut aliis diebus. Tunc pergant fratres se calciare, et caetera, sicut aliis diebus fieri solet. Pulsato ad terciam signo, factis tribus solitis orationibus, pulsato alio signo inchoet statim infans ymnum Dei fide qua uiuimus,[2] sed non dicatur ultimus uersus Gloria tibi Trinitas. Et pronunciata antiphona, dicantur psalmi regulares a beato Benedicto instituti, sine Gloria. Dictis psalmis, et percantata antiphona, curuati supra formas dicant in silentio Kyrieleison et caetera quae sequuntur ; collecta Respice, quaesumus, Domine. Post haec pulsetur solitum signum ad capitulum. Lectio sine Iube domne, uersus in silentio dicatur, legatur sententia de regula sancti Benedicti, sine Tu autem. Factoque ex ea sermone, correctis quae corrigi oportet, dicantur consuetudines, quae agendae sunt ab ipso capitulo usque ad crastinum capitulum. Dehinc ordinentur, quae ad seruitium totius diei ordinanda sunt. Quibus ordinatis surgant canentes alte Uerba mea,[3] si defunctum aut breue pro defuncto habeant.[*] In silentio autem dicant Pater noster ; A porta inferi ; Absolue, Domine. Pulsata tabula loquantur in claustro.

Cum tempus fuerit pulsetur signum ad sextam, et facta oratione, pulsatoque alio signo, inchoet infans

[*] habent A B
[1] HB VI 201
[2] For text of this (later superseded by *Nunc sancte nobis spiritus*) v. HB I 72v.
[3] Ps. 5. This was chanted by the monks when going from chapter to choir on days when prayers were appointed for an anniversary or one recently dead.

the confession. Then a signal is given by the abbot and the *Confiteor* is said. Then what follows is said in silence, *Couverte nos* etc, *Miserere mei Deus* without doxology, the collect *Domine Deus, qui ad principium*.[1] Then the seven psalms are said aloud without doxology, and with the usual litany ; then they shall sit in the cloister until Terce. When it is time for this the sacristan shall ring the smallest bell, as on other days. Then the brethren shall go to put on their shoes and do as on other days. When the bell rings for Terce and the customary three prayers have been said, another bell shall ring and one of the children straightway intone the hymn *Dei fide qua uiuimus*,[2] but the last verse *Gloria tibi Trinitas* shall not be said. When the antiphon has been given out, the regular psalms appointed in the Rule shall be said without the doxology. When the psalms are done, and the antiphon sung, they shall say in silence, bowing over their desks, *Kyrie eleison* and what follows, with the collect *Respice, quaesumus, Domine*. After this the customary bell shall ring to chapter ; there the reader shall begin without *Jube domne*, the versicle shall be said in silence and the portion of the Rule shall end without the *Tu autem*. When the sermon upon it is done, and the needful corrections have been made, the rites to be performed between this chapter and the next shall be announced and instructions given for all the services of the day. When these arrangements are made they shall rise chanting the psalm *Verba mea*[3] if they are commemorating one recently dead at home or elsewhere, but the *Pater noster, A porta inferi* and *Absolue Domine* shall be said in silence. The board shall then be rapped and there shall be talking in the cloister.

In due time the bell shall ring for Sext, and after a space for prayer, when another bell has rung, one of

ymnum, et caetera, sicut fecerunt ad terciam ; dehinc
pulsato signo, loquantur iterum in claustro. Tunc
secretarius pulset paruum signum minimum,[1] sicut in
duodecim lectionibus ante matutinalem missam. Cele-
107 bretur tunc ab ebdomadario minoris / missae missa
pauperibus, qui mandato interesse debent, ducente eos
fratre elemosinario, cooperantibus caeteris fratribus,
quibus iniunctum fuerit. Expleta missa communicet
sacerdos ipsos pauperes de oblatis non consecratis, signo
tantum sanctae crucis in nomine Domini super eas facto [2] ;
dehinc ducantur ad reficiendum. His actis, pulsato
signo ad nonam, facta oratione, pulsatoque alio signo
canatur nona ut tercia et sexta. Qua cantata induantur
infantes, et qui missam sunt celebraturi, sacerdos uidelicet uel abbas honorifice, diaconus dalmatica, subdiaconus tunica, duo ad responsorium, tres conuersi ad
candelabra et thuribulum. Interim auferantur formae
de choro, quae auferri solent. Pulsentur signa sicut in
festiuis * diebus, cantor ebdomadarius chorum teneat in
cappa, missa festiue celebretur. Gloria in excelsis Deo
minime dicatur,[3] nisi episcopus missam celebret et chrisma
faciat. Tunc etiam in fine missae Ite missa est dicitur.
Tot hostiae ponantur ad sacrandum, quot sufficere possint ipso die et in crastino ad communicandum.[4] Quatuor
his diebus nullus a communione se subtrahat, nisi sub-
trahendi rationabilis causa existat.[5] Celebrata fere missa

---

* festis A
[1] Bernard of Cluny II xv 310 ; where the monks put on new shoes,
giving the old pair to the poor.
[2] It is assumed they will not have received Eucharistic communion ;
cf. Bernard of Cluny II xv 310 : ' non enim congruum est, ut ita indis-
crete communicentur, quorum conscientia nescitur.'
[3] cf. Bernard of Cluny II xv 311. The *Gloria* is said on this day at all
Masses in the Roman rite. The point is not mentioned in Albers I and II.

the children shall intone the hymn, and all else shall be as at Terce ; then a bell shall ring and there shall again be talking in the cloister.[1] Then the sacristan shall ring the smallest bell for a brief space, as before the Morrow Mass on days of twelve lessons. Then the priest of the week at the low Mass shall celebrate Mass for the poor men who are to be at the Maundy ; the almoner and others charged with the duty shall lead them in. When the Mass is done the priest shall give to them of the wafers which were offered but not consecrated, over which only the sign of the cross has been made in the name of the Lord[2] ; after this they shall be led away and given refreshment. After this the bell shall ring for None, and prayer be made ; then another bell shall be rung and None chanted as Terce and Sext. Then the children and those who are to celebrate Mass shall vest. The priest or abbot shall have a rich vestment, the deacon shall wear a dalmatic and the subdeacon a tunicle ; there shall be two to sing the responsory, with three converses to carry candlesticks and thurible. Meanwhile the desks shall be removed from the choir as usual. The bells shall ring as on feast days, the cantor of the week shall lead the choir in a cope, and Mass shall be sung according to the festal rite. *Gloria in excelsis Deo* shall not be sung,[3] unless a bishop is celebrating and consecrating the chrism ; in this case at the end of Mass *Ite missa est* is said. Enough hosts shall be consecrated to suffice for communion for the day itself and the morrow.[4] On these four days no-one shall withdraw from communion without reasonable cause.[5]

---

[4] There was another discipline in the later Roman rite : Communion was (and still is) forbidden to all save the celebrant on Good Friday, and till recently there was a custom against receiving on Holy Saturday.

[5] Bernard of Cluny II xv 311 even says : ' etiam illi quibus tale quid in nocte contigerit ' should receive Communion.

reportentur in chorum formae, pulsetur tabula ad
uesperas. Expleta missa fiat oratio uespertina supra
formas. Interea sacerdos praecedente processione [1] cum
qua ad altare uenit, uadat ad locum constitutum decentis-
sime praeparatum, ibique reponat corpus Domini, incen-
sato ipso loco, et ante repositionem et post repositionem.
Ante quem locum lumen continue ardeat. Quo completo, uadant in refectorium accipere mixtum.[2] Ingressi
autem refectorium faciant ante et retro ante sedilia sua,
et considentes sumant mixtum de pane tantum et potu
quem super iusticias [3] * suas a refectorariis in sciphis
positum inuenerint.

Dum haec aguntur,[4] celerarius, et elemosinarius, et
caeteri quibus iniunctum fuerit, introducant pauperes in
claustrum, et faciant eos ordinate sedere alterum iuxta
108 alte/rum. Qui pauperes priusquam claustrum introeant,
pedes suos abluere debent aqua calida a camerariis
ministrata. Omnia uero in locis conuenientibus debent
esse praeparata quae ad mandatum opus sunt necessaria
scilicet, aqua calida a camerariis in uasis idoneis parata ;
alia quoque uasa, ac tersoria ad pedes, manutergia ad
manus, a celerario sciphi et potus, et si quae sunt huiusmodi. Praesto sint ad seruiendum famuli camerarii, et
aliorum ministeriorum, qui ad hoc sunt idonei. Qui
prius per eos quibus iussum fuerit bene debent esse
instructi, qualiter eos seruire oporteat. His ita ordinatis
cum uisum fuerit abbati surgat. Reliqui quoque fratres
surgentes ante et retro inclinent. Egressi refectorium
infantes diuertant cum magistris suis in scolam suam,
ibique stent mixtim cum magistris suis ante pauperes

---

* obbas C
[1] It will be noted that this procession is of ministers and assistants
only ; it is not mentioned in Bernard.
[2] The *mixtum* is allowed to all in view of the unusual exertions to come.

When Mass is ending the desks shall be carried back to the choir and the board be rapped for Vespers, and when Mass is over the prayer before Vespers shall be said as they kneel at their desks. Meanwhile the priest shall approach the altar in procession [1] and go to an appointed place fittingly prepared, and there lay the Body of the Lord, incensing the place before and after he lays down the Host. A lamp shall burn without ceasing before the spot. After this they shall go to the refectory for the *mixtum* [2]; entering, they shall make a double bow before their seats, and sitting down they shall partake of bread only, and of the draught which they find placed in jugs near their stoups [3] by the refectorians.

While this is happening,[4] the cellarer and almoner and others concerned shall lead the poor into the cloister and cause them to sit in order side by side ; before entering the cloister they shall wash their feet in warm water provided by the chamberlains. All necessaries for the maundy shall stand prepared in fitting places, that is, the chamberlains shall have warm water ready in ewers, together with other vessels and cloths and towels for feet and hands ; the cellarer shall provide jugs and drink and all else of that kind. The servants of the chamberlains shall be at hand, and suitable attendants from other departments, who shall previously have been well instructed as to their duties by those concerned. When all is ready the abbot shall rise at his pleasure ; the rest of the brethren shall rise also, making double obeisance. As they leave the refectory the children shall turn aside to their school with their masters ; these shall stand among the children before the poor who are

---

[3] The Cambridge (? Worcester) MS has the homely word *obbas*.
[4] The account of the twofold Mandatum that follows is more detailed than any of the earlier sources.

suos ; reliqui quoque fratres ueniant ante pauperes suos,
et stent ordinate ante eos sicut sunt priores singuli ante
singulos ; abbas uero duos habeat. Tunc prior iussu
abbatis percutiat tabulam tribus ictibus, et inclinantes
se flexis ad terram genibus adorent Christum in pauperibus. Abbas uel cantor incipiat antiphonam Dominus
Iesus,[1] et alias quae conueniunt. Singuli singulis abluant
pedes, tergant, et osculentur ore et oculis. Ablutis cunc-
torum pauperum pedibus, duo ex fratribus quibus
iussum fuerit ministrent abbati, unus aquam, et alter
manutergium ; famuli autem reliquis fratribus. Postea
accipiens abbas baccilia et manutergium a fratribus, qui
ei seruierunt, reliqui fratres a famulis, seruiant et ipsi
pauperibus. A quibus subsequentes fratres accipientes
ministrent et ipsi per ordinem. Quo peracto supradicti
seruitores ministrent abbati et reliquis fratribus sciphos
cum potu. Tunc prior percutiat tabulam tribus ictibus,
et dicatur ab omnibus moderata uoce : Benedicite ; et
data benedictione tribuant potum pauperibus osculantes
eorum manus, et receptis sciphis dent singuli singulis
pauperibus duos denarios,[2] aut quot abbas praeceperit,
iterum osculantes eorum manus. Ipsos denarios dare
109 debet fratribus celerarius aut camerarius secun/dum
quod abbati uisum fuerit. Fratres qui eo anno defuncti
sunt suos pauperes ad hoc mandatum habere debent ;
similiter et familiares illi, pro quibus uiuis in hoc mandato
pauperes debere poni abbas decreuerit. Quibus pauperibus supradicto modo seruiant fratres, quibus iniunctum
fuerit ; alter nullus praesumat. Quamdiu ad hoc mandatum cantant, id est, dum pauperum pedes ac manus

---

[1] Text in *Missale Westmon.* I 273
[2] Bernard of Cluny II xv 312 : ' dantur singulis pauperibus duo
denarii, quos Camerarii . . . ministrant.'

allotted to them ; the rest of the brethren shall likewise
go to the poor allotted to them and shall stand before
them in order of seniority ; the abbot shall have two
poor men. Then the prior shall strike the board thrice
at the abbot's command, and genuflecting and bowing
down they shall adore Christ in the poor. The abbot
or cantor shall then intone the antiphon *Dominus Jesus* [1]
and others suitable. Each one shall wash the feet of his
poor man, wipe and kiss them, and touch them with his
forehead. When the feet of all the poor are washed two
of the brethren as appointed shall wait upon the abbot,
one bearing water, the other a towel, and the servants
shall do likewise by the brethren. Then the abbot shall
take the basins and hand-towel from the brethren who
have waited on him, and the others shall take them from
the servants and shall themselves wait upon the poor.
Others taking their place in due order shall take their
turn in service. When this is done the forementioned
servants shall wait upon the abbot and the rest of the
brethren with stoups and liquor. Then the prior shall
strike the board thrice and all shall say in a moderate
voice *Benedicite*, and when the blessing has been given
they shall give drink to the poor, kissing their hands,
and receiving back the stoups shall each give to a poor
man two pence, [2] or whatsoever the abbot orders, again
kissing his hands. The money shall be given to the
brethren by the cellarer or chamberlain, as the abbot
thinks fit. The brethren who have died during the year
shall have their poor at this maundy ; similarly those
associates of the house for whom the abbot decided
during their lifetime that there should be a poor man.
These poor shall be served like the rest by those to whom
the abbot has given command ; let no other presume to
do it. So long as they are singing at this maundy, that

lauantur, sedere possunt qui uolunt, eo tamen modo,
quo sedetur in choro, uno scilicet sedente inter duos
stantes.[1] Dum autem propinatur potus, sedere possunt
omnes quicunque uolunt, alter iuxta alterum, non obseruato illo standi uel sedendi ordine. Inter haec secretarius
obseruare debet congrua interualla, quibus tabulam ad
uesperas pulsare debeat,[2] semel uidelicet lotis pedibus, et
semel lotis manibus. Propinato omnibus potu, reuersis
singulis in loca sua, prior ter percutiat tabulam. Tunc
abbas uel sacerdos mediocri uoce [3] dicat capitulum
Ostende nobis, Domine. Fratres omnes flexis ad terram
genibus respondeant Et salutare tuum da nobis ; dehinc
inclinati super genua sua tantum dicant Kyrieleison ;
Pater noster ; abbas uel sacerdos dicat mediocri uoce
Et ne nos ; Suscepimus, Deus, misericordiam tuam in
medio templi tui ; Tu mandasti mandata tua custodiri
nimis ; Domine, exaudi orationem meam, et clamor meus
ad te ueniat ; Dominus uobiscum ; Oremus : Adesto,
Domine Iesu Christe, officio nostrae seruitutis, et quia
tu pedes lauare dignatus es tuis discipulis, ne despicias
opera manuum tuarum, quae nobis retinenda mandasti ;
sed sicut his exteriora abluuntur inquinamenta corporum,
sic a te omnia nostra interiora lauentur peccata, quod
ipse praestare digneris. Ad cuius finem respondentes
omnes Amen, et inclinantes se ante et retro, uadant ad
aecclesiam mediocri uoce canentes psalmum Miserere
mei, Deus. Interim secretarius, et aliqui fratres secum,
110 percutiant tabulas gradatim, eoque modo / atque ordine,
quo signa pulsari solent in festiuis diebus.[4]

---

[1] This follows Bernard verbally
[2] From the *Gloria* of Maundy Thursday till that on Holy Saturday no
bells are rung.
[3] Bernard of Cluny II xv 312 : ' mediocriter tantum ut possit audiri.'
[4] Verbally from Bernard

is, while the feet and hands of the poor are being washed, those who wish may sit down, keeping to the custom in choir, that is, one shall sit between two who stand.[1] While the drink is being served, however, all who wish may sit, side by side and not observing the order of alternate standing. Meanwhile the sacristan should take note of fitting intervals at which the board may be struck [2] for Vespers, that is, for the first time when they have washed the feet and for the second time when they have washed the hands. When all have drunk and returned to their places, the prior shall strike the board thrice. Then the abbot or a priest shall recite in a moderate voice [3] the chapter *Ostende nobis, Domine*, and all the brethren, kneeling down, shall answer *Et salutare tuum da nobis* ; then all shall bow kneeling and say *Kyrie eleison, Pater noster*, and the abbot or priest shall say in a moderate tone *Et ne nos*, and then : ' We have received thy mercy, O God, in the midst of thy temple ; Thou hast commanded thy precepts, O Lord, to be exactly observed. O Lord, hear my prayer, And let my cry come to thee ; The Lord be with thee. Let us pray : Assist, we beseech thee, O Lord, this work of our service, and since thou didst vouchsafe to wash the feet of thy disciples, despise not the work of thy hands, which thou hast commanded us to imitate ; that as the outward stains are washed away by them, so all our inward sins may be washed away by thee. Which do thou thyself vouchsafe to grant.' At the end of this all shall answer ' Amen,' and doing double obeisance shall proceed to the church, singing in a moderate tone the psalm *Miserere*. Meanwhile the sacristan and other brethren standing with him shall beat the boards slowly, in the same manner as the bells are rung on feast days.[4]

When the psalm is done and the brethren are stand-

Dicto psalmo, et fratribus in ordine suo in choro
stantibus, statim puer incipiat antiphonam Calicem
salutaris [1] ; ad cuius inchoationem petitur uenia ab
omnibus supra formas. Dicto psalmo Magnificat, et
repetita antiphona sine finis melodia, curuati supra
formas dicant in silentio Kyrieleison ; Pater noster ;
preces, Ego dixi, Domine ; psalmum Miserere mei,
Deus ; collecta Respice, quaesumus Domine. Si aliquis
frater * de foris ueniens benedictionem petierit, omnibus
horis accipiat ipso die quo uenerit [2] his tribus diebus.
Tabulae refectorii coopertae sint. Ad cimbalum, et
super tabulam abbatis ponantur tabulae cum malleolis.
Uersus et benedictiones in refectorio, et Miserere mei,
Deus, post mensam humili voce dicantur ; lector sine
petita benedictione legat, et sine Tu autem, Domine,
terminet. Interim dum sunt in refectorio † fratres,
secretarii discooperiant omnia altaria, [3] et parent duo
analogia, unum quod in capitulo est, et alterum in
monasterio, quod ante collationem in refectorium depor-
tetur. Postquam fratres a mensa surrexerint, et de
monasterio ac dormitorio solito more redierint, lauent
sibi pedes, ut sabbato fieri solet ; praeparentur cuncta,
quae ad mandatum sunt necessaria. [4] Refectis seruitoribus, et pedibus ablutis, pulsetur tabula, et ad bibendum
in refectorium uadant.

Post haec egressis fratribus de refectorio, prior claustri,
iubente abbate, percutiat tabulam ad mandatum. Intro-
gressis in capitulum fratribus, priore claustri sedente in
loco abbatis, praecingant se linteis abbas et prior, et
inchoante priore claustri antiphonam Dominus Iesus, [5]

---

* frater *om.* A   † in refectorio sunt A
[1] *HB* I 96
[2] For the meaning of this *v. infra*, pp. 96–7
[3] Bernard of Cluny II xvi 314
[4] i.e. the second or monastic Mandatum
[5] Text in *Missale Westmon.* I 273

ing in order in choir, one of the children shall at once
begin the antiphon *Calicem salutaris* [1] ; when it is begun
all shall bow over their desks, and when the canticle
Magnificat has been recited, and the antiphon repeated
without the final modulation, bowing over the desks
they shall say in silence *Kyrie eleison, Pater noster*, with the
preces Ego dixi, Domine, the psalm *Miserere* and the collect
Respice quaesumus.   If any brother coming from without
shall ask for a blessing he shall receive it during this
triduum at all the hours on the same day that he arrives. [2]
The tables of the refectory are to be draped.   Boards
with small mallets shall be set by the gong and on the
abbot's table.   The verse and blessing in the refectory,
and the *Miserere* after the meal shall be said in a low
voice ; the reader shall read without asking a blessing
and shall end without *Tu autem, Domine*.   Meanwhile,
while the brethren are in the refectory, the sacristans
shall strip all the altars [3] and prepare two lecterns, one in
the chapter-house and the other in the church, which
shall be carried into the refectory before the collation.
After the brethren have risen from table, and have
retired from the church and dormitory as usual, they
shall wash their feet, as on Saturdays ; let all be prepared that is necessary for the maundy. [4]   When the
servers have eaten and their feet have been washed, the
board shall be struck and all shall go to take their drink
in the refectory.

After this when the brethren have left the refectory,
the claustral prior at the bidding of the abbot shall strike
the board for the maundy.   The brethren shall enter
the chapter-house, where the claustral prior shall sit
in the abbot's place, and the abbot and prior shall
gird themselves with linen cloths ;   and while the
claustral prior intones the antiphon *Dominus Jesus* [5] both

ueniant in capitulum, abbas ad dexteram, et prior ad
sinistram, sequentibus eos fratribus, qui ad seruitium
eorum ipsa die in capitulo fuerant ordinati, et utrique
flexis genibus lauent pedes fratrum, et tergant et osculentur. Camerarii praesto esse debent, qui madefactis
111 terso/riis alia ministrent, quotiens opus fuerit. Lotis
omnium qui in capitulo sunt pedibus, sedeant foris ante
capitulum prior, et praedicti seruitores cum eo ; quorum
pedes praecinctus tersorio abbas flexis genibus abluat, et
tergat, et osculetur, seruientibus sibi fratribus ad hoc
obsequium deputatis. Post haec redeat abbas in sedem
suam, ad quem prior praecinctus tersorio ueniens cum
fratribus sibi deputatis, lauet pedes eius, et tergat, et
osculetur, et ablutis pedibus suis statim deferat sibi
aquam ad abluendas manus, uno eorum qui sibi seruierunt tenente manutergium. Deinde redeunte priore
claustri in locum abbatis, exeat abbas, et accipientes
ipse et prior baccilia cum aqua, et manutergia, duo
fratres qui de coquina ipsa septimana seruiunt, qui inter
caeteros adiutores ad huius mandati obsequium ordinari
debent, seruiant omnibus ad abluendas manus, sicut
seruierunt ad abluendos pedes. His expletis exeat abbas
et prior, et seruitores eorum, et ante capitulum praebeat
eis abbas aquam ad abluendas manus, tenente manutergium uno eorum fratrum qui ad hoc obsequium ei
deputati sunt.

Quo peracto, praecedens abbas, et caeteri sequentes
eum, introeant capitulum, et faciant ante et retro, sicut
solet fieri die sabbati ab eis qui mandatum fecerunt.
Postea pergat abbas ad sedem suam, surgente conuentu
donec sedeat ; reliqui similiter ad loca sua. Cessante
autem cantu, et secretario percutiente tabulam ad
collationem, qui petita licentia ad eam percutiendam
perrexit, hora congrua ingrediatur diaconus capitulum,

shall enter the chapter, the abbot to the right and the prior to the left, followed by those of the brethren who have been appointed that day in chapter to attend them, and both on their knees shall wash the feet of the brethren, dry them and kiss them. The chamberlains should be at hand to provide fresh towels when the first are moist, as often as need arises ; when the feet of all in chapter have been washed the prior and aforesaid servers shall sit outside, and the abbot, girt with a towel, shall kneel and wash and kiss their feet, assisted by brethren appointed to the task. After this the abbot shall return to his seat, and the prior, girt with a towel, shall draw near with his appointed brethren, wash his feet, dry and kiss them, and when he has washed his feet shall at once bear water to the abbot to wash his hands, one of his assistants bearing the hand-towel. Then when the claustral prior returns to the abbot's seat the abbot shall retire, and he and the prior shall take basins with water and towels, while two brethren who do the kitchen service that week, and who are to be appointed among the other ministers at this maundy, shall minister to all at the washing of hands as they did at the washing of feet. When this is done the abbot and prior and their servers shall retire, and the abbot before the door of the chapter-house shall minister water for them to wash their hands, while one of the brethren appointed to this task shall hold the towel.

When this is done, the abbot shall lead the others into the chapter and do full obeisance, as those do who have performed the maundy on a Saturday. Then the abbot shall go to his seat, the convent rising till he is seated, and the rest shall likewise go to their places. When the singing is done, and the sacristan has rapped the board for collation, after asking permission to depart

qui post manuum suarum ablutionem ad se praeparan-
dum iuit, alba, et stola, et dalmatica * indutus, textum
euangelii portans, praecedentibus tribus conuersis portantibus candelabra, et thuribulum igne et thure refer-
tum.   Ipse enim diaconus antequam exeat de monasterio
ponere debet thus in ipso thuribulo.   Quibus ingredien-
tibus capitulum totus conuentus assurgat, stans donec
112 unus uersus de euangelico sermone † perlectus sit./
Cum autem tempus esse perspexerit,¹ innuat abbas
priori ut uadat percutere tabulam.   Et cum audierit
prior a diacono Surgite, eamus hic, percutiat tabulam,
sicut solet percuti cimbalum, quod dum fit, surgant
omnes ac praecedente diacono cum textu, et conuersis
cum candelabris et thuribulo, sequatur conuentus in
refectorium, sicut fit in sabbato ad caritatem.   Ibi
secretarius habeat analogium de aecclesia paratum, im-
positoque desuper textu, iterum mittat diaconus thus in
thuribulum, et incenset analogium et textum.   Et
sedente maiore priore in loco abbatis, ad eius nutum
incipiat diaconus lectionem ab eo loco ubi dimiserat.
Et percutiente refectorario tabulam uno ictu, abbas et
fratres, qui ad pedes lauandos ipsius adiutores extiterant,
uadant ad locum ubi potus caritatis paratus est, ferentes
uitreas phialas, aut sciphos fratrum in manibus suis.   Et
accepto uino in praedictis uasis, tacente lectore, praecedant ad gradum sicut mos est.   Refectorarius uero ex
quo accepto potu incipiant ire, paulatim percutiat
tabulam suam quousque ad gradum perueniant ; quo
cum peruenerint, ter aut quater festinantius percutiat,

---

* tunica C
† euangelio (sermone *om.*) A C
¹ For what follows cf. Porée, *Bec* II 603.   The deacon, who began to
read at Jo. xiii.1, ceases at xiv.31, to continue in the refectory.

for this purpose, at the right moment a deacon shall enter the chapter (he went out to prepare himself after his hands had been washed) vested in alb, stole and dalmatic and carrying the book of the gospels. Three converses shall go before him carrying candlesticks and a thurible with incense burning, for the deacon shall put incense in the thurible before leaving the church. When they enter the chapter all the convent shall rise and stand till the first verse of the gospel discourse has been read.

When the abbot sees the right moment has come [1] he shall nod to the prior to go to sound the board, and when the prior hears the deacon say ' Arise, let us go hence,' he shall strike the board, as the gong is wont to be sounded. When this is done all rise, and the community shall follow the deacon, carrying the gospel book, and the converses with candlesticks and thurible, to the refectory as they do on Saturdays when they go to the *caritas*. There the sacristan shall have a lectern from the church ready, and when the gospel book has been laid on it the deacon shall again put incense in the thurible and incense the lectern and the book. The great prior shall sit in the abbot's place, and at his nod the deacon shall begin to read from where he left off. Then the refectorian shall beat the board once, and the abbot and brethren who assisted him to wash the feet shall go to where the drink of *caritas* is ready, carrying glass vials or the stoups of the brethren, and receiving wine in the foresaid vessels they shall advance in the usual manner to the dais, the reader meanwhile remaining silent. When they have received the wine and begin to advance, the refectorian shall strike his board until they reach the dais ; when they arrive there he shall strike it three or four times rapidly and then cease.

et cesset. Tunc omnibus humili uoce dicentibus Benedicite, sacerdos ebdomadarius surgat, et eadem uoce
benedictionem faciat. Benedictione facta, porrigat abbas
priori potum et reliquis sicut sunt priores, osculans eorum
manus,[1] ministrantibus ei fratribus, qui cum ipso potum
ad gradum detulerunt. Ministrato potu maioribus et
infantibus post maiores, accedat abbas ad diaconum,
qui collationem legit, et expectato fine incoepti uersus
praebeat ei potum, dehinc tribus illis, qui de candelabris
et thuribulo seruiunt, seruitoribus abbatis candelabra et
thuribulum interim tenentibus. Qui et sciphos a diacono et ab eis recipientes portent ad tabulam abbatis,
et super eam ponant. His actis praedicti seruitores
abbatis, qui cum eo potum ad gradum detulerunt, ante
ipsum gradum simul ueniant, et ante et retro faciant,
113 et postea sessum uadant ; quibus abbas / similiter potum
ferat osculans eorum manus, ministrantibus illi fratribus
illis, qui ei ad lauandos pedes prioris et ipsorum serui-
torum ministrauerunt.

Hoc facto abbas ad sedem suam uadat, et ante eam
ante et retro faciat, assurgente sibi conuentu donec
sedeat ; prior uero surgens porrigat illi potum osculans
eius manum ; lecto sermone quantum abbati uisum
fuerit, innuente eo * diaconus lectionem absque Tu
autem, Domine, finiat, et clauso libro, ante et retro
faciat, et postea dalmaticam et stolam et manipulum
supra analogium ponat. Conuersi uero candelabra et
thuribulum super mensam abbatis ferant et ante ipsam
mensam ante et retro faciant. Post haec et diaconus et
conuersi ad ipsam mensam sedentes bibant, diaconus

---

* ei *ut uidetur perperam* D
[1] Bernard of Cluny II xvi 315, has been verbally copied from *ad gradum*
to *eorum manus.*

Then, when all say in a low voice *Benedicite*, the priest of the week shall rise and give the blessing in the same tone of voice. When the blessing has been given, the abbot shall give drink to the prior, and the rest in order, kissing their hands,[1] and assisted by the brethren who with the abbot carried the wine to the dais. When drink has been given to the seniors and to the children after the seniors, the abbot shall approach the deacon who is reading the collation, and when the verse which has been begun is done he shall offer him drink, and then shall offer it to the ministers with candlesticks and thurible ; meanwhile the abbot's servers shall hold these for them. Having received back their stoups from the deacon and ministers they shall carry them to the abbot's table and set them down ; this done, the foresaid servers of the abbot, who with him carried the wine to the dais, shall come together before the dais and make double obeisance and then go to their seats, whereupon the abbot shall bear drink likewise to them, kissing their hands, and waited upon by those who were with him when he washed the feet of the prior and ministers.

When this is done the abbot shall go to his seat, making full obeisance ; the community shall rise and stand till he is seated. Then the prior shall rise and offer him drink, having kissed his hand ; the Lord's discourse shall then be read until the abbot, by a sign to the deacon, brings it to an end ; the *Tu autem Domine* shall not be said, and when the book has been closed the deacon shall make double obeisance and then place his dalmatic, stole and maniple on the lectern, while the converses set their candlesticks and thurible on the abbot's table, making full obeisance before it. After this the deacon and the converses shall sit and drink at the abbot's table, the deacon sitting next to the abbot

iuxta abbatem, conuersi iuxta diaconum, sicut sunt
priores. Abbas uero lecto sermone statim percutiat uno
ictu tabulam, et postea tot uicibus, quot uicibus skillam
percuti consuetudo est sabbato ad caritatem post mandatum. Interim duo secretarii surgant et analogium et
dalmaticam, cum textu et stola et manipulo, ad monasterium ferant. Post haec abbas surgat, et humili uoce
dicat : Adiutorium nostrum in nomine Domini, et eadem
uoce conuentus respondeat : Qui fecit coelum et terram ;
deinde praecedente diacono cum conuersis candelabra
et thuribulum portantibus, sequatur conuentus ad
monasterium, secretario percutiente tabulam ad completorium, et facta confessione dicant completorium,
bini aut terni sub silentio.[1] Post completorium tres
orationes solito more faciant ; prior tabulam percutiat
tribus ictibus post orationes infantum, sicut skillam
pulsare solet. Notandum est autem in huius diei obsequio, quia si abbas sufficere ualet, omnium fratrum pedes
solus in hac die lauare debet ; testante enim beato
Benedicto, uices Christi agit in monasterio,[2] et maxime
in hoc ministerio.

FERIA SEXTA ante nocturna pulsetur tabula in claustro,
et ante celarium,[3] et ante domum infirmorum ad excitan-
114 dos / dormientes. Post orationes solitas, sicut in quinta
feria, quindecim psalmi dicantur, candelae extinguantur,
lectiones in primo et secundo nocturno * legantur, unde
lectae sunt in quinta feria. In tertio nocturno de epistola
ad Hebreos, Fratres festinemus ingredi, et caetera omnia

---

* nocturno et secundo A
[1] Compline was for long treated as a personal, semi-private devotion,
to be said in a low tone by pairs or small groups ; cf. Tolhurst, *HB* VI
174, and Porée, *Bec* II 603, quoting Bibl. Nat. MS lat. 1208 63 and 63v :
'dicant completorium duo et duo aut etiam plures sub silentio.'
[2] *Regula* II 4 ; LXIII 29. The clause referring to the abbot is not
found in Bernard of Cluny or the Constitutions edited by Albers.

and the converses in order next to the deacon. The abbot, when the reading is done, shall strike once upon the board, and then as many strokes as the bell is wont to be struck on Saturdays when they take drink after the maundy. Meanwhile two sacristans shall rise and carry the lectern, dalmatic, gospel book, stole and maniple into the church. Then the abbot shall rise and say in a low voice ' Our help is in the name of the Lord,' and the community shall reply in the same tone ' Who hath made heaven and earth.' Then, led by the deacon and converses carrying the candles and thurible, the community shall proceed to the church, while the sacristan strikes the board for Compline, and the *Confiteor* shall be said and Compline recited in a low voice by groups of two or three.[1] After Compline the three prayers shall be said as usual, and the prior shall strike the board thrice after the children's prayers, as the bell is wont to be sounded. Note also that in this day's office, if the abbot alone can wash the feet of all the brethren, he should do so, for St Benedict declares[2] that he holds the place of Christ in the monastery, and this is especially true of this service.

ON FRIDAY, before the Nocturns, the board shall be sounded in the cloister and at the entrance of the cellary[3] and infirmary to rouse those who are asleep. After the usual prayers the fifteen psalms shall be said, as on Thursday, and the appropriate number of candles extinguished, and the lessons of the first and second nocturn shall be read from the same passages as on Thursday. In the third nocturn they shall be taken from the Epistle to the Hebrews, *Fratres, festinemus ingredi*, and the rest

---

[3] Possibly brethren were sleeping there on guard. Lanfranc makes no mention of the monks who later slept by the shrine in so many monastic churches.

usque ad primam, sicut in quinta feria. Ad primam
pulsata tabula surgentes nudis pedibus uadant ad
monasterium,[1] et sic maneant omnes donec impleatur diei
officium, nisi iussu abbatis calcientur pro nimia asperitate
frigoris. Quod si euenerit, officio tantum intererunt
nudis pedibus.

Primam et omnes horas diei, praeter uesperas, usque
ad uesperas sabbati dicant sicut in quinta feria, excepto
quod in quinta feria in alto cantantur ymni, intonantur
psalmi, cantantur antiphonae ; in his uero duobus
diebus * haec omnia in silentio et in directum dicuntur ;
dicta prima septem psalmos et letaniam in alto dicant.
Postea sedeant omnes in claustro, et inchoante abbate,
dicant psalterium ex integro ; quo completo uadant ad
confessionem, qui uoluerint, usque ad horam officii.

Appropinquante hora tercia, pulsata tabula, sicut
solent pergant in dormitorium. Dehinc abluti, et pectinati, pulsata tabula uadant ad monasterium, et factis
solitis orationibus dicant terciam. Post terciam pulsata
tabula pergant in capitulum ; in quo uersus in silentio
dicatur, et sententia sicut in quinta feria de regula
legatur. Post sermonem narrentur et ordinentur quae
agenda sunt usque ad crastinum capitulum. Exeuntes
de capitulo, sedeant in claustro, non loquentes, sed
cantantes aut legentes.

Dicta nona induantur sacerdos et leuita et reliqui qui
ad officium sunt seruituri. Procedant ad altare sacerdos
et leuita soli, sacerdos in casula, diaconus in stola,
nullaque praemissa supplicatione dicat sacerdos, Oremus
et diaconus, Flectamus genua; et ad alteram collectam[2]

---

* diebus duobus A
[1] So as to be barefoot when ' creeping to the Cross.'
[2] cf. *Missale Westmon.* I 273. In the Roman rite the office, after silent
prayer, begins with the lesson from Osee VI 1–6.

until Prime shall be as on Thursday. When the board is sounded for Prime all shall go barefoot to the church [1] and remain unshod until the office of the day is done, unless at the abbot's bidding they put on their shoes owing to extreme cold. In this case they shall be unshod only at the office of the day.

Prime and all other day hours, save Vespers, until Vespers on Saturday, shall be said as on Thursday, save that on Thursday the hymns shall be sung at a high pitch, the psalms intoned and the antiphons sung, whereas on the other two days all shall be said in a low voice and without modulation. When Prime is done the seven psalms and litany shall be said in a high voice. After this all shall sit in the cloister and recite the whole psalter, the abbot beginning it ; when this is done those who wish shall go to confession before the office begins. When nine o'clock approaches the board shall be sounded as usual and they shall go to the dormitory. Then, when they have washed and combed themselves, the board shall be sounded and they shall go to the church, where they shall recite Terce after the usual prayers. After Terce the board shall be sounded and they shall go to chapter, where the versicle shall be said in a low voice, and a passage from the Rule read as on Thursday. After the discourse the arrangements for the day till next chapter shall be read out, and going forth from the chapter-house they shall sit in the cloister, not speaking but chanting or reading. When None has been said the priest and deacon and other ministers shall vest. The priest and deacon approach the altar alone, the priest in a chasuble, the deacon in a stole, and with no previous prayers the priest shall say *Oremus*, and the deacon *Flectamus genua*, and in similar wise at the second collect.[2] The altar shall be covered with a single linen cloth.

similiter.   Altare sit desuper coopertum * uno tantum
lintheamine.   Singulos tractus duo in albis canant.
115 Passio absque Do/minus uobiscum legatur ; ad quam
nec candelabrum, nec thuribulum ; et cum peruentum
fuerit ad locum ubi dicitur Partiti sunt uestimenta mea
sibi,¹ sint duo de indutis iuxta altare hinc et inde trahentes
ad se duos pannos, qui ante officium super altare missi
fuerant, linteo tamen remanente subtus missale.   Lecta
passione dicantur orationes solennes, sicut in missali
continentur.   Pro cunctis ordinibus flectantur genua,
nisi pro Iudeis.²

His expletis, deposita casula et stolis, reuertantur
sacerdos et leuita in chorum in albis.³   Tunc duo sacerdotes, quibus cantor iusserit, induti albis accedant ad
crucem, quae debet esse praeparata et cooperta ad altare
matutinale,   quam   accipientes   ferant   eam   paulatim
progredientes, et cantantes uersus Popule meus ; duo
leuitae in albis stantes ad gradus ante altare maius
respondeant Agios o theos ⁴ ; chorus autem dicat Sanctus
Deus ;   sacerdotes Quia eduxi uos ;   leuitae Agios ;
chorus Sanctus ;   sacerdotes Quid ultra ; leuitae Agios ;
chorus Sanctus.   Tunc sacerdotes crucem ferentes ueniant
ante altare et cum finierint Sanctus, statim discooperientes
eam incipiant ambo antiphonam Ecce lignum ; et tunc
demum omnes flectant genua.   Repetatur antiphona
cum uersibus psalmi Beati immaculati,⁵ quantum cantori
uisum fuerit.   Dehinc canantur alia ad hoc seruitium
pertinentia quantum opus fuerit.   Tapetia sint extensa
ante altare, super quae prosternantur primum domnus

---

* coopertum desuper A

¹ Jo. xix. 24.   This direction is not in Bernard.

² i.e. the *Flectamus genua*, etc., is not sung by the deacon before the
prayer for the Jews ; this rubric is in the Roman missal also.

³ The ceremony of creeping to the Cross is not an original part of the
office of Good Friday.

Two cantors in albs shall sing each tract, and the Passion shall be read without *Dominus vobiscum*, and without candles and incense, and when the words are reached ' They have divided my garments among themselves,[1]' two ministers in albs by the altar shall pull off towards themselves on right and left two cloths which were put on the altar before the office ; the linen cloth, however, shall remain under the missal.   When the Passion has been read the solemn prayers shall be said, as in the missal.   They shall genuflect at the prayers for all degrees of men, save for the Jews.[2]

When these are done the priest and deacon, putting off the chasuble and stole, shall return to choir in albs.[3] Then two priests, chosen by the cantor and vested in albs, shall approach the cross, which should be prepared beforehand and veiled, on the altar of the Morrow Mass. Taking it, they shall bear it a little forward, singing the verse *Popule meus*, while two deacons in albs, standing before the steps of the high altar, shall answer *Agios o theos*.[4]   Then the choir shall sing *Sanctus Deus*, the priests *Quia eduxi vos* and the deacons *Agios* ; then the choir *Sanctus*, the priests *Quid ultra*, the deacons *Agios* and the choir *Sanctus*.   Then the priests bearing the cross shall come before the altar, and when they have finished the *Sanctus* they shall straightway uncover it and both begin the antiphon *Ecce lignum*, and then all shall kneel.   The antiphon is repeated with verses of the psalm *Beati immaculati*,[5] as many as the cantor thinks fit.   Then other antiphons belonging to this office shall be sung as may be necessary.   Carpets shall be laid before the altar, and on these the abbot and the vested ministers shall prostrate

---

[4] These ' Reproaches ' are in modern usage recited by the priest and sung by the choir while the congregation is worshipping the Cross.
[5] Ps. 118 (119)

abbas, et induti ; interim in locum eorum, qui tenent
crucem, succedentibus aliis, deinde caeteri, sicut est ordo
eorum. Et non prolixe adorantes iaceant, sed breuiter
et pure orantes [1] ; postea unusquisque osculetur pedes crucifixi, et post reuertatur in chorum. Quod si conuene-
rint aliqui uel clerici, uel laici uolentes adorare crucem,
portetur eis crux in alium locum ubi aptius adorent eam.
Quae si per chorum transierit, flexis ad terram genibus
adoretur a fratribus, non simul omnibus, sed sicut
116 portabitur coram eis. Adorata ab omni/bus cruce,
portitores eius eleuantes eam incipiant antiphonam,
Super omnia ligna cedrorum,[2] et sic uadant ad locum
ubi eam collocare debent. Tunc omnes petant ueniam
flexis ad terram genibus.

His ita gestis, sacerdos resumpta casula cum stola, et
diaconus stola, praecedentibus conuersis cum candelabris,
et thuribulo, uadant ad locum ubi quinta feria corpus
Domini fuit repositum ; et posito incenso in thuribulo
incenset illud, et sic tradat diacono ad reportandum. In
eundo et redeundo conuersos sequatur diaconus, sacerdos
extremus ueniat. Cum appropinquant altari adorent
omnes fratres flexis genibus corpus Domini.[3] Collocato
super altare Christi corpore, facta in calice uini et aquae
commixtione, dicta a sacerdote cum diacono confessione, facta suppliciter a sacerdote ad altare oratione,
incenset sacerdos corpus Christi, et calicem ; deinde
dicat mediocri uoce, Oremus ; Praeceptis salutaribus,
et caetera usque Et ne nos inducas in temptationem, et
chorus respondeat, Sed libera nos a malo.[4] Dehinc
sacerdos in silentio Libera nos, quaesumus, Domine, et

----

[1] cf. *Regula* XX 8 : ' brevis debet esse et pura oratio.' This allusion
is not found in Bernard.

[2] Text as a responsory in *HB* III 251v.

[3] i.e. when the Blessed Sacrament has been carried back to the High
Altar.

[4] cf. *Missale Westmon.* I 288

themselves ; meanwhile others shall approach to take the place of those holding the cross, and then others still, in due order. They shall not lie in adoration for long, but praying briefly and simply,[1] and then each one shall kiss the feet of the crucifix and return to choir. If any clerics or layfolk be there, who wish to adore the cross, this shall be carried to them in another place more suitable for their worship, and if it is borne through the choir the brethren shall do reverence on their knees, not all at once but as the cross is borne by them. When the cross has been worshipped by all, those who bear it shall lift it up and begin the antiphon *Super omnia ligna cedrorum*,[2] and so shall go to the place where they are to set it up. Then all shall kneel on the ground and bow.

After this the priest shall resume his chasuble and stole, and the deacon his stole, and, preceded by converses with candlesticks and thurible, they shall go to the place where the Lord's body was laid on Thursday ; incense shall be put in the thurible and the priest shall incense the Host and hand it to the deacon to bear back. Going and returning the converses shall precede the deacon, and the priest shall come last. When they approach the altar all the brethren shall adore the body of the Lord on their knees[3] ; when the body of Christ is placed on the altar, wine and water shall be poured into the chalice, the priest and deacon shall say the *Confiteor*, and the priest, having prayed bowing before the altar, shall incense the body of Christ and the chalice. Then he shall say in a moderate tone of voice *Oremus* ; *Praeceptis salutaribus moniti* and the rest up to *Et ne nos inducas in tentationem*; and the choir shall answer *Sed libera nos a malo*.[4] Then the priest shall say in silence *Libera nos, quaesumus, Domine* and the rest, down to *in unitate Spiritus*

caetera, usque In unitate Spiritus Sancti Deus ; et post,
moderata uoce, Per omnia saecula saeculorum, et
respondente choro Amen, nichil amplius dicat. Missaque
in calicem sicut solet particula Dominici corporis,[1] communicet se, et fratres omnes, sine osculo pacis. Com-
municatis omnibus, pulsetur tabula, et fiat oratio
uespertina. Qua completa, exeant in claustrum, et
lauent pedes de aqua calida, et calcient se diurnalibus
suis. Postea, pulsatis tabulis, redeuntes in chorum,
dicant uesperas in silentio, eisdem sicut in quinta feria
psalmis, antiphonis, precibus, collectis, nisi quod pro
psalmo Uoce mea,[2] qui dictus est quinta feria, hac die
dicitur psalmus Benedictus Dominus Deus meus.[3]

Dictis uesperis, et pulsata tabula, eant in refectorium,
ubi reficiantur pane tantum et aqua et herbis crudis.[4]
Cibi fratrum coquantur in coquina sicut caeteris diebus,
117 et inde/portentur ad elemosinam.[5] Solitus quoque potus
detur pauperibus. Reficiente conuentu, secretarii adiunctis sibi sacerdotibus, quot necessarii fuerint et quibus
iussum fuerit, remaneant in aecclesia ad abluenda altaria
omnia, quae prius lauanda sunt aqua, deinde uino.
Refectis seruitoribus, postquam de monasterio et dormitorio in claustrum redierint, pulsata tabula, fratres eant
in refectorium propter seruandum ordinem, quasi ad
bibendum, et bibant aquam qui uoluerint, alium potum
minime. Illis exeuntibus de refectorio, et in claustro
residentibus, facto congruo interuallo, pulsetur tabula,
et uadant omnes ad collationem. A qua iubente abbate,
percussa a priore tabula, surgentes pergant in refectorium
ad caritatem bibendam.

[1] i.e. is as usually done in the Canon at the *Pax Domini*
[2] Ps. 141 (142)
[3] Ps. 143 (144)
[4] Bernard of Cluny II xvii 317 : ‘ panis et herbae crudae sumuntur.’
cf. Albers I 54
[5] i.e. food of the usual kind taken on other days

Sancti Deus, and then, in a moderate voice, *Per omnia saecula saeculorum*. After the choir have answered *Amen* he shall add no more, but, putting the fragment of the Host in the chalice as usual,[1] he shall give Communion to himself and all the brethren, omitting the kiss of peace. When all have received Communion the board shall be struck and the evening prayer take place. When this is done they shall go out into the cloister and wash their feet in warm water, and put on their day shoes. Then, when the boards have been sounded, they shall return to choir and say Vespers in silence, using the same psalms, antiphons, prayers and collects as on Thursday, save that in place of the psalm *Voce mea*[2] of Thursday the psalm *Benedictus Dominus Deus*[3] is said on this day.

When Vespers are done, and the board has been sounded, they shall enter the refectory, where they shall eat bread only, with water and uncooked herbs.[4] The food of the brethren shall be cooked as usual in the kitchen and then given in alms[5]; the accustomed measure of drink shall likewise be given to the poor. While the community are at their meal, the sacristans and as many priests as may be needed and as have been warned shall remain in the church to wash all the altars, which shall be washed first with water and then with wine. When the servers have eaten and the brethren have returned to the cloister from the church and dormitory, the board shall be sounded and they shall go into the refectory as if to drink, so that the usual order may be followed, and those who wish may drink water, but no other drink. When they leave the refectory and are seated in the cloister, after a due interval the board is struck and all go to the collation. Rising from this at the word of the abbot, when the board has been struck by the prior they shall go to the refectory to drink the *caritas*.

SABBATO SANCTO percutiatur tabula ante nocturna, sicut in sexta feria, et caetera similiter fiant usque ad primam. In tercio nocturno legatur de epistola Pauli apostoli, Christus assistens pontifex futurorum. Ad primam surgant in nocturnalibus suis. Primam, et septem psalmos et letaniam, et caeteras horas usque ad uesperas dicant sicut in sexta feria. In capitulo legatur sententia de regula sancti Benedicti, et disponantur quae agenda sunt usque ad pascale capitulum. Ante capitulum, et post capitulum, debent secretarii monasterium et omnia altaria ornare,[1] cereos ubicunque esse debent collocare, cereum ad benedicendum in loco suo stabilire. In quo a cantore scribi debet quotus annus ille sit ab incarnatione Domini, et crux designari infixis in quinque locis quinque granis incensi.

Post nonam induantur qui officium sunt celebraturi, et ad officium specialiter seruituri, et infantes omnes, sacerdos alba et stola, caeteri albis. Induti in chorum redeant. Dehinc procedant ad sacrandum ignem, canentes psalmum quinquagesimum.[2] Primus omnium secretarius qui hastam portat, in qua sacratum ignem reportet ; dehinc portitor aquae benedictae ; post hos qui portant crucem et thuribulum ; dehinc sacerdos, 118 qui ignem sacraturus est ; post / quem infantes ; dehinc reliqui induti, post quos alii fratres, sicut procedunt in dominicis diebus. Sacrato igne, proiciat sacerdos aquam benedictam super eum, et postea ex carbonibus ipsius ignis impleatur thuribulum, quo impleto, imponat sacerdos thus, et incenset ignem. Tunc accendatur cereus,[3] quem portare in hasta debet secretarius. Accendatur

---

[1] Bernard of Cluny II xviii 317
[2] i.e. the *Miserere*. The blessing of the new fire and the paschal candle are in the *Missale Westmon.* II 573ff.

ON HOLY SATURDAY the board shall be sounded before Nocturns, as on Friday, and all shall be done similarly till Prime. In the third nocturn the lessons shall be from the Epistle of St Paul *Christus assistens Pontifex futurorum*. They shall rise for Prime in their night shoes and shall say Prime and the seven psalms and litany, and the other hours up to Vespers, as on Friday. In chapter a passage from the Rule shall be read, and arrangements shall be made for all things up to the chapter of Easter Day. Before chapter and after the sacristans shall decorate the church and all the altars [1] ; they should place tapers everywhere, and set up the candle that is to be blessed in its place. On it the cantor should write the date of the year from the Incarnation, and a cross should be made by the five grains of incense set in it.

After None those who are to celebrate the office shall vest, together with those who are to serve and all the children ; the priest shall wear alb and stole, the others albs, and then they shall return to choir. Then they shall proceed to bless the new fire, singing the fiftieth psalm.[2] The sacristan shall go first, carrying the staff on which he shall bring back the blessed fire ; then the bearer of holy water, then the bearers of the cross and thurible, then the priest who is to bless the fire ; then the children and then the others who are in albs, finally the other brethren, walking as on Sundays. When the fire is blessed the priest shall sprinkle it with holy water, and then the thurible shall be filled with coals from the fire ; when the thurible is full the priest shall put incense in it and incense the fire. Then the candle [3] shall be lighted and carried on the staff by the sacristan. A

---

[3] The candle (now threefold on a single staff) lighted from the new fire is not the Paschal candle.

et candela in laterna ut si forte in eundo extinguatur
cereus ex ea accendatur ; hanc laternam portare debet
unus de magistris puerorum.

Ad hanc processionem candelabra non portantur.
Eumdem ordinem seruent in redeundo, quem habuerunt
in eundo. Reuertentes dicant hos psalmos : Deus, in
nomine tuo ; Miserere mei, Deus, miserere ; Deus
misereatur nostri ; Deus in adiutorium [1] ; in sede episcopali canatur a duobus pueris ymnus Inuentor rutili. [2]
Ignis sanctificatus qui in claustro remansit a famulis
celararii colligatur, et ex hoc igne omnes foci in omnibus
officinis prius extincti iterum accendantur. Plurima
monachorum coenobia [3] faciunt hanc ad sanctificandum
ignem processionem in quinta feria et sexta,* secretario
praeferente cereum in hasta, uel uirga, in quinta feria,
priore in sexta, abbate in sabbato. Processione in chorum
reuersa sine candelabris et thuribulo, sacerdos indutus
casula procedat ad altare ; diaconus uero stola et
dalmatica indutus ueniat ante abbatem, et petat ab eo
benedictionem ; dehinc uadat ad cereum, et benedicat
eum, nec ante benedictionem, nec post benedictionem
ante et retro faciens ; unus autem ex conuersis cum
tempus fuerit, indicante cantore, deferat abbati ignitis
carbonibus plenum thuribulum ; in quod † thure iniecto
accedat ad diaconum, et iuxta eum sit, ut cum tempus
fuerit, accipiat diaconus ab eo thuribulum, et incenset
cereum. Secretarius vero sit paratus, ut cum dictum
fuerit Rutilans ignis accendit,[4] statim accendat cereum.

---

* et sexta feria A
† quo A B C
[1] Ps. 53 (54), 56 (57), 66 (67), 69 (70)
[2] Text (not in Roman rite) is in *Missale Westmon.* II 578
[3] e.g. Cluny ; cf. Bernard of Cluny II xv 310, and Albers I 48, II 47.
[4] These words occur in the *Exultet.* In Bernard of Cluny II xv 317,
as in the Roman rite, the deacon lights the candle.

candle shall also be lighted in a lantern, so that if by chance the blessed candle is extinguished in the procession it may be relighted thence ; this lantern shall be carried by one of the masters of the children.

At this procession candlesticks shall not be carried, and the same order shall be kept in going and returning. On the return they shall say the following psalms : *Deus in nomine tuo ; Miserere mei Deus, miserere mei ; Deus misereatur nostri ; Deus in adjutorium,*[1] and in a cathedral church two children shall sing the hymn *Inventor rutili.*[2] The blessed fire that remains in the cloister shall be collected by the cellarer's servants, and from this fire all the hearths in all the household offices, which had previously been extinguished, shall be rekindled. Many monasteries [3] make this procession with the blessed fire on Thursday and Friday as well ; in such a case the sacristan carries the candle on its staff or rod on Thursday, the prior on Friday and the abbot on Saturday.

When the procession, without lights and incense, has returned to the choir, the priest in his chasuble goes to the altar, while the deacon, vested in stole and dalmatic, approaches the abbot and asks a blessing of him ; he then goes to the candle and blesses it, doing obeisance neither before nor after the blessing. When the moment arrives the cantor shall give a sign to one of the converses, who shall place before the abbot a thurible full of burning coals ; on these incense shall be cast, and the converse shall then approach the deacon and stand by him, so that at the fitting time the deacon may take from him the thurible and incense the candle. The sacristan shall be ready to light the candle as soon as the words are reached *Rutilans ignis accendit.*[4]

119   Benedictione peracta, diaconus deposita dalmatica et/
stola ad suum locum in chorum reuertatur. Cereus uero
non extinguatur usque in crastinum post uesperas ;
lectiones statim inchoentur [1] : sacerdos absque diacono * [2]
dicat orationes ad altare sicut sunt per ordinem ; ultima
oratione dicta cantor, et alter frater, quem uoluerit,
induti cappis incipiant in choro letaniam ternam, hoc
modo : cantores Kyrieleison ; dexter chorus similiter
respondeat Kyrieleison ; deinde sinister, et caetera
eodem modo usque ad finem letaniae ; ternos sanctos
de unoquoque ordine dicant.[3] Ad singula sanctorum
nomina uterque chorus inclinet, cantores ad nullum.[4]
Incepta letania fratres accedant ad formas, sicut in
duodecim lectionibus ; ad terciam sacerdos reuertatur
in secretarium, et deposita casula et stola, redeat in
chorum. Cum dixerint cantores, Omnes sancti, orate
pro nobis, exeant de choro sacerdos, leuita, subdiaconus,
tres conuersi, et induat se sacerdos casula, leuita dalmatica, subdiaconus tunica. Finita letania, pronuncient
cantores tribus uicibus alta uoce Accendite,[5] et tunc
primum accendantur candelabra, et caetera luminaria,
quae ante altare, et circa altare sunt, et cantores incipiant
festiuum † Kyrieleison ; et sacerdos cum processione
solita ad altare procedat, et signa tunc pulsari incipiant,
nec desinant, usque ad finem Kyrieleison. Et tunc

---

* diacono *codd. omn.* cantu *Reyner*
† festiue C
[1] i.e. the Prophecies
[2] It is to be noted that *Missale Westmon.* 288ff., has no *flectamus genua*
(always sung by the deacon) before the prayers. In the Roman rite, where
flectamus genua is found, the celebrant is assisted by deacon and subdeacon,
and presumably Reyner or another deliberately altered the word to suit
the passage to the only practice familiar to him.
[3] The Latin of the last clause could also be translated 'invoking three
saints of each class' (i.e. martyrs etc.).
[4] So Bernard of Cluny II xviii 318

When the blessing is done the deacon shall put off his dalmatic and stole and return to his place in choir, but the candle shall not be put out until after Vespers on the morrow. Straightway after this the lessons [1] shall begin, and the priest shall say the prayers in order at the altar without the deacon[2] ; when the last prayer has been said the cantor, and another brother of his choice, vested in copes, shall begin the litany, which shall be chanted in three parts, as follows : the cantors sing *Kyrie eleison*, the right-hand choir shall answer likewise *Kyrie eleison*, and then the left-hand choir, and so on until the end of the litany, invoking each saint thrice.[3] Both choirs shall bow at the name of each saint, but the cantors shall not do so.[4] When the litany is begun the brethren shall go to their desks as on feasts of twelve lessons, and after the third invocation the priest shall return to the sacristy, put off his chasuble and stole and return to choir. When the cantors have sung *Omnes sancti, orate pro nobis,* the priest, deacon, subdeacon and three converses shall leave the choir, and the priest shall vest in a chasuble, the deacon in a dalmatic and the subdeacon in a tunicle.

When the litany is done the cantors shall sing thrice in a loud voice ' Kindle the lights,' [5] and then, and not before, shall the candles and other lights before and about the altar be lighted, and the cantors shall begin *Kyrie eleison* in the festal tone, and the priest with the procession as usual shall go to the altar, and the bells shall then begin to be rung, not ceasing till the end of

---

[5] This direction is found in *Missale Westmon.* II 598, but not in the Roman rite. In modern usage the lamps are rekindled during the *Exultet.* Bernard of Cluny II xviii 318 (cf. Albers I 56) directs that the bells should be rung at this point and should not cease till the *Gloria.*

primum det cantor cappas iis qui Alleluia et tractum
cantaturi sunt. Finito Kyrieleison, incipiat sacerdos
Gloria in excelsis Deo. Quando legetur euangelium,
non teneantur candelabra, sed solum thuribulum : in
hac consuetudine concordant omnes fere principales
monachorum aecclesiae, quae nostro tempore maioris
auctoritatis sunt,[1] sicut et in eo quod offerenda, et Agnus
Dei, et Communio ad hanc missam non dicuntur, licet
caetera festiue dicantur. In quibusdam quoque non
improbandae auctoritatis coenobiis, nec ante sacerdotem
ad altare procedentem hac die candelabra portantur.

120   Celebrata fere missa sacerdote incipiente Per Domi/-
num nostrum, incipiant pulsari duae skillae ad uesperas,
ut mos est in maximis festiuitatibus. Responso Deo
gratias ad Ite missa est, fiat oratio uespertina ; qua facta
vadant infantes in refectorium, si aliqui adeo parui sunt,
ut usque post uesperas expectare non possint. Interim
pulsentur maiora signa duo et duo, ad extremum pulsatis
omnibus signis, canantur uesperae ut decet solenniter.
Ebdomadarius cantor incipiat Alleluia ex aliqua antiphona ex qua cantor praeceperit. Psalmi Confiteantur [2] ;
capitulum Si consurrexistis ; responsorium Angelus
Domini locutus est ; ymnus Ad cenam Agni ; uersus
Resurrexit Dominus ; ad Magnificat, Uespere autem
sabbati ; collecta * : Deus qui hanc sacratissimam
noctem.[3] Post uesperas, procedant ad crucifixum.[4]

* collectam *ut uidetur perperam* D
[1] cf. Bernard of Cluny II xviii 318
[2] Ps. 144, second part (145, second part), 145 (146), 146 (147, v. 1–11),
147 (147, v. 12 to end). Lanfranc here prescribes First Vespers of Easter
of the normal type. Originally there were no Vespers on Holy Saturday,
but when the nocturnal ceremonies and Mass were advanced into the
day, time was found for an abnormally short Vesper office immediately
following the Mass. This was the Roman practice ; it appears in the
Regularis Concordia, and has survived to the present day. Lanfranc, however, as also, two centuries later, the provincial chapter of the black monks
(Pantin, *Chapters* I 96, of the date 1278), imposes the monastic type—
with what success, does not appear.

the *Kyrie*. Then, and not before, the cantor shall give copes to those who are to sing the Alleluia and tract. When the *Kyrie* is done the priest shall intone *Gloria in excelsis Deo*. When the gospel is being read, candlesticks are not borne but only the thurible ; this is the custom in almost all the principal monasteries of greatest authority in our time,[1] as it is also that the *Offertory* and *Agnus Dei* and *Communion* are not said at this Mass, though all else is as on festal days. In some monasteries of no small repute, also, on this day lights are not carried before the priest as he goes to the altar.

When the Mass is ending and the priest begins *Per Dominum nostrum*, two bells shall begin ringing for Vespers, as on the greatest feasts. When *Deo gratias* has been answered after *Ite Missa est* the evening prayer shall be made ; when this is done the children go to the refectory, if there be any so young as not to be able to wait till after Vespers. Meanwhile the greater bells shall be rung two by two, and finally, when all the bells have been rung together, Vespers shall be sung as solemnly as possible. The cantor of the week shall begin Alleluia from an antiphon selected by the cantor. The psalms shall be *Confiteantur*,[2] the chapter *Si consurrexistis*, the responsory *Angelus Domini locutus est*, the hymn *Ad coenam Agni prouidi*, the versicle *Resurrexit Dominus*, the antiphon at the Magnificat *Vespere autem sabbati*, the collect *Deus qui hanc sacratissimam noctem*.[3] After Vespers they shall go in procession to the crucifix.[4]

---

[3] i.e. the collect of the Mass. In the Roman rite the Vespers are woven into the Mass and the Postcommunion prayer is used.

[4] Bernard of Cluny II xviii 318. The procession normally went to the altar of Our Lady.

DIE SANCTO pascae ante uigilias matutinas pulsentur omnia signa ; dehinc duo et duo sicut mos est. Ad inuitatorium quatuor in cappis, psalmi a beato Benedicto instituti, id est, Domine in uirtute tua,[1] et caeteri. Ad lectiones circumferantur thuribula, sicut in die dominicae natiuitatis institutum est.[2] Totum denique officium more monachorum agatur.[3] Processio ad crucifixum post matutinas laudes, et post uesperas, per totam istam * septimanam uadat. Missa matutinalis hac die cum una collecta ; processio in cappis. Ad uesperas psalmi regulares, id est Dixit Dominus[4] et reliqui, qui diebus dominicis dici solent. Super psalmos, antiphonae quae ad matutinas laudes dictae sunt.

Tribus sequentibus diebus,[5] ante uigilias pulsentur signa duo et duo ; ad inuitatorium tres in cappis ; psalmi feriales dicantur, sex sub una antiphona, et sex sub alia ; duo et duo primum et secundum responsorium; tertium tres ; laudes sub una antiphona. Ad thuribula duo sacerdotes cappis induti ad laudes et ad uesperas. Missa matutinalis cum una collecta ; ad maiorem omnes sint cappis induti. Ad uesperas, per totam ebdomadam, sub una antiphona di/cantur psalmi, qui in die pascae ad uesperas dicti sunt.

Tribus sequentibus diebus, ad inuitatorium duo in froccis ; ad nocturna psalmi feriales, tres lectiones de pronunciato euangelio ; maior missa, et caetera omnia sicut in duodecim lectionibus. In hac ebdomada non

---

* illam C om. A
[1] i.e. the Sunday psalms of the monastic office, 20 (21) etc., not those of the Roman rite.
[2] Bernard of Cluny II xix 319; v. supra, p. 12
[3] i.e. not according to the 'canonical' Roman rite.
[4] Ps. 109–12 (110–13)

ON EASTER DAY, before the night choirs, all the bells shall be rung for Matins, then by two and two as usual. At the invitatory there shall be four in copes, and the psalms as in the Rule, that is, *Domine in virtute tua* [1] and the rest. During the lessons thuribles shall be borne round, as is laid down for Christmas. [2] All the rest of the office shall be according to the monastic rite. [3] There shall be a procession to the crucifix after Lauds and Vespers throughout the week. The Morrow Mass shall be said this day with a single collect, and the procession shall be in copes. At Vespers the ordinary psalms shall be said, that is *Dixit Dominus* [4] and the others which are usually said on Sundays. The antiphons shall be those said at Lauds.

On the three following days [5] the bells for the night choirs shall be rung two by two ; at the invitatory there shall be three in copes ; the ferial psalms shall be said, six under one antiphon and six under another ; the first and second responsories shall be sung by two, the third by three ; Lauds shall be said with a single antiphon. Two priests vested in copes shall bear thuribles at Lauds and Vespers. The Morrow Mass shall have one collect and at the High Mass all shall wear copes. The psalms at Vespers throughout the week shall be said under a single antiphon, and they shall be as on Easter Sunday.

On the three following days there shall be two in tunics at the invitatory ; the ferial psalms shall be said and three lessons from the gospel of the day. The High Mass and all else as on feasts of twelve lessons. During this week there shall be no talking in the cloister. The

---

[5] In modern usage Monday and Tuesday, and these only, are of the first rank, and on these days the office in the main follows that of Easter Sunday.

loquantur in claustro. Missa matutinalis Resurrexi [1] ;
omnes horae cum antiphonis canantur. Sabbato tantum
ad uesperas psalmi cum Alleluia [2] dicantur.

OCTAUA DIE ad inuitatorium tres in cappis. Ad
lectiones legantur pascales sermones ; in tercio nocturno
pronuncietur euangelium Cum esset sero.[3] Missa matutinalis Quasi modo geniti.[4] Processio in albis ; maior
missa Resurrexi, ad quam sint omnes cappis induti.

Feria secunda ponatur ad legendum liber actuum
apostolorum [5] usque ad sequentem dominicam. Ad
utrumque nocturnum, et ad omnes horas alleluia dicatur
usque ad ascensionem Domini. Post capitulum, pulsata
tabula, loquantur in claustro. Post nonam, cum exierint
de refectorio, pergant in capitulum, et supplicent ante
et retro, pulsetque prior tabulam tribus ictibus,[6] dicatque ter, Deus, in adiutorium meum intende : Domine,
ad adiuuandum me festina ; et conuentus idem ter
respondeat adiungentes Gloria Patri ; Kyrieleison ;
Christe eleison ; Kyrieleison ; Pater noster ; et prior,
Et ne nos ; Adiutorium nostrum in nomine Domini ;
conuentus Qui fecit coelum et terram ; et a priore dicto
Benedicite, post loquantur in claustro. Hic loquendi
ordo teneatur usque ad idus Septembris priuatis diebus,
nisi ieiunium fuerit.[7]

A* DOMINICA prima post octauas Pascae, legatur
apocalipsis, et canatur hystoria Dignus es, Domine,[8]

---

    * *om.* A
    [1] i.e. the Mass of Easter Sunday ; the High Mass would follow the
proper of each day ; cf. Bernard of Cluny II xix 321.
    [2] i.e. *Alleluia* replaces the Easter antiphon   [3] Jo. xx.19
    [4] This is the proper Mass of Low Sunday
    [5] Albers II 23
    [6] Bernard of Cluny II xx 324
    [7] Bernard of Cluny II xx 323

Morrow Mass shall be *Resurrexi*,[1] and all Hours sung with antiphons. Only on Saturday shall the psalms at Vespers be said with *Alleluia*.[2]

ON THE OCTAVE OF EASTER there shall be three in copes at the invitatory. For lessons Easter sermons shall be read, and in the third nocturn the gospel *Cum esset sero*.[3] The Morrow Mass shall be *Quasi modo geniti*.[4] There shall be a procession in albs, and the High Mass, at which all shall wear copes, shall be *Resurrexi*.

On the Monday following the Acts of the Apostles shall be begun[5] and continued till the following Sunday ; at both nocturns and at all Hours *Alleluia* shall be said until the Ascension. After the chapter the board shall be sounded and there shall be talking in the cloister. After None, when they leave the refectory, they shall enter the chapter-house and make a double inclination. The prior shall then beat the board thrice[6] and say thrice *Deus in adjutorium meum intende, Domine, ad adjuvandum me festina*, and the community shall thrice answer likewise, adding *Gloria Patri, Kyrie eleison, Christe eleison, Kyrie eleison, Pater noster*. The prior shall say *Et ne nos ;* *Adjutorium nostrum in nomine Domini*, and the community shall answer *Qui fecit coelum et terram*, and when the prior has said *Benedicite* they shall talk in the cloister. This order of talking shall obtain on ferial days until the thirteenth of September, save on days of fasting.[7]

ON THE FIRST SUNDAY after the octave of Easter the Apocalypse shall be read and the lesson sung *Dignus es Domine*,[8] for two weeks. From the third Sunday till

---

[8] Albers II 23. *hystoria* here = responsory. For the text, *v. HB* II. 109

duabus septimanis. A dominica tercia usque ad ascensionem Domini legantur septem canonicae epistolae, et canatur hystoria Si oblitus.[1]

DIEBUS rogationum dictis matutinis pro defunctis, fratres ad lectos redeant, et qui uolunt plus solito 122 dormiant.[2] His / enim diebus meridianis horis non dormiunt,[3] nec aliquo sonitu, ut aliis diebus mos est, mane excitantur, sed cum tempus congruum uisum fuerit,* excitare debent infantes magistri eorum, quam quietius possunt ; quibus in claustro legentibus, surgant sine mora, qui in lectis adhuc quiescunt. Post primam, et familiares psalmos primae, et septem psalmos et letaniam, dicatur missa de ieiunio ad maius altare ; post cuius primam orationem dicantur aliae quae ad maiorem missam cotidianis diebus dici solent, addita in fine alia, id est, Sanctorum tuorum intercessionibus. Omnes offerant ; ad pacem solus prior, aut qui in loco prioris est, uadat. Sententia de regula legatur in capitulo et ordinetur processio. Post terciam sumant mixtum pueri, et infirmi, qui ieiunare non possunt. Cantata sexta uadant in dormitorium, sicut alio tempore, quando meridianis horis in lectis quiescere solent, et facto paruissimo interuallo pulsetur skilla ; dehinc nudis pedibus de dormitorio descendant, manus abluant, ad aecclesiam uadant, orationem faciant. Qua facta incipiat infans antiphonam Exsurge, Domine. Interim pulsentur duo signa. Cantata antiphona dicat sacerdos, Ostende nobis, Domine, misericordiam tuam ; sequatur Kyrieleison ;

---

* uisum fuerit congruum A
[1] In *HB* II 113v, this is the eleventh, not the first, responsory.
[2] cf. Albers II 52, but what follows is apparently from Bernard of

Ascension Day the seven canonical epistles shall be read, and the responsory *Si oblitus* [1] be sung.

ON THE ROGATION DAYS, after Matins of the Dead, the brethren shall return to bed, and those who wish shall sleep longer than usual.[2] For on these days no sleep is taken in the afternoon,[3] and they are not roused in the morning by an alarum, as on other days, but at a fitting hour the masters shall waken the children as quietly as possible, and when these are reading in the cloister those who are still abed shall rise without delay. After Prime and the psalms for relations and the penitential psalms and litany, the Mass of the fast-day shall be said at the high altar ; after the first prayer shall be said the others which are wont to be said at High Mass on ordinary days, with the addition of the one *Sanctorum tuorum intercessionibus.* All shall make an offering, but the prior, or his substitute, shall alone go for the kiss of peace. A passage of the Rule shall be read in chapter, and a procession be made. After Terce the children and the sickly, who cannot fast, shall receive the *mixtum.* When Sext has been sung they shall go to the dormitory as at other times, when they are wont to rest in bed in the noonday, and after a very short interval the small bell shall be rung. Then they shall come down from the dormitory barefoot, wash their hands, go into church and pray. When this is done one of the children shall begin the antiphon *Exurge Domine,* while two bells are rung. When the antiphon is done the priest shall say *Ostende nobis Domine misericordiam tuam,* and there shall follow *Kyrie eleison, Pater noster* and the psalm *Deus*

Cluny II xxii 327 : ' et plus solito dormiunt.' This is on account of the coming exertion.

[3] This follows Bernard verbally, as do many of the passages following.

Pater noster, psalmus Deus misereatur nostri.[1] In crastino,
Deus in adiutorium meum.[2] Dehinc sacerdos, Et ueniat
super nos, collectam pro peccatis. Postea sonantibus
signis exeant processuri canentes, incipiente cantore,
quae ad processionem pertinent ; praecedant famulis
cum uexillis, sequatur conuersus cum aqua, post quem
alius cum cruce ; dehinc subdiaconus, ferens textum,
post quem fratres laici, dehinc infantes cum magistris,
post quos cantores, extremis prioribus et praecedentibus
iunioribus, sicut est ordo eorum. In egressu monasterii
sint famuli camerarii, habentes ibi baculos praeparatos
quos tribuant fratribus ad se sustentandos.[3]

123   Cum peruenerint ad aecclesiam ad quam ituri sunt,
inci/piat cantor antiphonam, uel responsorium de sancto
in cuius honorem fundata est ipsa aecclesia. Intrantes
fratres reddant baculos praedictis famulis ab eisdem
iterum recepturi exeuntes. Finito incepto cantu, dicat
statim sacerdos capitulum de sancto illo, et collectam,
cum Dominus uobiscum, alta uoce et solenniter ; infans,
Benedicamus Domino. Quo dicto inclinantes se faciant
orationem. A qua facto signo surgentes inclinent ante
et retro. Dum haec fiunt, sacerdos, et leuita, et caeteri,
qui circa altare seruituri sunt, praeparare se debent ad
celebrandam missam, secretarius quoque pallio et hones-
tis pannis altare decenter parare ; omnia enim quae ad
hoc seruitium sunt necessaria, instantia secretarii illuc
prius debent esse delata. Paratis omnibus celebretur iterum missa de ieiunio. Post primam orationem dicatur
oratio de sancto illo cuius est aecclesia, nullaque amplius.

  [1] Ps. 66 (67)
  [2] Ps. 69 (70)
  [3] cf. Albers I 67 : ' famuli . . . unus hinc, unus illinc,' and Bernard
of Cluny II xx 328 : ' duo famuli sylvarum custodes.'

misereatur nostri.[1] On the following day the psalm *Deus in adiutorium meum* [2] is said. Then the priest shall say *Et veniat super nos* and a collect for the remission of sins. Then, while the bells ring, they shall go out in procession singing what pertains to the procession, the cantor intoning the chant. The servants with banners shall lead, then a converse with holy water, then another with a cross, then the subdeacon with a gospel book, followed by the lay brethren, then the children with their masters, then the cantors and the brethren with the seniors last and juniors first, in order. As they go out of the church the servants of the chamberlain shall stand with staves ready to give to the brethren for their support.[3]

When they reach the church which is their goal, the cantor shall begin the antiphon or responsory of the saint in whose honour the church was founded. As the brethren enter they shall hand their staves to the fore-mentioned servants, to receive them again as they go out. When the chant they are singing is done, the priest shall say at once the chapter and collect of the saint, with *Dominus vobiscum*, solemnly in a loud voice, and one of the children shall sing *Benedicamus Domino*. After this they shall bow down and pray. Rising from this at a signal they shall make double inclinations ; while all this is being done, the priest and deacon, and others who are to be servers at the altar, should prepare themselves to celebrate Mass, while the sacristan makes the altar ready in fitting wise with clean linen and a frontal. All necessary things for the service shall have been previously carried thither at the instance of the sacristan. When all is ready the fast-day Mass is again celebrated ; after the first prayer the prayer of the patron saint of the church shall be said, and no other be added.

Celebrata fere missa, duo fratres qui cappis induti
debent dicere Agnus Dei ad portas monasterii, inclinantes
se ante et retro regrediantur ; sumentes secum aliquos
ex famulis, quibus iussum fuerit, et dicentes inter se
letaniam quam conuentus in reditu cantaturus est.

Expleta missa [1] accedant statim fratres, quibus iussum
fuerit, et stantes in medio pronuncient letaniam.[2] Interim
sacerdos, et qui ad missam seruierunt, expediant se, et sic
reuertantur in chorum.   Post Sanctum Ioannem,[3] et
Omnis chorus prophetarum, pronuncient illum sanctum
duabus uicibus in cuius nomen est aecclesia dedicata.
Postea inclinantes se omnes ante et retro, regrediantur
eo ordine, quo uenerunt.   Cantores letaniae producant
aut breuient ipsam letaniam secundum quantitatem
itineris.   Qui in redeundo pergere debent post infantes,
ante reliquum conuentum cantorum.[4]

Cum autem processio rediens ante monasterii introitum uenerit, statione facta letaniam finiant ; qua finita
124 cantores eius in ordinem suum redeant, et praedicti duo
cantores / qui praecesserant, cappis induti, nudis pedibus
ante portas monasterii stantes dicant : Agnus Dei, qui
tollis peccata mundi, miserere nobis.   Chorus similiter
respondeat ; cantores, Suscipe deprecationem nostram,
qui sedes ad dexteram Patris ; chorus, Agnus Dei, sicut
supra ; cantores Gloria Patri, et Filio, et Spiritui Sancto :
sicut erat in principio, et nunc, et semper, et in saecula
saeculorum, Amen.   Interim praecedentibus qui uexilla
portant, et caetera quae superius dicta sunt, sequantur
cantores, et reliquus conuentus.   Dicto Gloria, respondeat

---

[1] In modern usage the Rogation procession and litanies precede the Mass.
[2] For a long version of the Litany, v. HB V G 66ff.
[3] i.e. the invocation to St John the Baptist.   The accusative follows
the preposition.
[4] All the MSS read as in the text.   If *cantorum* is a correct reading it
would seem that the group of singers who answer the invocations is con-

When Mass is ending, two of the brethren in copes, who are to intone *Agnus Dei* at the door of the monastic church, shall return, having made a double inclination. They shall take with them, as arranged, some of the servants, and shall say as they go the litany which the community are to sing on their return journey.

When Mass is over,[1] brethren who have been charged with this task shall approach and, standing in the midst, shall sing the litany.[2] Meanwhile the priest and servers shall unvest and return to choir. After the invocation of St John [3] and all the choir of prophets, they shall invoke twice the patron saint of the church. Then, making a double inclination, they shall return in the order in which they came. Those who are chanting the litany shall draw it out or shorten it to suit the length of the way ; they shall walk after the children and before the rest of the group of cantors.[4]

When the procession on its return arrives before the door of the church, they shall halt and finish the litany ; then the cantors shall return to their places, and the aforementioned two cantors who have gone ahead shall stand barefoot in copes before the doors of the church and say *Agnus Dei, qui tollis peccata mundi, miserere nobis.* The choir shall repeat this, and the cantors shall say *Suscipe deprecationem nostram, qui sedes ad dexteram Patris* ; the choir shall then say *Agnus Dei* as above, and the cantors *Gloria Patri.* Meanwhile those who carry the banner and the other things as set out above shall move forward, followed by the cantors and the rest of the community. When the *Gloria* is done the community shall answer *Agnus Dei* as above. As the community enters the church the bells shall be rung ; the cantors

trasted with the two who sing the Litanies, e.g. the two sing *Sancta Maria* and the others answer *Ora pro nobis.*

conuentus Agnus Dei, ut supra. Conuentu intrante
monasterium pulsentur signa ; cantores, Exaudi Deus ;
conuentus, Uoces nostras ; cantores, Exaudi, Christe,
conuentus, Miserere nobis ; cantores, Exaudi Deus ;
conuentus, Orationem populi tui, Cunctis fratribus
chorum ingressis, collocata cruce et reliquis*, quae
portata sunt, in locis suis, praedicti duo cantores in
medio chori stantes pronuntient letaniam : Sancte
sanctorum Deus, miserere nobis ; priores a parte altaris
sint, reliqui post eos, sicut est ordo eorum. Expleta letania
pulsetur signum ad nonam, factaque oratione nonae,
uadant in claustrum lauare pedes ; quibus lotis, reuertentes in chorum, pulsato alio signo, cantent nonam.

Ad uesperas secunda et tercia feria, pulsentur signa,
sicut priuatis diebus ; inter signa dicantur psalmi, Deus
auribus nostris [1] ; post uesperas de omnibus sanctis,
dicantur uesperae mortuorum ; uigilia mortuorum his
diebus non agatur si processio extra claustrum perrexerit,
alioquin agatur sicut solet.

His tribus diebus ad nocturna, capitula et collectae
de resurrectione, et ad uesperas secundae et terciae
feriae. Ad matutinas uero laudes et ad terciam, et ad
sextam, et ad nonam, capitulum et collectae de ieiuniis.
Si in his tribus diebus festiuitas duodecim lectionum
euenerit, totum seruitium noctis et diei de ipsa festiuitate
agatur. Dicta tercia, et pulsatis omnibus signis, missa
ipsius festiuitatis sicut alio tempore solenniter celebretur.
Processio uadat sicut aliis diebus excepto quod calciati
125 et sine baculis ibunt. Missa / ieiunii ad monasterium,
quo processerint, celebretur. Si autem festiuitas trium
lectionum euenerit, commemoratio ipsius tantummodo
fiat ad uesperas, et ad matutinas laudes et ad priorem
missam de ieiunio.

* reliquiis C   [1] Ps. 43 (44)

shall sing *Exaudi Deus* and the community *Voces nostras* ; the cantors *Exaudi Christe* and the community *Miserere nobis* ; the cantors *Exaudi Deus* and the community *Orationem populi tui*. When all the brethren have entered the choir and the cross and all else that was carried have been set in their places, the two cantors already mentioned shall stand in the middle of the choir and intone the litany *Sancte sanctorum Deus, miserere nobis* ; the seniors shall be nearest to the altar, and the rest behind them in order. When the litany is done the bell for None shall ring, and when the None prayer is over they shall go to the cloister to wash their feet, after which they shall return to choir, another bell shall ring and None be sung.

At Vespers on this Monday and Tuesday the bells shall ring as on ferial days ; while they are ringing the psalm *Deus auribus nostris* [1] shall be said ; after Vespers of All Saints those of the Dead shall be said ; Vigils of the Dead shall not be said on these days if the procession has gone outside the cloister, otherwise they shall be said as usual. On these three days the chapters and collects at Matins shall be of Eastertide, and also at Vespers on Monday and Tuesday. At Lauds, however, and at Terce, Sext and None, the chapter and collect shall be of the fast-day. If a feast of twelve lessons occurs on one of these three days all the night and day office shall be of the feast, and after Terce, when all the bells have been rung, Mass of the festival shall be solemnly celebrated as at other seasons. The procession shall be made as on the other days, save that they shall go shod and without staves. The Mass of the fast-day shall be celebrated at the church to which they go. If a feast of three lessons occurs, a commemoration only shall be made of it at Vespers and Lauds and the first Mass of the fast-day.

SABBATO in uigilia pentecostes, surgentes a meridiana, abluti et pectinati ad aecclesiam ueniant, et oratione facta, induantur officium celebraturi, et ad officium seruituri. Agatur officium festiue sicut in sabbato sancto[1]; cantor, et alius frater, quem uoluerit, induti cappis pronuncient letaniam ternam, sicut in uigilia pascae. Cum pronunciatum fuerit Accendite, accendatur cereus benedictus, et reliqua luminaria, unus enim cereus solummodo ante illam horam debet esse accensus ante altare. Cum inceperint Kyrieleison, pulsentur omnia signa. Sequatur Gloria in excelsis. Ad euangelium teneantur candelabra, et thuribulum. Post missam pulsatis duobus maioribus signis faciant orationem. Nonae etiam duo cantores in cappis. In crastino, et totis octauis agatur sicut in paschali solennitate, et octauis paschalis solennitatis, nisi quod octaua huius festiuitatis die, utraque missa est Spiritus Domini.[2]

FERIA SECUNDA, si nulla festiuitas sit, dicatur missa Domine in tua misericordia.[3] Hac ebdomada inchoanda sunt ieiunia, quae regula praecipit,[4] quarta et sexta feria, usque ad idus Septembris ; nisi rationabilis causa existat, cur abbas, uel prior, bis reficiendi licentiam tribuat. Post capitulum ipsis ieiuniorum diebus, sedeant in claustro loquentes. Secretarius uero non pulsabit minimum signum sicut consuetudo est post capitulum ad apparatum missae. Post terciam pergant infantes, et minuti sanguine, et infirmi, quibus licentia data est, accipere mixtum. Post sextam agatur meridiana ; a qua

---

[1] Albers I 72 ; II 53
[2] The first Sunday after Pentecost was elsewhere appropriated as the feast of the Holy Trinity, e.g. at Cluny (cf. Albers II 54, and Bernard of Cluny II xxv 333), though Farfa (Albers I 78) has the Pentecost office. Ethelwold's *Regularis Concordia* (c. viii) has the feast, which was reintroduced at Canterbury, during the first years of Archbishop Thomas Becket.

ON SATURDAY, THE VIGIL OF PENTECOST, rising from the siesta they shall go to the church after they have washed and combed themselves, and, after a space for prayer, those who are to celebrate or to serve the office of the day shall vest. The office shall be of festal rite as on Holy Saturday [1] ; the precentor, and another brother of his choice, vested in albs, shall intone the litany, to be sung with three invocations, as on the vigil of Easter. When *Accendite* is sung, the blessed candle shall be lighted and the rest of the lamps ; until this, only one candle is to be lighted before the altar. When the *Kyrie* is begun all the bells shall be rung ; *Gloria in excelsis* shall follow. Lights and incense are borne at the gospel. After Mass two great bells are rung and there is a space for prayer. At None there shall be two cantors in copes. The following day and the whole octave shall be celebrated as at Eastertide and its octave, save that on the octave day of Pentecost both Masses are *Spiritus Domini*. [2]

ON MONDAY, if no feast occurs, the Mass *Domine in tua misericordia* [3] shall be said. In this week the fast as prescribed by the Rule [4] shall begin, on Wednesdays and Fridays, until September 13th, unless there be a reasonable cause for the abbot or prior to give permission for a second meal. After chapter on these fast-days they shall sit for conversation in the cloister, but the sacristan shall not ring the smallest bell as is usually done after chapter as a signal for vesting for Mass. After Terce the children, and those who have been bled, and the sick who have permission, shall go to partake of the *mixtum*. After Sext the siesta shall take place, and when they rise

---

[3] i.e. that of the first Sunday after Pentecost
[4] *Regula* XLI 5

surgentes, nudis pedibus in claustrum ueniant, afferentes
calciamenta sua. Post haec abluti et pectinati ueniant
in aecclesiam, et facta oratione, pulsatisque duobus
126 signis, inchoet infans Exurge Domine, et / caetera, sicut
longe superius dictum est. Hic ordo seruandus est feria
quarta et sexta, usque ad festiuitatem omnium sanctorum, nisi sit uigilia, cuius missa solenniter celebretur,
tunc enim processio ex toto dimittitur.

DOMINICA prima post octauas pentecostes canantur
ymni ad nocturna, et ad matutinas laudes, Nocte surgentes ; Ecce iam noctis ; qui canendi sunt dominicis
diebus, usque ad dominicam primam mensis Octobris.[1]
Ponantur ad legendum libri regum, et paralipomenon
usque ad dominicam primam mensis Augusti. Hystoria,
Deus omnium.[2]

DOMINICA prima mensis Augusti ponant Salomonem,
usque ad dominicam primam mensis Septembris. Responsoria, In principio.[3]

DOMINICA prima mensis Septembris ponant Iob, Tobi,
Iudith, Hester, Hesdram, usque ad dominicam primam
mensis Octobris.

AB IDIBUS Septembris priuatis diebus agantur continue ieiunia, quae regula praecipit,[4] atque ipsa die iduum
incipiant ieiunare sicut sanctus * Benedictus instituit, una
tantum uice loquantur in claustro usque ad calendas
Octobris, id est, post capitulum usque ad terciam. Post
sextam in dormitorium uadant, et post paruissimum

---

* beatus A B C
[1] Albers II 54. These are the two short summer hymns, discontinued
at the end of September (v. supra, p. 3). For texts, v. HB II 134v, 135v.
[2] HB II 134v

from this they shall go into the cloister barefoot, carrying their shoes. Then, having washed and combed themselves, they shall enter the church, and after a space for prayer, when two bells have been rung, one of the children shall intone *Exurge Domine* and the rest, as set out a long way back. This arrangement is to hold on Wednesdays and Fridays until the feast of All Saints, unless a vigil with its solemn Mass occurs ; in such a case the procession is omitted entirely.

ON THE FIRST SUNDAY after the octave of Pentecost, at Matins and Lauds, the hymns *Nocte surgentes* and *Ecce iam noctis* are sung,[1] and so on Sundays till the first Sunday of October. At Matins the lessons from Kings and Paralipomenon are read until the first Sunday of August, with the sung responsory *Deus omnium.*[2]

ON THE FIRST SUNDAY OF AUGUST the books of Solomon begin and continue till the first Sunday of September, with the responsories *In principio*[3] etc.

ON THE FIRST SUNDAY OF SEPTEMBER begins the Book of Job, which, with Tobias, Judith, Esther and Esdras, continues till the first Sunday of October.

FROM THE THIRTEENTH OF SEPTEMBER, on ferial days, fasting begins as in the Rule,[4] and the thirteenth itself, as appointed by St Benedict, is a fast-day ; talking shall take place in the cloister but once daily until the first of October, that is to say, after chapter until Terce. After Sext they shall go to the dormitory, and after a very short interval, when the smallest bell has been rung,

---

[3] *HB* II 138
[4] *Regula* XLI 13

interuallum, pulsato minimo signo, descendant, lauent,
ad monasterium pergant, factaque oratione, dictaque
letania, missam celebrent. Celebrata fere missa pulsetur
signum ad nonam. Post missam facta oratione, pergant
seruitores accipere mixtum. Quibus reuertentibus pulsato alio signo canatur nona.

QUINQUE sunt praecipuae festiuitates,[1] id est, natale
Domini, resurrectio eius, pentecostes, assumptio sanctae
Dei genetricis Mariae,[2] festiuitas loci ; seruatis omnibus,
quae de sabbato sancto[3] dicta sunt, in harum festiuitatum
uigiliis ornetur totum monasterium, et omnia altaria,
127 secundum facultatem loci, sicut honestius fieri potest./
Mundentur officinae et claustrum. Sedilia refectorii,
capituli, claustri tegantur bancalibus. Sternatur iuncus.

Ad missam ieiunii[4] induantur honeste, qui eam sunt
celebraturi. Sacerdos honorifice,[5] diaconus dalmatica,
subdiaconus tunica. Tres conuersi, cantor ebdomadarius
cappa, duo fratres ad responsoria. Ante missam pulsentur signa, sicut in festis diebus, letania minime dicatur.
Kyrieleison festiuum canatur, una tantum collecta
dicatur. Si festiuitas in hac die euenerit, missa matutinalis de ea cantetur. Ad nonam duo maiora signa pulsentur. Ad uesperas duo minima, dehinc gradatim duo
et duo, ad extremum omnia. Inter signa, luminaria
monasterii omnia accendantur. Ante singula altaria,
quae extra presbyterium sunt, singula luminaria ardeant.
Antiphonas super psalmos, quibus cantor praeceperit,
incipiant. Responsorium quatuor in cappis canant.
Antiphona ad Magnificat ter dicatur ; abbas et prior,

---

[1] Bernard of Cluny I 1 244, has Christmas, Easter, Pentecost, SS Peter
and Paul, and the Assumption. The fourth was of course Cluny's patronal
feast.   [2] 15 August   [3] v. supra, p. 46
[4] Missa jejunii, i.e. Mass of the vigil.
[5] Bernard of Cluny I 1 244 : ' festivis atque auratis vestimentis.'

they shall come down, wash and go to the church, where, after prayer and the litany said, they shall celebrate Mass. When the Mass is ending the bell shall ring for None. After Mass and prayer the servers shall go to partake of the *mixtum* ; when they return another bell shall ring and None be sung.

THERE ARE FIVE PRINCIPAL FESTIVALS,[1] that is, Christmas ; Easter ; Pentecost ; the Assumption of Mary, holy Mother of God [2] ; and the feast of the house. All shall be done as noted on Holy Saturday [3] ; on the vigil of these feasts the whole church shall be decorated, together with all the altars, as richly as possible according to the means of the house. All offices and the cloister shall be cleaned ; the seats in refectory, chapter and cloister shall be draped, and rushes strewn on the floor. At Mass on the vigil [4] the celebrants shall be richly vested ; the priest in a fine chasuble,[5] the deacon in a dalmatic, the subdeacon in a tunicle. Three converses shall minister, the weekly cantor shall wear a cope, and there shall be two brethren to sing the responsory. Before Mass the bells shall ring as on festal days, and the litany shall not be said. A festive *Kyrie* shall be sung, and a single collect. If a feast occur on this day the Morrow Mass shall be of the feast. Two of the greater bells shall ring for None ; for Vespers the two smallest, then gradually the rest, two by two, and finally all together. While the bells are ringing for Vespers all the lights in the church shall be kindled, and a light shall burn before every altar outside the presbytery. The cantor shall appoint those who are to intone the antiphons, and four in copes shall sing the responsory. The antiphon at the Magnificat shall be sung thrice ; the abbot and prior in copes shall incense both altars in the presbytery ; both together shall incense

cappis induti, incensent utraque presbyterii altaria ante
et desuper utrique simul, singuli singula latera.* Parati
sint duo alii sacerdotes ebdomadarii, scilicet maioris et
minoris missae,† qui thuribula de eorum manibus accipiant, et hinc et inde per altaria, quae extra sunt, circumferant. Qui reuertentes in chorum, abbati prius, priori
postea, ferant, post eis qui responsorium cantauerunt,
non ambo simul, sed unus hinc, et alter inde ; dehinc
duo conuersi in albis caeteris fratribus. Abbati de libro
seruiat, qui thuribulum de eius manu accepit. In his
uigiliis tabulae refectorii debent esse coopertae.

IN CRASTINO, ante nocturnas uigilias, ad excitandos
fratres pulsentur omnia signa ; dehinc gradatim duo et
duo, ad extremum omnia. Ad inuitatorium quatuor in
cappis. Terna responsoria in tribus nocturnis duo et
duo ; quartum quatuor ; octauum quinque ; duodecimum sex canant. In tribus nocturnis dum legitur
tertia lectio, duo sacerdotes, cappis induti, incensent
altaria maius et minus ; dehinc ferant abbati et priori
128 et caeteris fratribus per ordinem ; / octauum et duodecimum responsorium post Gloriam a capite repetantur ;
pronunciato euangelio altare discooperiatur, et omnia
luminaria accendantur. Ad Te Deum laudamus duo
maiora signa pulsentur ; lecto euangelio, collecta dicta,
pulsatis omnibus signis, inchoet sacerdos matutinas
laudes ; dehinc in uestiarium reuersus casulam et stolam
deponat, et sic in alba cum manipulo in chorum redeat.
Incepto ymno exeat, manipulum deponat, cappam induat, et cum alio fratre similiter ‡ induto sicut ad hester-

---

* altaria C
† missae et minoris A
‡ + cappa A B

p. VII

"The monasticism was ... of the
Abbey of Fleury-sur-Loire!

the altar from in front and from above, and separately the two ends. Two other priests of the week shall be at hand, those of the High and Low Mass, to receive the thuribles from the hands of abbot and prior and carry them about the altars outside the presbytery. Returning, they shall incense first the abbot and prior and then those who have sung the responsory, not both together but one on this side and the other on that ; then two converses in albs shall incense the other brethren. He who took the thurible from the abbot's hand shall hold the book for him. On these vigils the tables in the refectory should be covered with cloths.

ON THE MORROW, before the night choirs, all the bells shall ring to waken the brethren, then in stages two by two, and finally all together again. At the invitatory there shall be four in copes. There shall be three responsories in the three nocturns sung by two voices ; four shall sing the fourth, five the eighth and six the twelfth. In all three nocturns, while the third lesson is being sung, two priests in copes shall incense the high altar and lesser altar, and then abbot, prior and other brethren in order. The eighth and twelfth responsories shall be repeated from the beginning after the *Gloria.* When the Gospel has been sung the altar shall be uncovered and all the lights kindled. At the *Te Deum* the two largest bells shall be rung ; when the Gospel has been read and the collect said, and all the bells rung, the priest of the week shall begin Lauds ; then, returning to the vestry, he shall lay aside his chasuble and stole and so return to choir in an alb and with his maniple ; when the hymn begins he shall go out, lay aside the maniple, put on the cope, and with another brother likewise in a cope go with thuribles to all the

nas uesperas cum thuribulis per altaria uadat, duobus
conuersis cum eis indutis in albis. Si abbas euangelium
legerit, post euangelium, indutus cappa, in chorum
reuertatur. Antiphona ad Benedictus ter dicatur. Ad
primam duo maiora signa pulsentur. Tres cerei ante
altare accendantur, similiter ad terciam et sextam et
nonam ; capitulum breuiter peragatur.

Missa matutinalis cum una collecta et praefatione
dicatur. Dum sacerdos in canone est, remanentibus
infantibus cum magistris suis in choro, qui ante missam
debent esse induti, caeteri pergant induere se, qui
accipientes a secretario uestimenta extra secretarium se
induant. Si uero locus paruus * est, exeant aliqui in
claustrum uel capitulum, et ibi induant se.¹ Meliores
uero albae tribuantur prioribus et honestioribus personis ;
unusquisque mox ut indutus fuerit, reuertatur in chorum,
missa peracta, si dies dominicus non fuerit, cessante
maiore signo, quod incepta ultima collecta missae pulsari coepit, fiat oratio terciae. Post orationem, pulsato
alio signo, cantetur tercia.

Si uero dies dominicus fuerit, expleta matutinali
missa, non pulsato adhuc terciae signo, fit aqua benedicta,
sicut aliis dominicis diebus fieri solet ; dum cantant
Asperges me, pulsetur maius signum ad terciam. Aspersa
aqua benedicta, uadat sacerdos per officinas cum portitoribus aquae et crucis. Cessante signo, fiat oratio
terciae. Qua expleta, pulsato alio signo, canatur tercia.
129 Sacerdos interim, / qui per officinas iuit, reuertens ante
introitum monasterii, dicat orationem solitam ; dehinc
intrans ante unum de altaribus,† via sanctorum.²

* paruus locus A   † + dicat C
¹ Albs are put on here ; copes later after Terce, v. infra, p. 58.
² From Bernard of Cluny I xlv 236, we learn that the prayer beginning *Via sanctorum omnium, Domine,* was said by the Armarius (precentor)
or president of the choir, standing before the high altar, immediately
before Terce.

altars as at Vespers the day before ; two converses in albs shall accompany them. If the abbot reads the Gospel he returns to choir after it, wearing the cope. The antiphon at the *Benedictus* shall be said thrice. For Prime two large bells shall ring and three candles burn before the high altar, and the same shall be done at Terce, Sext and None. The chapter shall be speedily finished.

The Morrow Mass shall be said with one collect and preface. While the priest is saying the canon, and while the children, who have been vested before Mass, remain with their masters in choir, the others go to vest, and receiving their vestments from the sacristan they shall put them on outside the sacristy. If the space is not large enough, some of them shall go into the chapter-house or cloister and vest there.[1] The best albs shall be given to the priors and the monks of dignity ; everyone, so soon as he is vested, shall return to choir, and when the Mass is over, if it be not a Sunday, and the big bell, which began to ring when the final collect was begun, has ceased, the prayer before Terce shall be made. After prayer, when another bell has rung, Terce shall be sung.

Should it be a Sunday, however, when the Morrow Mass is ended the bell is not rung for Terce at once, but there is a blessing of holy water, as usual on Sundays ; while *Asperges me* is sung the big bell shall be rung for Terce. When the holy water has been sprinkled, a priest shall go through the whole monastery with the bearers of holy water and the cross. When the bell ceases the prayer of Terce is made, and when this is done, and another bell has rung, Terce shall be sung. Meanwhile the priest who has gone round the house and returned to the door of the church shall say the customary prayer, and then, going before one of the altars, he shall say *Via sanctorum*.[2]

Dicta tercia, distributis cappis, dispositis in choro
a cantore qui ea, quae portanda sunt, portare debent,
exeant omnes hoc ordine processuri. Primum conuersus
ferens situlam cum aqua benedicta ; dehinc duo portantes duas cruces ; post quos duo cum duobus candelabris accensis desuper cereis ; alii duo ferentes duo
thuribula igne et thure plena ; hos sequantur duo subdiaconi tunicis induti, portantes duos euangelii textus ;
post quos infantes cum magistris suis ; extremi abbas,
et priores, praecedentibus aliis binis et binis, sicut est
ordo eorum. Cum processio de choro incipit exire,
pulsentur duo maiora signa, non cessatura usque dum
processio in chorum sit reuersa, cessentque alia signa.
Procedentes per maiores ianuas monasterium introeant,
et ante crucifixum stationem facient. Qua facta, expleto
cantu quem inceperant, incipiat abbas, uel cantor, quod
ad ipsum diem pertineat, et sic sonantibus omnibus
signis chorum introeant, eisque cessantibus missam
incipiant.

Ante missae introitum sternatur unum aut duo tapetia
per transuersum chori, ubi stare debeat cantor, et caeteri,
quos ad se uocauerit ad regendum chorum. Omnes
cerei, qui in coronis sunt, et caetera luminaria, quae in
choro et presbyterio, et ante crucifixum sunt, accendantur.
Cantor prouideat quot et qui, quae singulariter cantanda
sunt, cantent. Ad sequentiam duo maiora signa pulsentur. Communio, si opus fuerit, repetatur cum uersu
et Gloria Patri. Expleta missa, pulsentur omnia signa ;
unusquisque uestimentum suum et cappam, utraque
bene plicata, deferat secretario ad arcam.

Festiuae mappae super tabulas refectorii sint extensae,

When Terce has been said and copes have been given out and the cantor has allotted their places in choir to those who are to be bearers in the procession, all shall go in procession as follows—first a converse, bearing the bucket with holy water ; then two bearers with crosses ; then two with candlesticks and lighted candles ; then two bearing thuribles with lighted coals and incense ; then two subdeacons in tunics carrying two gospel books ; then the children with their masters ; finally the abbot and priors, following the brethren who walk two by two in order. When the procession begins to leave the choir, the two great bells shall be rung and shall not cease until the procession returns to the choir and the other bells cease. Going through the great door they shall then enter the church and halt before the crucifix ; then, when they have finished the chant that has been begun, the abbot or cantor shall intone the chant of the day, and so, while all the bells ring they shall enter the choir, and when the bells stop they shall begin Mass.

Before the introit one or two carpets shall be laid down at the crossing of the choir, where stand the cantor and the others whom he has chosen to lead the choir. All the tapers on the circlets, and the other lights in choir and in the presbytery and before the crucifix, shall be lighted. The cantor shall arrange who, and how many, are to sing the solo chants. At the sequence two great bells shall ring ; the Communion shall be repeated with its verse and *Gloria* if necessary. When Mass is over, all bells shall be rung, and each one shall give back his alb and cope, properly folded, to the sacristan at the chest.

Festal tablecloths shall be spread in the refectory,

ita ut ante pendeant. Sint et cotidianae, lotae tamen, super quas manducent fratres. Manutergia [1] etiam 130 candida et / honesta super tersoria quotidiana sint extensa ; quae manutergia post capitulum a camerariis sunt extendenda. Nullus tamen fratrum debet ibi manus tergere, nisi solummodo ad refectionem primam, et sero ad cenam.

Ad nonam duo maiora signa pulsentur. Ad uesperas agatur de signis et caeteris,* sicut actum est ad uesperas praecedentis diei. Post cenam refectis seruitoribus colligant refectorarii mappas festiuas, et bene plicatas reddant celerario conseruandas ; camerarius uero honestiora tersoria accipiat et custodiat.

SUNT ALIAE festiuitates, quae magnifice celebrantur, quamuis non aequaliter superioribus ; sunt autem hae [2] : epiphania,[3] purificatio sanctae Mariae,[4] festiuitas sancti Gregorii,[5] annunciatio Christi,[6] octaua dies paschalis solemnitatis, festiuitas sancti Aelfegi martyris,[7] ascensio Christi, festiuitas sancti Augustini Anglorum archiepiscopi,[8] octaua pentecostes dies, natiuitas sancti Joannis baptistae,[9] passio apostolorum Petri et Pauli,[10] translatio sancti Benedicti,[11] natiuitas sanctae Mariae,[12] festiuitas sancti Michaelis,[13] festiuitas omnium sanctorum,[14] festiuitas sancti Andreae,[15] dedicatio aecclesiae.

Harum omnium festiuitatum praecedentibus diebus ornentur altaria, presbyterium, chorus, membra monasterii ex utraque parte chori ; pulsentur signa sicut in

---

* cereis A C
[1] These were probably soft towels, as opposed to the rough everyday ones.
[2] Bernard of Cluny I 1 243, has a somewhat different list.
[3] 6 January   [4] 2 February   [5] 12 March
[6] 25 March
[7] 17 April. Lanfranc had for a time been sceptical of the merits of Old English saints, particularly St Alphege (Aelfheah, ob. 1012), but had been reassured by Anselm. *v. Vita Lanfranci*, in Giles, *Lanfranci Opera*, 310, and Knowles, *Monastic Order*, 119.

hanging down over the tables in front. The everyday cloths shall be there likewise, for the brethren to eat upon, and these shall be newly washed. White towels of fine quality [1] shall be spread by the chamberlains after chapter over the everyday ones, but no brother should dry his hands with them save before dinner and supper.

For None two of the great bells shall ring, and at Vespers bells and all else shall be as at Vespers the previous day. After supper, when the servers have had their meal, the refectorians shall collect the festal cloths and return them duly folded to the cellarer to store, while the chamberlain receives and stores the better towels.

THERE ARE OTHER FESTIVALS which are kept with solemnity, though not so solemnly as the above ; these are they[2]: Epiphany[3]; Purification of Our Lady[4]; the feast of St Gregory[5]; the Annunciation[6]; the octave of Easter; the feast of St Alphege the martyr[7]; the Ascension ; the feast of St Augustine of England, the archbishop[8]; the octave of Pentecost; the birthday of St John the Baptist[9]; the day of martyrdom of SS Peter and Paul[10]; the translation of St Benedict[11]; the birthday of Our Lady[12]; the feast of St Michael[13]; the feast of All Saints[14]; the feast of St Andrew[15]; and the Dedication of the church.

On the day before all these feasts the altars, presbytery, choir and parts of the church on each side of the choir shall be decorated ; bells shall be rung as on the principal feasts ; two-thirds of the tapers in the circlet

---

[8] 26 May   [9] 24 June   [10] 29 June
[11] 11 July, when the feast of the translation of the body of the saint at Fleury was celebrated, and kept with the more solemnity since the day of St Benedict's death fell in Lent (21 March)
[12] 8 September   [13] 29 September   [14] 1 November
[15] 30 November

praecipuis festis * ; accendantur duae partes cereorum
coronae presbyterii, et omnia luminaria quae circa maius
altare sunt, et cereus ante crucifixum ; antiphonae, si
propriae habentur, quibus cantor praeceperit, super
psalmos imponant. Sin autem, cum una antiphona de
ipsa festiuitate canantur ; responsorium duo in cappis.
Antiphona ad Magnificat bis dicatur ; duo sacerdotes
cappis induti ad thuribula, sicut superius de praecipuis
festiuitatibus dictum est.

Missae uigiliarum ascensionis Christi, Ioannis baptistae, apostolorum Petri et Pauli, omnium sanctorum
festiue celebrentur. Si quaelibet harum uigiliarum, uel
131 alia aliqua, / quae festiue celebretur, dominica die
euenerit, totum seruitium noctis, et missa matutinalis
de dominica agatur ; maior uero missa, cum alleluia
post responsorium, de uigilia dicatur, excepta dominicae
natiuitatis uigilia, in qua si ita euenerit in tercio nocturno
de ipsa uigilia cantatur et legitur. In crastino ante
nocturnas uigilias pulsentur signa, bina et bina, dehinc
simul omnia. Ad inuitatorium tres in cappis, tria
responsoria in tribus nocturnis duo et duo canant,
quartum tres, octauum quatuor, duodecimum quinque,
quod post Gloriam a capite repetatur. Pronunciato
euangelio altare discooperiatur, luminaria, sicut ad
uesperas praecedentis diei, accendantur. Antiphona ad
Benedictus bis dicatur, et thuribula similiter circumferantur. Ad primam, duo signa pulsentur, tres cerei
accendantur, similiter ad terciam et sextam et nonam.
Ornentur sedilia, extendantur mappae et tersoria, sicut
supra dictum est. Missa matutinalis de ipsa solennitate
cum una collecta, nisi sit festiuitas alicuius sancti, unde
commemoratio fiat ; quod si euenerit, matutinalis missa

---

* festiuitatibus A

in the presbytery and all the lamps about the high altar and the taper before the crucifix shall be lighted ; the antiphons, if they are proper to the feast, shall be given out by those to whom the cantor gives the task ; if they are not proper, the psalms shall be sung under a single antiphon of the feast. Two in copes shall sing the responsory, the antiphon at the *Magnificat* shall be repeated once ; and two priests in copes shall bear thuribles as on the principal feasts.

The Masses of the vigils of the Ascension, St John the Baptist, SS Peter and Paul and All Saints shall be celebrated with festal rite. If any of these vigils or any other days with festal celebration occur on a Sunday, the whole night office and the Morrow Mass are of the Sunday, but the High Mass is said of the vigil, with the Alleluia after the Gradual, save on the vigil of Christmas when, should this happen, all of the third nocturn is of the vigil. On the following day before the night choirs the bells are rung two by two and then all together. At the invitatory there shall be three in copes ; the three first responsories in the three nocturns shall be sung by two against two, the fourth by three, the eighth by four and the twelfth by five, and this last shall be repeated from the beginning after the *Gloria*. When the Gospel has been read the altar shall be uncovered and the lamps lighted as at Vespers on the peceding day. The antiphon at the Benedictus shall be recited twice, and the incensing shall be as before. At Prime two bells shall ring, three candles shall be lighted, and the same at Terce, Sext and None. The seats shall be covered and tablecloths and towels provided as above. The Morrow Mass shall be of the solemnity of the day with a single collect, unless there occur the feast of a saint to be commemorated ; if this happens the Morrow Mass

11

erit de sancto, et collecta prima, secunda de ipsa solennitate, et non amplius. Sacerdotes ad missas priuatas similiter collectam unam. Dicta matutinali missa, canatur tercia, celebretur missa in cappis, excepta purificatione sanctae Mariae, in qua ad missam sint omnes albis induti propter cereos, praeter cantorem, et eos qui circa eum sunt, quos cappis etiam indutos esse oportet.[1] Excipiuntur quoque beati Gregorii,[2] et dominicae annunciationis[3] festiuitates, quando intra quadragesimam celebrantur. In his enim similiter sint omnes albis induti, praeter supradictos, et eos qui responsorium et tractum cantant. Hi namque praecipiente cantore, accedentes ad cantandum cappas in choro induant, et cum percantauerint uenientes in uestiarium eas ibi deponant. Cantor quot, et quos uoluerit ad se uocet. Numerus cantantium responsorium et Alleluia et caetera quae 132 cantanda sunt, in arbi/trio cantoris sit. Celebrata missa pulsentur omnia signa. Si aliqua harum festiuitatum dominica die euenerit, dicta matutinali missa, fiat aqua benedicta, et processio per claustrum, sicut solet dominicis diebus, omnes tamen sint albis induti. Ad nonam pulsentur signa duo, et agantur uesperae sicut praecedenti die. Festiuitatem beati Gregorii inter superiores ideo computamus, quia nostrae, id est, Anglorum gentis apostolus est.[4]

Si dominicae annunciationis festiuitas aliqua quadragesimae dominica euenerit, in crastinum differatur; alioquin seruitium dominicae diei restaurari non posset. Uesperae usque ad capitulum de dominica agantur, capitulum de festiuitate dicatur. Post primam collectam commemoratio dominicae diei fiat. Si sabbato euenerit,

---

[1] Bernard of Cluny II ix 297, says this was an innovation of Abbot Hugh of Cluny. The candle droppings would harm the fine stuffs; it would moreover be awkward to hold a candle when wearing a stiff cope.
[2] 12 March

shall be of the saint, with the first collect of the saint and the second, the only other one, of the solemnity. Priests saying private Masses shall say one collect only. When the Morrow Mass is done Terce shall be sung and Mass celebrated in copes, save on the Purification, on which day all at Mass shall wear albs, on account of the candles, save for the cantor and those about him who shall wear copes.[1] The same exception holds on the feasts of St Gregory[2] and the Annunciation,[3] when they are kept in Lent. On these likewise all shall wear albs save for those mentioned above, and those who sing the Gradual and Tract. These, at the motion of the cantor, shall put on their copes in choir when about to sing, and when they have done shall take them off and lay them in the vestry. The cantor shall choose as many as he wishes, and whom he wishes, to stand with him. The number of those singing the Gradual and Alleluia and other pieces rests with the precentor. When the Mass is done all the bells shall ring. If any of these feasts fall on a Sunday, after the Morrow Mass the water is blessed and there is the usual Sunday procession in the cloister, but all shall wear albs. For None two bells are rung, and Vespers are celebrated as on the previous day. The Feast of St Gregory is counted among the greatest because he is the apostle of our people, that is, of England.[4]

If the Annunciation falls on a Sunday in Lent it is put off till the following day, otherwise the office of the Sunday would fall out. Vespers shall be of the Sunday up to the chapter, the chapter shall be of the feast. After the first collect there shall be a commemoration of the Sunday. If the feast come on a Saturday the whole

---

[3] 25 March
[4] This is one of the few recognizable touches of Lanfranc's own hand.

totum diei seruitium de ipsa solennitate agatur. Post primam uespertinam collectam, collecta de dominica agatur, excepto sabbato ante palmas, in quo si haec festiuitas euenerit, de ipsa festiuitate agatur seruitium usque ad capitulum uespertinum. Ipsa die duo fratres in froccis responsorium cantent, unus sacerdos cappa indutus altaria incenset. Post primam collectam commemoratio festiuitatis fiat. Si uero tercia feria post palmas euenerit, festiuitas quidem, sicut dictum est, celebretur, sed fratres in crastino radantur, et tunc post capitulum et post sextam in claustro loquantur. Qui autem ipso die balneari non poterunt, in crastino qui uoluerint balneentur. Si uero quinta feria, uel sexta, uel sabbato ante pasca, uel in paschali solennitate, uel tribus sequentibus diebus * euenerit, in quintam feriam post paschalem solennitatem differatur. Festiuitas ista tunc ita solenniter agatur sicut paschalis solennitas, excepto quod pro skilla ante nocturnas uigilias ad excitandos fratres classicum non pulsetur, nec processio fiat. Antiphonae et responsoria, quae in hac festiuitate in quadragesima canerentur, in hoc quoque tempore, cum adiunctis alleluia canantur ; uersiculi quoque 133 omnes cum finali alleluia dicantur. / Inuitatorium alleluia, alleluia, secundum melodiam inuitatorii Aue Maria ; cantica de aduentu Domini.¹

DIE ASCENSIONIS Christi fiat processio in albis, uel extra claustrum circa curiam monasterii, † praecedentibus uexillis et reliquiis, cum reliquis, quae ad festiuam processionem praecedere solent, uel per claustrum sine uexillis. Ex quo incipit processio exire pulsentur duo signa, sicut superius dictum est.

---

* *om.* A   † monasterii curiam A   ¹ i.e. Isaias xl.10-17, etc.

office shall be of the feast. After the first collect at Vespers the Sunday collect shall be said, save on Saturday before Palm Sunday ; if this feast fall on that day, the office of the feast is continued only until the chapter of Vespers. On the day itself two brethren in cowls shall sing the responsory ; one priest in a cope shall incense the altars. After the first collect there shall be a commemoration of the feast. If the Annunciation fall on Tuesday in Holy Week it shall be kept, as set out above, but the brethren shall shave on the following day and then there shall be talking in the cloister after chapter and after Sext. Those who cannot bathe on the feast day shall bathe, if they wish, the next day. If, however, this feast occur on the Thursday, Friday or Saturday of Holy Week, or on Easter Sunday or one of the three following days, it shall be put off until the Thursday after Easter. In such a case the feast shall be kept as solemnly as Easter, save that the peal of bells shall not be used instead of the small bell to wake the brethren for the night choirs, and there shall be no procession. The antiphons and responsories, which would be sung on this feast if it came in Lent, shall be used in Paschal time also, with *Alleluia* added ; similarly, the versicles shall all have a final *Alleluia*. The invitatory shall be *Alleluia, Alleluia,* to the melody of the invitatory *Ave Maria* ; the canticles shall be those of Advent.[1]

ON ASCENSION DAY there shall be a procession in albs, and it may either go outside the cloister round the great court, with banners and relics and all else pertaining to a festal procession, or it may go through the cloister without banners. As the procession starts two bells shall be rung, as above.

In DIE natiuitatis sanctae Mariae. Ad uesperas, psalmi Dixit Dominus ; Laetatus sum ; Nisi Dominus aedificauerit domum ; Memento Domine Dauid,[1] cum antiphona De fructu uentris tui, qui psalmus cum hac antiphona quartus dicitur in omnibus festiuitatibus sanctae Mariae.

In FESTIUITATE sancti Michaelis psalmi ad uesperas Dixit Dominus ; Confitebor ; Beatus uir ; aliud Confitebor [2] ; cum antiphona In conspectu angelorum.

UIGILIA omnium sanctorum, ad uesperas psalmi cum antiphonis de ipsis psalmis, qui cotidie ad eorum memoriam solent dici [3] ; preces Post partum uirgo, et caetera. Cum dictum fuerit Adducentur uirgines post eam,[4] adiungatur Pro fratribus nostris absentibus ; Mitte eis, Domine, auxilium de sancto ; Domine, exaudi orationem ; Domine, Deus uirtutum ; Dominus uobiscum ; post collectam commemoratio solummodo de sancta cruce. In crastino ad laudes similiter preces Post partum uirgo ; ad uesperas psalmi, et super psalmos antiphonae, sicut praecedente * die. Dictis uesperis, pulsentur omnia signa, et productius solito canantur uesperae pro defunctis, nisi in crastino sit dies dominicus, uel quaelibet festiuitas duodecim lectionum ; collecta una, Fidelium Deus. Sequente autem nocte ad uigiliam mortuorum pulsentur similiter omnia signa. Ipsa die sacerdotes omnes celebrent missas pro omnibus fidelibus defunctis.[5]

---

* precedenti A
[1] Ps. 109 (110), 121 (122), 126 (127), 131 (132). So also Bernard of Cluny II xxx 348. In the monastic breviary the psalms are : 109 (110), 112 (113), 121 (122), and 126 (127).
[2] Ps. 109 (110), 110 (111), 111 (112), 137 (138) ; the last psalm was chosen on account of the second verse (from which the antiphon is taken) : ' In conspectu angelorum psallam tibi.'

ON OUR LADY'S BIRTHDAY the psalms at Vespers shall be *Dixit Dominus ; Laetatus sum ; Nisi Dominus ;* and *Memento Domine,*[1] with the antiphon *De fructu ventris tui ;* and this psalm and antiphon shall be sung in the fourth place on all festivals of saint Mary.

ON THE FEAST OF ST MICHAEL the psalms at Vespers shall be *Dixit Dominus, Confitebor, Beatus vir* and the other *Confitebor*[2] with the antiphon *In conspectu angelorum.*

ON THE VIGIL OF ALL SAINTS the psalms at Vespers shall be the psalms and antiphons accompanying them which are wont to be said daily at the commemoration of All Saints,[3] with the *preces, Post partum virgo* and the rest. When the verse *Adducentur regi virgines post eam* has been said,[4] there shall be added : *Pro fratribus nostris absentibus ; Mitte eis, Domine ; Domine, exaudi orationem ; Domine, Deus virtutum ; Dominus vobiscum.* After the collect there is a commemoration of the Cross only. Similarly on the following day at Lauds the *preces Post partum virgo* shall be said. At Vespers the psalms with their antiphons as on the previous day.

When Vespers are done, all the bells shall be rung and Vespers for the dead shall be sung more slowly than usual, unless the next day be a Sunday or a feast of twelve lessons ; there shall be a single collect, *Fidelium Deus.* During the night that follows all the bells shall be rung similarly for the vigils of the dead. On the day itself all the priests shall celebrate Masses for all the faithful departed,[5] while for all those who are not priests

---

[3] i.e. some of the antiphons ordinarily occurring in the daily office of All Saints are used in the office of this vigil, and are not repeated afterwards ; cf. Tolhurst, *HB* VI 34ff., 115ff.

[4] Bernard of Cluny II xxxii 353

[5] A Cluniac devotion, of which St Odilo was the originator or patron ; cf. Bernard of Cluny II xxxii 354.

Qui uero sacerdotes non sunt, iniungantur eis in capitulo psalmi pro missis. Agatur missa matutinalis festiue, pulsentur omnia signa, cappa sit in choro. Leuita et
134 subdiaconus casulis induantur ; duo infantes responso-/rium in albis, duo maiores fratres tractum similiter in albis, tres conuersi ad thuribulum et candelabra. Septem diebus plena officia, usque ad triginta dies Voce mea et Verba mea.[1]

In FESTIUITATE dedicationis aecclesiae * cerei accensi ad priores uesperas per omnia altaria, quae ipsa die sacrata fuerunt, non extinguantur usque in crastinum post completorium. Cantica Laetare Ierusalem ; Vrbs fortitudinis : Non uocaberis ultra.[2] Ipsa die celebretur missa per unumquodque altare si numerus sacerdotum tantus est. Dicta tercia agatur processio festiua in albis, aut circa monasterium, si locus aptus est, aut per claustrum, praecedentibus quae festiuam processionem praecedere solent, et ingrediatur monasterium per maiores ianuas, fiatque statio ante crucifixum. Psalmi ad uesperas, qui in festiuitate uirginum dici solent. Haec festiuitas octauas habet.

Sunt ALIAE terciae dignitatis festiuitates, quae non tantopere celebrantur. Hae autem sunt[3] : festiuitates sancti Vincentii ; conuersio sancti Pauli ; Philippi et Iacobi ; inuentio sanctae crucis ; Iacobi apostoli ; sancti Petri in calendis Augusti ; Laurentii martyris ; octaua dies assumptionis sanctae Mariae ; Bartholomei

---

* ecclesiae dedicationis A
[1] Ps. 141 (142) and 5
[2] Isaias lxvi.10 ; xxvi.1 ; lxii.10
[3] The dates are : 22 January, 25 January, 1 May, 3 May, 25 July, 1 August, 10 August, 22 August, 24 August, 28 August, 29 August, 14 September, 21 September, 28 October, 11 November, 21 December.

psalms shall be allotted instead of Masses at chapter. The Morrow Mass shall be celebrated with festal rite ; all bells shall be rung and there shall be a cope in choir. Deacon and subdeacon shall wear chasubles ; two children shall sing the responsory in albs, and two senior brethren similarly attired shall sing the tract ; three converses shall bear thurible and candles ; for seven days the full office of the dead shall be said, and for thirty days the *Voce mea* and *Verba mea*.[1]

ON THE FEAST OF THE DEDICATION OF THE CHURCH tapers shall be lighted at first Vespers at all the altars which were consecrated on the day of dedication, and shall not be put out until after Compline on the following day. The canticles shall be *Laetare Jerusalem, Urbs fortitudinis* and *Non vocaberis ultra*.[2] On the day itself Mass shall be celebrated at every altar if the number of priests allows. After Terce there shall be a festal procession in albs, either round the church, if the place is suitable, or round the cloister ; all shall be done that usually precedes a festal procession ; the church shall be entered by the main doors and there shall be a halt before the crucifix. The psalms at Vespers shall be those usually said on feasts of virgins. This feast has an octave.

THERE ARE OTHER FEASTS of the third rank, which are not celebrated so solemnly. These are[3] : the feasts of St Vincent ; the Conversion of St Paul, Philip and James ; the Finding of the Holy Cross ; James the Apostle ; St Peter on the first of August ; Laurence the martyr ; the octave day of the Assumption of St Mary ; Bartholomew

apostoli ; Augustini doctoris ; decollatio Ioannis baptistae ; exaltatio sanctae crucis ; Mathei apostoli ; Symonis et Iudae ; beati Martini ; Thomae apostoli ; et si quae aliae festiuitates ita celebrari instituantur.

Pridie ante has festiuitates parentur duo presbyterii altaria, presbyterium, et chorus. Ad nonam, et ad uesperas, pulsentur signa sicut priuatis duodecim lectionibus, nisi quod maiora signa pulsari debent. Tria candelabra ante altare, et caetera luminaria, quae circa altare sunt, accendantur. Uesperae cum una antiphona de ipsa festiuitate canantur, nisi praecedat festiuitas de qua dicantur uesperae usque ad capitulum. Responsorium si propria hystoria est, duo fratres canant in 135 froccis suis ; si non est propria hystoria, sicut / in festiuitatibus quorundam apostolorum, aut si iam cantata est, quemadmodum octaua die assumptionis sanctae Mariae, duo pueri dicant * breue responsorium. Sacerdos indutus cappa incenset altaria, conuersus sit in alba. In crastino ad inuitatorium duo in cappis. Tria responsoria in tribus nocturnis singuli singula ; quartum responsorium duo, octauum tres, duodecimum quatuor, quod post Gloriam repetatur. Pronunciato euangelio, discooperiatur altare, et accendantur luminaria, sicut pridie ad uesperas. Ad Te Deum laudamus duo mediocria signa pulsentur. Post lectum euangelium, sacerdos in chorum redeat in alba. Ad laudes, duo pueri breue responsorium, siue sit propria hystoria siue non. Et ad uesperas similiter. Ad primam, pulsetur unum de maioribus signis ; accendantur duo cerei ante altare, et per omnes horas usque ad uesperas. Ad missam in choro omnes sint albis induti † praeter cantorem et eos,

* canant A C   † *om.* A

the Apostle ; Augustine the doctor ; the Beheading of John the Baptist ; the Exaltation of the Holy Cross ; Matthew the Apostle ; Simon and Jude ; blessed Martin ; Thomas the Apostle ; and any other feasts appointed to have like rank.

On the day before these feasts the two altars of the presbytery, together with the presbytery and choir, shall be decked out. At None and at Vespers the bells shall be rung as on ordinary feasts of twelve lessons, save that greater bells shall be rung. The three candelabra before the altar and the other lights about the altar shall be lighted. Vespers shall be sung under a single antiphon of the feast, unless it is preceded by another feast of which the Vespers are said as far as the chapter. If the responsory is a proper one, two brethren shall sing it in their tunics ; if it is not proper, as happens on some feasts of apostles, or if it has already been sung, as on the octave day of the Assumption, two children shall sing the short responsory. The priest in a cope shall incense the altars, with a converse in an alb. On the following day there shall be two in copes for the invitatory. The three first responsories in the three nocturns shall be sung by one only ; the fourth by two, the eighth by three and the twelfth by four, and this shall be repeated after the *Gloria*. When the gospel has been read, the altar shall be uncovered and the lights kindled as at Vespers on the day before. At the *Te Deum laudamus* two bells of moderate size shall be rung. After the gospel has been read, the priest shall return to choir in his alb. At Lauds two children shall sing the short responsory, whether it be a proper one or no, and similarly at Vespers. At Prime one of the larger bells shall be rung, and two tapers shall be lighted before the altar ; this shall be done at all hours until Vespers. At

qui secum erunt, qui etiam cappis induti chorum regere debent. Ad nonam, pulsetur signum sicut ad primam. Antiphonas super psalmos ad uesperas imponant iuuenes, quibus cantor praecepit. Caetera agantur, sicut ad uesperas praecedentis diei.

AD PRIORES uesperas inuentionis sanctae crucis hymnus Vexilla regis.[1] In crastino inuitatorium, et duo nocturna de martiribus,[2] tercium de sancta cruce ; cantica Domine audiui,[3] quod diuidatur in tres Glorias : prima Gloria est ante uersum Pro iniquitate ; secunda ante uersum Egressus es. Ymnus ad laudes Lustra * sex.[4] Missa matutinalis de martiribus, maior de sancta cruce, psalmi ad uesperas Dixit Dominus ; Confitebor ; Beatus uir ; Laudate pueri [5] : hymnus Vexilla regis.

IN EXALTATIONE sanctae crucis simile seruitium est seruitio inuentionis eiusdem, nisi quod in hac sancta crux adoratur, in illa minime.[6] In hac itaque solennitate, dicta tercia, sternatur presbyterium tapetibus, usque ad maius altare ; quo facto exeant de parte matutinalis altaris duo fratres in albis, quibus cantor praeceperit, 136 portantes crucem cooper/tam, donec ueniant super gradum, qui ante altare est propior ipsi altari ; tunc a portantibus discooperta cruce, et ab eisdem incepta antiphona Ecce lignum crucis,[7] omnes flectant genua, ac

* Lustra D A   Lustras B   Lustris C
[1] This and the hymn of Lauds are portions of the celebrated poem of Venantius Fortunatus (ob. 610). Text in *HB* I 85ff., and *Oxford Book of Medieval Latin Verse*, no. 17.
[2] i.e. SS Alexander and companions, whose feast, an ancient institution, occurs on the same day, 3rd May.
[3] Habakkuk iii.1ff.
[4] See critical note. The first words of the stanza read in the original (as indeed the trochaic metre demands) *Lustra sex qui jam peracta*, where the neuter accusatives are presumably in apposition to *tempus* ; the difficulty of construction and ignorance of the metre led to the substitution of the simpler ablative absolute. The MSS readings reflect the perplexity of the scribes.

Mass all in choir shall be in albs save the cantor and those with him, who shall lead the choir wearing copes as well. At None the bell shall ring as for Prime. At Vespers those of the young monks who are so directed by the cantor shall begin the antiphons ; all else shall be done as on the previous day at Vespers.

AT FIRST VESPERS of the Finding of the Holy Cross the hymn shall be *Vexilla regis*.[1] The following day the invitatory and two nocturns shall be of the martyrs,[2] the third of the Holy Cross ; the canticles shall be *Domine audivi*,[3] which shall be divided into three *Glorias* : the first *Gloria* is before the verse *Pro iniquitate,* the second before *Egressus es.* The hymn at Lauds is *Lustra sex*.[4] The Morrow Mass is of the martyrs, the High Mass of the Holy Cross ; the psalms at Vespers are *Dixit Dominus, Confitebor, Beatus vir, Laudate pueri*,[5] the hymn *Vexilla regis*.

FOR THE EXALTATION OF THE HOLY CROSS the service is similar to the service for the Finding, save that in the former the Holy Cross is worshipped, and not on the latter day.[6] On this solemnity, therefore, when Terce has been said, carpets shall be laid in the presbytery up to the high altar ; after this two brethren, chosen by the cantor, and wearing albs, shall proceed from near the morrow altar bearing a veiled cross and go to the step before the high altar and nearest to it. The cross shall then be unveiled by the bearers, and when they intone the antiphon *Ecce lignum crucis*[7] all shall bend their

---

[5] Ps. 110–13 (111–14)
[6] In classical Latin *hic* = ' the latter,' and *ille* = ' the former,' but the sense here demands that the meanings should be reversed. cf. also Bernard of Cluny II xxxi 349, where the adoration takes place on the feast of the Exaltation.
[7] As on Good Friday, *v. supra*, p. 40

deinde super tapetia prostrati toto corpore adorent eam,
et osculentur pedes crucifixi, sicut sunt priores. Cantata
antiphona supra dicta, incipiat cantor antiphonam
Crucem tuam adoramus,[1] quam repetant per singulos
uersus psalmi Deus misereatur nostri.[2] Deinde alia quae
conueniunt, si opus fuerit. Adorata cruce, praedicti duo
fratres, qui eam tenent, incipiant simul alta uoce antiphonam Super omnia,[3] et flectentibus omnibus genua,
fixaque cruce in loco suo, pulsatis signis celebretur missa.
Ad introitum In nomine Domini omne genu flectatur ;
euangelium Nunc iudicium est mundi.[4]

QUINQUE DIES dominici sunt, qui communia quaedam
inter se habent separata caeteris diebus dominicis [5] :
dominica uidelicet prima de aduentu Domini, dominica
prima septuagesimae, dominica prima quadragesimae ;
dominica in medio quadragesimae, dominica in palmis.
In his duo inuitatorium canant in albis ; sacerdos lecto
euangelio exutus in uestiario casula et stola, reuertatur
in chorum in alba cum manipulo, exiturus incepto
ymno, et incepta antiphona ad Benedictus similiter in
alba intraturus, et incensum per altaria portaturus ;
chorus ab hesterna die debet esse paratus, et per chorum
iuncus sparsus. Ad utrasque uesperas, et ad laudes, duo
fratres in froccis responsorium canant. Tabulae refectorii sint coopertae, honesta * manutergia sint extensa
super tersoria, sicut in omnibus festiuitatibus in quibus
inuitatorium in cappis canitur. Quae extendantur et
colligantur sicut superius dictum est.

---

* honestae B
[1] For text, in form of a responsory, v. HB III 250v
[2] Ps. 66 (67)
[3] For text, v. HB III 251v

knees and then, prostrate upon the carpets, shall adore the cross and kiss the feet of the crucifix in due order. When the above antiphon has been sung the cantor shall intone the antiphon *Crucem tuam adoramus*,[1] which shall be repeated after each verse of the psalm *Deus miseratur nostri* [2]; then shall follow such other suitable chants as may be needful. When the adoration of the cross is done, the two foresaid brethren who hold it shall together before the altar with a loud voice intone the antiphon *Super omnia*,[3] and while all bend the knee, the cross is set in its place, then the bells are rung and Mass is celebrated. The introit is *In nomine Domini omne genu flectatur*; the gospel, *Nunc judicium est mundi*.[4]

THERE ARE FIVE SUNDAYS which have certain common features distinguishing them from other Sundays [5]; they are the first Sunday of Advent, Septuagesima Sunday, the first Sunday in Lent, the Sunday in the middle of Lent and Palm Sunday. On these days the invitatory is sung by two in albs ; the priest after he has read the gospel puts off his chasuble and stole in the vestry and returns to choir in an alb with maniple, to retire again when the hymn at Lauds is begun ; and when the antiphon at the *Benedictus* is begun he re-enters clad as before to bear incense about the altars. The choir shall have been decked the day before, and rushes spread therein. At both Vespers and at Lauds two brethren in tunics sing the responsory. The refectory tables shall be covered and fine towels hung over the common towels, as on all feasts on which the invitatory is sung in copes. The towels are hung and collected again as has been set out above.

[4] Jo. xii.31
[5] Bernard of Cluny I xlix 242

IN OMNIBUS festiuitatibus duodecim lectionum, quae-
cumque sint, et in omnibus diebus, qui infra octauas
137 sunt, in quibus in claus/tro non loquuntur monachi,
quamuis ipsi dies trium lectionum sint, et in omnibus
uigiliis, in quibus missae pulsatis omnibus signis festiue
aguntur, et in omnibus sabbatis ieiuniorum quatuor
temporum, cum cantor inchoauerit Gloria Patri ad
officium,[1] sacerdos ingrediatur ad altare ferens missale
manibus suis, praecedentibus tribus conuersis cum candelabris et thuribulo, subdiacono post eos cum textu, sub-
diaconum sequente diacono, et posito missali super altare
faciat orationem suppliciter inclinatus ; diaconus quoque
retro post eum similiter faciat ; [2] factaque oratione signet
se sacerdos, et osculetur textum euangelii, quem subdiaconus super altare positum habere debet : diaconus
quoque similiter signans se faciat ante et retro, et ueniens
ad sinistram sacerdotis osculetur cornu altaris ; dehinc
faciant simul confessionem, qua facta imposito a sacerdote
thure in thuribulo, tribuat diaconus sacerdoti thuribulum,
humiliter osculans brachium eius. Accepto thuribulo
sacerdos incenset altare ante et desuper, reddatque
diacono ; diaconus incenset utraque altaris latera, et
altare matutinale, et sic reddat conuerso ; qui deferens
in chorum offerat primum cantori, et ipsis qui cum eo
sunt, dehinc in dextro choro omnibus per ordinem, et
sic in sinistro ; deinde infirmis, qui extra chorum sunt ;
duo uero conuersi qui tenent candelabra ante altare non
dimittant ea, usquequo inchoetur Kyrieleison, quo
inchoato, depositis candelabris reuertantur in chorum.

[1] i.e. the *Gloria* following the first singing of the introit.
[2] As will be noticed, there are several differences between the rite
here described and that of the Roman use. The practices of the text are
almost identical with those in Bernard of Cluny I xxii 183, and with that
given for the Ordinary of the Mass in *Missale Westmon.* II 489–990, where
the *Confiteor* is said by the celebrant at the left (i.e. gospel) ' horn ' of the
altar.

ON ALL FEASTS OF TWELVE LESSONS, of whatever rank they be, and on all days within an octave on which there is no talking in the cloister, even though they are days of three lessons, and on all vigils on which the Masses are celebrated in festal rite with all bells rung, and on all Saturdays of the Ember Days—on all these days, when the cantor begins the *Gloria* of the introit,[1] the priest shall come in to the altar bearing the missal in his hands, preceded by three converses with candlesticks and thurible ; they are followed by the subdeacon with the gospel book, and after him comes the deacon. When the missal has been set on the altar the priest shall say the prayers bowing down, and the deacon behind him shall do likewise.[2]   When the prayers are done the priest signs himself with the Cross, and kisses the gospel book, which the subdeacon shall have resting on the altar.   The deacon likewise crosses himself and makes a double obeisance, and coming up to the left of the priest kisses the altar at the end.   Then together they say the *Confiteor*, and when this is done the priest puts incense in the thurible and the deacon hands the thurible to the priest, humbly kissing his arm ; the priest then incenses the altar in front and above, and returns the thurible to the deacon.   The deacon incenses both ends of the altar and the morrow altar, and then returns the thurible to the converse, who bears it into the choir and incenses the cantor first, and those with him, then all in order on the right of the choir, and then those on the left.   Then he incenses the sick, outside the choir.   Meanwhile the two converses who bear the candlesticks before the altar do not put them down till the *Kyrie* is begun.   When this is intoned, setting down the candlesticks they return to choir.

At the gospel in like manner the thurible is brought

12

Ad euangelium similiter deferatur thuribulum ad sacerdotem. Post euangelium, dum canitur offerenda uel
uersus offerendae, conuersus afferat thuribulum cum
acerra cantori, quicunque ille sit, qui chorum tenet, si
festiuitas sit duodecim lectionum, uel festiui dies sint
trium lectionum intra octauas superius descriptas. Cantor uero cum uiderit tempus esse, ponat incensum in
thuribulo, et mittat diacono ad altare, et diaconus
tribuat sacerdoti, nisi abbas, uel episcopus in choro sit,
uel missam celebret : quod si euenerit ad ipsum deferatur
138 thuribulum / cum acerra, ad introitum et ante euange-
ium, a diacono et conuerso ; post offerendam, a cantore
et conuerso.

Circa finem missae, cum peruentum fuerit ad prioris
collectae Per Dominum nostrum, deponant duo conuersi
candelabra ante altare, et sic cum eo qui thuribulum
tenet reuertantur in uestiarium. Expleta missa sequatur
sacerdos praecedentem diaconum * ferentem missale.

Si FESTIUITAS trium lectionum eueniat in aliqua die
dominica,[1] uel in alia festiuitate alicuius sancti, quae
propriam hystoriam habeat, uel si propriam hystoriam
non habet, in albis tamen, uel in cappis sit, commemoratio de festiuitate trium lectionum solummodo fiat
ad priores uesperas, et ad matutinas laudes, et missa
matutinalis de ea canatur. Si uero hystoria iam alia die
dominica cantata est, aut illa alia festiuitas duodecim
lectionum hystoriam propriam non habet, nec in albis
nec in cappis fit, antiphona de festiuitate, de qua tres
lectiones fierent, ad cantica pronuncietur, et deinceps
totum seruitium usque ad finem ultimae collectae de ea
agatur. Post Benedicamus † fiat commemoratio festiui-

---

* diaconem *ut uidetur perperam* D † + Domino A C
[1] For the complications caused by the grading of feasts and their con-
currence, *v.* Tolhurst, *HB* VI 145ff.

to the priest. After the gospel, while the offertory is sung, or the versicle of the offertory, a converse shall bear the thurible with the incense-boat to the cantor, whoever he may be who is leading the choir, if it is a feast of twelve lessons, or a festal day of three lessons in an octave as aforesaid. When the cantor sees the time has come, he shall put incense in the thurible and despatch the deacon to the altar, and the deacon shall hand it to the priest, unless the abbot or a bishop be in choir or be celebrating Mass, in which case the thurible shall be taken to him along with the incense-boat, at the introit and before the gospel by the deacon and converse, and after the offertory by the cantor and converse.

Towards the end of Mass, when the end of the first collect is reached, the two converses shall set their candlesticks before the altar and so return with the thurible to the vestry. When Mass is over the priest shall follow the deacon, who goes before him bearing the missal.

IF A FEAST OF THREE LESSONS occur on a Sunday,[1] or on another feast of a saint which has a proper ' history,' or, if it has not, yet is kept in albs or in copes, a commemoration of the feast of three lessons is made only in first Vespers and Lauds, and the Morrow Mass is of that feast. But if the ' history ' has already been chanted on a previous Sunday, or if the feast of twelve lessons neither has a proper ' history ' nor is kept in albs or copes, then the antiphon of the feast of three lessons shall be given out at the canticles, and thenceforward all the office until the end of the last collect shall be of it. After *Benedicamus Domino* there shall be a commemoration of the feast of which eight lessons have been recited. Likewise all the hours shall be of this feast, together

tatis de qua octo lectiones fuerint ; omnes quoque horae de illa dicantur, sermo in capitulo, et missa maior ; matutinalis vero unde laudes fuerunt.

Si festiuitas alicuius sancti, de qua duodecim lectiones fiunt, eueniat in die dominica, de qua hystoria iam cantata sit, aut subsequente die dominica cantari possit, totum seruitium noctis et diei de sancto agatur ; missa tantum matutinalis de dominica dicatur ; tertium enim nocturnum de dominica die nunquam erit, nisi praecedentia duo de ea fiant.

In omnibus dominicis diebus, et in prima die dominicae natiuitatis ad maiorem missam tantum, et in die dominicae circumcisionis,[1] et * epyphania, et in prima die paschalis solennitatis, et in die ascensionis, et in prima die pentecostes, et in festiuitate omnium sanctorum, et in dedicatione aecclesiae, et in omnibus festiuitatibus beatae Mariae, et in die passionis apostolorum Petri et Pauli, et in caeteris festi/uitatibus aliorum apostolorum, dicatur ad maiorem missam Credo in unum Deum ; nam ad matutinalem missam in conuentu nunquam dicitur.

Quotiens disponitur ut aliqua persona cum festiua processione suscipiatur,[2] tangatur ter breuiter unum de maioribus signis, ut hoc signo conueniant omnes fratres in aecclesiam ad induendum se. Et cum omnes cappis induti fuerint, si tanta capparum copia est, aut casulis et dalmaticis, si cappae desint, et pueri tunicis, expectent sedentes in choro, donec procedant. Secretarius interim extendat unum tapetem, et desuper pallium ante maius altare super priorem gradum, et similiter faciat ante

139

---

* + in A C   [1] 1 January
[2] cf. Bernard of Cluny I xxxiii 217–19 (similar but not identical) and Albers I 170–1.

with the sermon in chapter and the High Mass ; but the Morrow Mass shall follow the feast kept at Lauds.

IF THE FEAST OF A SAINT which has twelve lessons shall occur on a Sunday, of which the ' history' has already been recited, or can be recited on a future Sunday, all the office of day and night shall be of the saint ; the Morrow Mass alone shall be of the Sunday. The third nocturn shall never be of the Sunday unless the preceding two nocturns have been of it also.

THE CREDO SHALL BE SAID at High Mass on all Sundays, on Christmas Day at High Mass only, on the Circumcision,[1] on the Epiphany, on Easter Sunday, on Ascension Day, on Whit Sunday, on the feast of All Saints, on the dedication of the church, on all feasts of the blessed Mary, on the day of martyrdom of the apostles Peter and Paul, and on the other feasts of apostles. At the conventual Morrow Mass it is never said.

WHENEVER IT HAS BEEN DECIDED to receive a visitor [2] with a solemn procession, one of the greater bells shall be thrice tolled for a short space, that warned by this all the brethren may gather in the church to vest. When all are vested in copes, if there is a sufficiency of these, or otherwise in chasubles and dalmatics, with the children wearing tunics, all shall sit waiting in choir till the procession begins. Meanwhile the sacristan shall lay a carpet, with a pall over it, on the top step before the High Altar, and shall do likewise before the crucifix in the centre of the church. Then, when notice is given that the visitor is approaching, two of the great bells shall be rung. Then some of the seniors shall take holy

crucifixum in medio aecclesiae ; his ºperactis cum indicatum fuerit iam prope adesse personam, pulsentur duo
maiora signa.

Tunc aliqui de maioribus accipiant aquam benedictam, et caetera quae ad festiuam processionem portari
solent, hos praecedentes sequantur abbas, et caeteri, ut
sunt priores. Pueri cum magistris suis extremi ueniant,
et in ordine suo stent inter duos choros, cum facta fuerit
statio ad susceptionem personae. Quae cum suscipitur,
det ei abbas aspersorium cum aqua in manum, si episcopus fuerit ; aliam personam aspergat ipse ; dehinc
porrigatur ei incensum similiter ab abbate, textus a
priore. Dum haec fiunt, pulsentur omnia signa. Cantor
uero incipiat cantum, qui conueniat personae, dehinc
reuertatur processio ; pueri cum magistris suis primi
ingrediantur aecclesiam, hos sequantur reliqui sicut in
statione fuerunt ; extremus ueniat abbas cum suscepta
persona, praecedentibus eos supradictis portitoribus.

Ingressi monasterium faciant stationem ante crucifixum. Pueri uero similiter stent inter utrosque choros.
Praedicti portitores paulatim progrediantur per medium
eorum, et stent ante crucifixum uersis uultibus ad eum.
Interim oret suscepta persona. Finito cantu, surgente ea
ab oratione, incipiat cantor antiphonam, uel respon-
140 sorium de sancto, in / cuius honore fundata est aecclesia.
Tunc praecedant praedicti portitores deposituri in locis
suis ea quae portant statim cum ad altare uenerint.
Sequantur infantes, post hos reliqui, eo ordine quo
superius dictum est. Ingressi chorum stent a parte
altaris ex utraque parte sicut sunt priores. Oret iterum
suscepta persona ; finito quod cantatur, surgat, et si
episcopus est qui suscipitur, post datam benedictionem
osculetur omnes fratres per ordinem. Fratres uero, quia
induti sunt, non flectant genua ante eum, sicut solent

water and all else that is usual in a solemn procession ; they shall be followed by the abbot and the rest in order. The children with their masters shall come last, and when the ranks are formed to receive the visitor they shall stand in order between the two choirs of monks.

At the reception the abbot, if a bishop is being received, gives him the sprinkler of holy water ; otherwise he himself sprinkles the visitor ; then incense is proffered by the abbot, and the gospel book by the prior ; while this is done all the bells are rung. The cantor shall then begin a chant that is suitable to the person who is being received, and the procession returns ; the children and their masters are the first to enter the church, followed by the rest in the order in which they were previously standing ; last of all comes the abbot with the person who has been received, preceded immediately by the bearers of incense and holy water.

When they have entered the church they halt at the crucifix, the children standing as before between the two choirs, while the bearers go forward a little in their midst and stand facing the crucifix. Meanwhile the visitor is praying, and when the chant is done and he has arisen the cantor shall begin the antiphon or responsory of the patron saint of the church. Then the bearers go forward, and as soon as they have reached the high altar they put what they are carrying down in the usual place ; the children and the rest shall follow in the order given above. When they have entered the choir they shall stand near the altar in order of seniority on each side of the presbytery. The visitor shall kneel again in prayer, and when the chant is done he shall rise, and if he be a bishop shall give his blessing before kissing all the brethren in order. As the brethren are vested, they shall not genuflect before him, as they

facere cum osculantur episcopum uel abbatem uel
principem terrae, sed humiliter inclinantes se procedant
ad osculum eius. Si spiritualis persona fuerit, et abbas
expedire iudicauerit, disuestitis * fratribus, et in capitulo
sicut solent considentibus, ducatur illuc praedicta persona, et, petita benedictione, legatur ante eam lectio
diuina ; qua finita cum Tu autem Domine, sermonem
si uoluerit de ea faciat. Si abbas fuerit, qui suscipitur,
ante introitum capituli egredientes fratres osculetur. Si
uero capitulum non intrauerit, seruata competenti hora
in claustro osculetur eos.

ABBAS cum eligitur, omnes fratres, uel maior et melior[1]
pars in eius electionem consentire debent. Electus autem
si extra monasterium consecratur, cum redierit cum
festiua processione suscipiatur. Ipse uero in utraque
statione prostratus iaceat. Finito cantu secundae stationis,[2] episcopus, si adest, uel legatus eius, in loco et
statione abbatis eum statuat. Quo statuto, si episcopus
abest, incipiat prior Te Deum laudamus, quod dum
cantant, accedant omnes fratres sicut sunt priores ad
osculum eius, bis flectentes genua, semel ante osculum,
et semel post osculum. Ex illa die in omni loco singulari
141 reuerentia honorandus est./

In primo capitulo ubi sederit, omnes qui intra monasterium obedientias habent, et res monasterii seruant,
suarum obedientiarum claues ante pedes eius ponant.
Ipse uero recommendet eis ipsas obedientias, si non

---

* diuestitis B C

[1] This phrase, in which *melior* was ultimately supplanted by *sanior*, was
technical in elections. The *major pars* was not necessarily in a numerical
majority, but was *major* because of the seniority and respectability of those
composing it ; hence it was also the *melior pars*. It is never made clear,
however, how there could be any recognisable criterion of a ' majority,'
save numbers, unless all agreed to appoint ' electors.'

[2] The two halts were before the crucifix at the entrance to the choir,
and before the high altar.

ordinarily do when kissing a bishop, abbot or secular prince, but shall come forward to kiss him after a low bow. If the visitor be an ecclesiastic, and the abbot judge it fitting, the brethren shall unvest and sit as usual in chapter ; the visitor shall then be led in and, after a blessing asked, a passage of the Scripture shall be read ; after this has ended with *Tu autem Domine*, he shall, if he wish, make a sermon upon it. If it be an abbot who is received, he shall stand at the door of the chapter-house and kiss the brethren as they come out. If he does not go into the chapter-house, he shall salute them at a convenient time in the cloister.

IN THE ELECTION OF AN ABBOT all, or at least the larger and more weighty part of the community,[1] must agree upon their choice. If the abbot-elect is blessed away from home, he shall be received with a solemn procession on his return. At the two halting-places he shall lie prostrate, and when at the second halt [2] the chant is done the bishop, if present, or his representative shall set the abbot in his stall and place. When this is done the prior (in the absence of the bishop) shall intone the *Te Deum*, and while this is being sung all the brethren shall approach in order to the kiss of peace, genuflecting before and after the kiss. Henceforward the abbot is to be treated with especial honour everywhere.

On his first attendance at chapter all who have obediences in the monastery and keep the goods of the house shall lay before his feet their keys of office ; if the abbot has decided to make no change he shall entrust the offices to them again. When he bows after beginning an antiphon all the community shall bow, as also

aliter ordinandas esse decreuerit. Inclinari debet a
toto conuentu cum post inceptam antiphonam inclinat,
cum in tabula in capitulo nominatur, si ibi praesens est,
cum in psalmo, uel in alio aliquo fallitur in choro, pro
quo ueniam petat. Eunte eo ad legendum, uel redeunte
a legendo, assurgat ei totus conuentus. Transeunte eo
per claustrum, uel per quemcumque locum, assurgant
ei omnes ante quos transit, quoad usque pertranseat.
Cum capitulum introierit, fratribus iam in eo considentibus, de omnibus gradibus omnes descendant donec
idem consideat.¹ Ubicunque sit, ibi debet esse ordo et
disciplina ; quapropter in quocumque loco fuerit, siue
in claustro, siue extra claustrum, cum reprehendit aliquem fratrem inordinate agentem, siue loquentem, mox
ille coram eo humiliter ueniam petat, sicut in capitulo,
et tamdiu stet ante illum donec illum iubeat sedere. Et
si uiderit illum irasci tamdiu satisfaciat ante ipsum
ueniam petendo, quousque illum reddat placatum. Abbas
tamen prouidere debet ne hoc faciat coram saecularibus
hominibus.

Ubicunque sederit nullus iuxta eum sedere praesumat,
nisi ipse iusserit. Iussus uero sedere ad genua eius se
flectat, et osculetur, et sic humiliter iuxta eum sedeat.
Quicunque ei in manum aliquid dederit, uel de manu
eius aliquid acceperit, osculetur manum ipsius. Intraturo
in refectorium duo fratres seruiant ei de aqua et manu-
tergio. Quamdiu in choro fuerit, nullus infantibus,
nisi eo iubente, audeat disciplinam inferre. Quamdiu
dormierit in lecto suo mane nullus sonitum audeat facere.²
Magister tamen infantum si uiderit transire horam, qua

---

¹ This phrase, and the use of *suppedaneus* (= footpace) below imply that
in chapter at this period the monks sat on a series of steps, facing or en-
circling an open space of floor.
² At this time the abbot still slept in the common dormitory, but by
1150 all but a very few abbots in England had removed to quarters of

when he is named in the list in chapter (if he be present)
and when he does penance for a fault in psalmody, or
any other fault in choir. When he goes to read, or
returns from reading, the whole community rises. When
he passes through the cloister or any other place, all
before whom he passes shall rise until he be past. When
he enters the chapter-house and the brethren are already
seated, all shall descend the steps until he is seated.[1]
Wherever he be, strict order and discipline should be
kept ; therefore, wherever he be, either within or without the cloister, if he take a brother to task for acting or
speaking contrary to good order, he who is reprimanded
shall at once humbly do penance as in chapter, and
stand before him until he bid him be seated. And if
the brother see him to be in anger he shall make satisfaction, doing penance before him, until he be appeased.
But the abbot shall take care that he do not this before
seculars.

Whenever the abbot is seated no-one shall presume
to sit by him unless bidden ; when told to be seated
the brother shall bow down to the abbot's knees and
kiss them, and so humbly sit by him. Whosoever gives
him anything or receives anything from him shall kiss
his hand. When he enters the refectory two of the
brethren shall wait upon him with water and towel.
When he is in choir none shall dare to punish the
children save at his bidding.

In the early morning no-one shall dare to make a
sound so long as he is in bed asleep.[2] If the master of the
children see that the hour is passing at which the signal
is wont to be given by the prior, he should rise and

their own. Lanfranc's text comes almost verbally from Bernard of Cluny
I lxxiv 275.

sonitus a priore fieri solet, surgat, et quam quietius
142 possit infantes excitet, uirga tantummodo tangens/
pannos, quibus cooperti sunt. Quo facto exeuntes de
dormitorio lauent se, et pectant, et factis solitis orationibus in scholam suam redeant, et cum silentio sedeant
donec abbas de lecto surgat.

Cum alicubi extra monasterium moram faciens,
mandat conuentui salutationes seu orationes, omnes qui
in capitulo sunt inclinent, flexis usque ad suppedaneum
scabellum genibus. Eodem modo fit pro papae uel regis
salutatione. Pro aliarum uero personarum salutationi-
bus, humiliter inclinetur tantum. Cum autem alicui
fratri mandat huiusmodi aliquid, ubicunque dicatur ei
ipsa salutatio, continuo humiliter inclinet, flexis ad
terram genibus.

Quicunque frater ad eum extra claustrum uenerit,
primum dicat Benedicite, deinde indicet propter quam
causam uenerit. Nec sedere coram eo, nec recedere ab
eo audeat sine eius licentia ; accepta ab eo recedendi
licentia, primum dicat Benedicite, deinde recedat.

Omnis totius monasterii ordinatio ex eius arbitrio
pendeat.[1] Si quid nouum, necessitate cogente uel ratione
suadente, eo absente in monasterio ordinatum fuerit,
cum redierit indicetur ei, et postea fiat sicut ipse praeceperit. Si de monasterio exierit, et uel una nocte extra
moratus fuerit, mox ut redierit cuicunque fratri * abstinentia in capitulo iniuncta fuerit, absolutus erit.

Cum de hac uita decesserit, de proximo inuitandus
est abbas uel episcopus ad sepeliendum eum. Praeter
omnia, quae aliis defunctis fratribus fieri solent, addantur
ei haec : circumdentur ei sacerdotalia indumenta, et
uirga pastoralis ponatur in eius dextro brachio ; Verba

* frater C fratrum E

rouse the children as quietly as may be, simply touching with his rod their bedclothes. This done, they shall leave the dormitory, wash and comb their hair, and after the usual prayers return to their school, sitting in silence till the abbot rises.

When he is making a stay outside the monastery, and sends the community greeting or asks for prayers, all in chapter shall bow, bending their knees to the footpace. The Pope and the King are saluted in this manner also, but for other persons only a profound bow is made. When the abbot sends a command to any brother, whenever the message reaches him he is straightway to do obeisance kneeling.

If a brother go to him without the cloister he shall first say *Benedicite* and then say for what cause he has come. He shall not venture to sit before him nor to depart without his permission. When this is granted, he shall first say *Benedicite* and then depart.

All the ordering of the monastery shall depend upon his will.[1] If in his absence a change be made out of necessity or for good reason, he shall be told about it on his return, and the matter shall be ordered as he shall bid. If he go out of the monastery and spend but one night outside, when he returns a brother shall be freed from any fast that has been laid upon him in chapter.

When he departs this life, a neighbouring abbot or bishop should be invited to bury him. In addition to all that is done by custom for other brethren who die, the following shall be done : he shall be clad in a priest's vestments and the pastoral staff be set in his right hand. The *Verba mea* shall be said for him for a whole year,

---

[1] cf. *Regula* LXV 22-7 : ' Ideo nos vidimus expedire . . . in abbatis pendere arbitrio ordinationem monasterii.'

mea per unius anni circulum pro eo dicatur; et iusticia[1]
eius per totum ipsum annum ad mensam abbatis cotidie
cum tribus pulmentis danda pauperibus ponatur. Omni
143 anno anniversarius dies mortis eius festiue celebretur./

SERUATA abbati in omnibus reuerentia, prior, qui et
praepositus in regula nominatur,[2] honorabilior est reliquis
ministris domus Dei. Ipse solus caeterorum ministrorum
primum suae partis locum habet in choro, in capitulo,
in refectorio. Ipsi soli seruit sacerdos de thuribulo post
abbatem ad uesperas et ad matutinas laudes, quotiens-
cunque ad easdem horas circumfertur thuribulum per
chorum. Ea quoque, quae extra claustrum sunt, si
abbas deest, iuxta ipsius arbitrium disponuntur. Si
abbas longius a monasterio fuerit, ipse deponere potest
eos, quos intellexerit non iuxta proficuum aecclesiae res
sibi commissas tractare. Quotiens res expostulat, tenet
aut teneri iubet capitulum de omnibus seruientibus,[3] qui
intra officinas monasterii conuersantur, et secundum
merita delinquentium, eo iubente, uindictae inferuntur.
Intrante eo capitulum omnes ei assurgant, stantes in
suppedaneis donec consideat. Quod si tardauerit, et
prior claustri in loco superiori prius sederit, intrare non
debet. Si causa fuerit quae differri non possit, aut non
debeat, ingresso eo prior claustri ex altera parte prior
omnibus sedeat. Transeunte eo per claustrum, uel per
chorum, non assurgitur illi. Uolenti eo sedere in claustro
ubi alii fratres sedent, assurgunt ei tantum iuxta quos
sedere uult ; ubicunque extra claustrum fratres sedentes
inuenerit, assurgunt ei omnes.

---

[1] The word *justitia* had many senses (*v.* Ducange), among them being
that of a jug of certain capacity (*v. supra*, p. 31) or (as here) the fixed daily
allowance of liquor.

[2] cf. *Regula* LXV De praeposito monasterii. The word *prior* in the
Rule is frequently used of the abbot, never of the provost.

and his measure of wine [1] for the whole year shall be set daily on the abbot's table, along with three dishes, all to be given to the poor. Each year the anniversary of his death shall be celebrated with solemnity.

SAVING THE REVERENCE due in all things to the abbot, the prior, who is called the provost in the Rule,[2] is to be honoured above the other servants of God's house. He alone of the other officials takes precedence of his side of the choir in choir and chapter and refectory. He alone is incensed by the priest after the abbot at Vespers and Lauds, whensoever the choir is incensed at those hours. He shall also dispose of external matters in the abbot's absence. If the abbot be far away, he may depose from office those whom he learns to be handling their business in a way contrary to the profit of the monastery. When need arises he holds, or causes to be held, a chapter of all servants who work in the offices of the monastery, and punishment is inflicted at his order according to the deserts of those culpable.[3] When he enters the chapter-house all rise and stand on the footpace till he sits down. If he is late and the claustral prior be already seated in the chief place, he shall not enter. If there be a matter which cannot, or should not, be put off, the claustral prior shall on his coming take the first place on the other side of the chapter-house. When he passes through the cloister or the choir those whom he passes do not rise ; should he wish to sit in the cloister with the other brethren those only rise with whom he wishes to sit ; but when he finds brethren seated outside the cloister they all rise.

---

[3] Although these were appropriated to certain offices (e.g. *famuli camerarii* on Maundy Thursday, *supra*, p. 31), they were still under the direct supervision of the head of the house. Later, the obedientiary concerned was their master in all things.

PRIOR CLAUSTRI,[1] quocunque maior prior eat, si fieri possit, in claustro uel circa claustrum semper debet esse, et ordinem claustri omni sollicitudine seruare. Cum abbas et maior prior absunt, si contingat quemlibet fratrum ex infirmitate laborare, potest ei praecipere in domum infirmorum ire, et si tanta egritudo est, carnem comedere. Ad ipsum maxime pertinet infirmos fratres uisitare, et quid agant, et quid uelint cognoscere, et in omnibus quae uel corporibus, uel animabus eorum necessaria sunt, consulere. Absente maiore priore capitulum seruientium debet tenere, et secundum culpas 144 uindictas / inferre, sed non est sui iuris quemlibet addere uel auferre.

Sui quoque officii est omni die post completorium,[2] suscepta, dante ebdomadario sacerdote, a fratribus aqua benedicta, remanere donec omnes pertranseant in aliquo congruo loco, unde bene possit obseruare qui sint, qui non reuerenter incedunt, et qui in exitu aecclesiae, ut mos est, non uelant capitiis capita sua, et multa huiusmodi. Egresso toto conuentu, accepta absconsa si nox est, uadit per criptam et caetera membra monasterii, ubi suspicio potest esse, per claustrum, capitulum, caeterasque officinas subtiliter obseruando, ne aliquis frater, qui non debeat, ibi remanserit, et ne forte hostia claustri uel armariorum non firmata remanserunt. His ita expletis uadit in domum infirmorum, eodem modo consideraturus, utrum omnes in lectis suis iam collocati sint, et habeant se silenter, et omnibus modis regulariter,

---

[1] The *prior claustri* was the effective domestic superior concerned immediately and solely with the monks of the cloister *qua tales*. In modern times the title of claustral prior has been used incorrectly of the second-in-command of an abbey (Lanfranc's *major prior*) as opposed to the conventual prior of a lesser house. In the later middle ages a frequent English usage gave the titles ' first,' ' second ' and ' third ' priors instead of ' great prior '

THE CLAUSTRAL PRIOR [1] should, if it is possible, always be in or about the cloister, wherever the great prior may be, and he should watch over the discipline of the cloister with all care. When both abbot and great prior are away and any of the brethren fall sick, he may bid him go into the infirmary and, if his illness be severe, eat fleshmeat. To him above others it falls to visit the sick brethren and to learn what they do and what they want, and to provide all things necessary for them, body and soul. When the great prior is away he should hold the servants' chapter, and allot penalties in proportion to faults, but he has no power to introduce or remove anyone.

It is his business also each day after Compline,[2] when the priest of the week has sprinkled the brethren with holy water, to stay behind in a suitable spot till all have passed, so as to note who they are who do not walk reverently, and who do not put up their hoods, as the custom is, on leaving the church, and many details of this kind. When all the community has left, he should take a dark lantern if it be night and go through the crypt and other such parts of the church as may harbour irregularity, through the cloister, also, chapter-house and other offices, looking carefully to see that no brother remain there who should not, and marking whether the door of the cloister and its cupboards be perchance unlocked. This done he goes to the infirmary to note in like wise if all are now in their beds and are quiet, and if all is according to rule and custom. Then

---

and 'subprior,' and the functions of the claustral prior were performed by one of these. There are differences here from Bernard of Cluny I lxxiii 270.

[2] cf. Bernard of Cluny I iii 141

sicut mos est. Reuertens quoque in dormitorium hoc idem consideret.

In hieme autem ad interuallum, quod fit inter nocturna et matutinas laudes, si maior prior abest, eandem circam facit, quam maiorem priorem debere facere superius dictum est, cum in tractatu mensis Novembris de hoc interuallo sermo fuisset.[1] Facit et aliam circam, cum tardantibus uesperis seruitores nocte in refectorio cenant, et fratres qui maiori cenae * interfuerunt, accensis luminaribus in capitulo eos expectant ; circumit enim tunc superius dicta loca, obseruans ne aliqui, qui cum caeteris in capitulo sedere debeant, ociosis uerbis aut alicui uanitati intendant. Quod cum accidit, si tanta noctis obscuritas est, accendantur luminaria in monasterio, claustro, dormitorio ut exeuntes ab utraque cena uideant quo procedant. Seruitores uero surgentes a cena ante capitulum tunc ad monasterium uadant. Et dum transeunt ante capitulum incuruati eant, quoadusque pertranseant. Ante introitum tamen capituli se erigant, et solito more ad orientem uersi humiliter 145 inclinent. Fratres quoque, qui in capitulo sedent,/ surgentes a sedibus suis illis transeuntibus humiliter se inclinare debent.

Quaecunque maior prior, dum in monasterio est, concedere potest uel prohibere, ulcisci culpas uel indulgere, haec quoque prior claustri absente eo facere potest, exceptis maioribus causis, quas uel ipsius maioris prioris uel abbatis iudicio reseruare debet ; ubicunque uel in refectorio uel in capitulo, siue in claustro, siue extra claustrum, assurgi debet maiori priori ut superius dictum est, absente ipso maiore priore, huic assurgi similiter debet.

---

* + non C E   [1] See above p. 7

returning to the dormitory he shall take the same note there also.

In winter, during the interval between Matins and Lauds, he shall, if the great prior be away, make the round which the other should make, as has been said above when this interval was dealt with in connection with the November time-table.[1] He makes also another round when Vespers are late and the servers are at supper in the refectory, and the brethren who were at first table wait for them in the chapter-house with lights burning. It is then he makes his round of the places already mentioned, noting if any who should be sitting with the others in chapter give themselves to idle talk or frivolities of any kind. At such times if night has fallen lights should be set in the church, cloister and dormitory, so that those going out from either table at supper may see their way. When the servers rise from supper they go into church past the chapter-house. And as they pass the chapter-house they shall bow profoundly. But at the door of the chapter-house they shall draw themselves up and bow profoundly towards the east in the usual manner. The brethren who are sitting in the chapter-house shall rise and bow profoundly to them as they pass.

All permissions, prohibitions, punishments and remissions that may be given by the great prior when he is at home may be given by the claustral prior in his absence, save for grave matters which he should reserve for judgment by the great prior or the abbot. On whatever occasions in the refectory, chapter-house, cloister or elsewhere the brethren rise to do reverence to the great prior, as said above, they shall in his absence do likewise to the claustral prior.

CIRCUMITORES monasterii,[1] quos alio nomine circas
uocant, iuxta sancti Benedicti praeceptum[2] certis horis
circumire debent monasterii officinas, obseruantes in-
curias et negligentias fratrum, et statuti ordinis praeuari-
cationes.

Isti eligantur de totius monasterii melioribus et
prudentioribus, qui nec maliciose pro priuato odio unquam clamorem de quolibet faciant, nec pro priuata
amicitia negligentias aliquorum taceant. Numerus
eorum sit secundum facultatem loci, et necessitatem rei ;
hi religiose et ordinate maxime in circumeundo debent
incedere, et exemplum religionis uidentibus ostendere ;
dum circumeunt, nulli signum faciant, nulli quacunque
occasione loquantur, studiose tantum negligentias et
offensiones inspiciant, et tacite praetereuntes, de eis
postea in capitulo clamores faciant. Cum autem extra
claustrum inueniunt aliquos fratres loquentes simul,
assurgant eis ipsi loquentes, dicatque eis unus eorum, si
ita est, quia per licentiam loquuntur ibi. Circumitores
uero nec uerbo nec signo ei respondeant, sed modeste
pertranseuntes, intenta aure subaudiant, ne ipsa uerba
146 sint inutilia, quae non oporteat dici. Cum autem / cum
famulo, seu cum quolibet alio * laico inueniunt aliquem
fratrem loquentem, non est mos ut ipse frater assurgat
cuilibet eorum, aut dicat eis quicquam.

Nunquam cum circumeunt debent simul ire, sed unus
hac, et alter illac, secundum quod iniunctam curam inter
se diuiserint, et abbas uel prior eis ordinauerit. Officinas
monasterii nunquam pro hac cura egrediantur,[3] sed per

---

* alio quolibet A
[1] This passage comes almost verbally from Bernard of Cluny I xiv 144.
[2] *Regula* XLVIII 39 : ' Let one or two of the elders be deputed to go
about the monastery during the hours when the brethren devote themselves
to reading, etc.'

THE ROUNDSMEN OF THE MONASTERY,[1] who are called also the *circas*, shall according to the command of St Benedict[2] go at certain times the rounds of the monastery's offices, noting the carelessnesses and negligences of the brethren, and the breaches of regular discipline. They shall be chosen from the worthiest and most prudent of the whole monastery, such as will never denounce any from malice or personal dislike, nor pass over any negligences for friendship's sake. Their number shall vary with the size and needs of the community. On their rounds they shall behave most religiously and orderly, giving an example of religious observance to all beholders ; they shall make no sign, and speak no word to any person on any pretext, but they shall straitly regard negligences and faults and nothing else, and, passing by in silence, shall denounce them afterwards in chapter.

If when they are outside the cloister they come upon brethren talking together, the latter shall all rise and one of them shall say (if it is indeed the case) that they have permission to speak there. The roundsmen shall answer neither by word or sign but shall pass quietly on their way ; they shall however mark carefully whether the talk is of useless matters that need not be spoken of. If they come upon a brother speaking with a servant or with any other lay person, it is not customary for the brother to rise or to say anything to them.

On their rounds they shall never go together, but one this way and the other that, according as they have divided their duties among themselves, or as the abbot or prior has given command. While on this task they shall never go outside the monastery buildings[3] but

---

[3] Bernard of Cluny I iv 144 : ' nunquam de claustro exire debent ; possunt tamen . . . aliquando intra officinas . . . stantes, per ostium . . . foris aspicere, ut videant vagantes, etc.'

ostia earum prospiciant, si forte aliqui fratres per curiam
uadant uagantes, aut stent uel sedeant fabulantes.   Hae
sunt horae, quibus ex consuetudine circumire debent,
quamuis et aliis horis, si abbas uel prior ita oportere
iudicauerit.   Completis tribus orationibus, quas conuentus facit ante psalmos, quos ante nocturna dicere solet,
tunc enim, accensa candela in absconsa, unus eorum in
dormitorio debet circumire lectos omnium, et omnia
sedilia in necessariis sollicite considerans, ne forte aliquis
frater dormiens ibi remanserit ;   dehinc reuertatur in
monasterium, et circumeat omnia altaria in criptis, et
quae ex utraque parte chori subtus sunt, caeteraque
monasterii loca ubi suspicio poterit esse, diligenter
obseruans, ne aliquis frater ibi dormiat uel iaceat uel
inordinate sedeat.   Sanguine uero minuti, et egri et
debiles non clamantur in capitulo, si ea hora inueniantur
sedendo quidem, sed non iacendo quiescere.   Caeteros
uero cum dormientes inuenerit, non eos quocunque
modo tangat, sed modeste atque ordinate sonitum
tantummodo quo excitentur faciat.

Circa medietatem secundi nocturni, et in laudibus
paululum ante Laudate Dominum de coelis,[1] accensa
candela in absconsa, circumeat praedicta monasterii
loca, obseruans omnia quae superius dicta sunt.   In die
autem circumeant * post offerendam minoris et maioris
missae, et post cenam, cum bis fratres reficiunt, et post
prandium, cum semel.   Vadant et in fine uigiliae
defunctorum.   Surgant etiam sepe de prandio aut cena,
non omnes quidem, sed aliqui, cum suspicantur se
147 inuenturos aliquid negligentiae ; / hoc uero non longe
a refectorio fiat, ut si opus fuerit statim possint occurrere

---

* circumeat C   [1] i.e. Ps. 148–50 at the end of Lauds

shall look out through the doors to see if haply any of the brethren are strolling about the courtyard, or are loitering or sitting down to gossip.

The following are the usual times for them to go on their rounds, though the abbot or prior may judge other times also to be suitable. When the three prayers are done, which are said by the community before the psalms which precede Matins, then one of them, taking a candle in a dark lantern, should go round all the beds in the dormitory and carefully examine all the compartments of the rere-dorter, lest a brother be fallen asleep there. Then he shall return to the church and go round all the altars in the crypts and those below the choir on each side, and all other such places in the church as may harbour irregularity, carefully noting if any brother be sleeping there, or lying down, or sitting in a way forbidden by rule. But if any of those who have been bled, or who are sick or feeble, be found at that time at rest seated but not lying down, they are not denounced in chapter. As for others, if he find them sleeping he shall not touch them in any way but shall simply make some slight recognized sound to wake them.

Towards the middle of the second nocturn, and at Lauds shortly before the *Laudate* psalms,[1] one shall light a dark lantern and go round the foresaid places in the church, noting all as above. By day he shall go round after the offertory at the Morrow and High Masses, and after supper if they are taking two meals, but after dinner if they have but one. They shall also go round at the end of vigils of the dead. They shall also often rise from dinner or supper (not all of them, but some only) if they have a suspicion that they may find some fault, but they shall not go far from the refectory, so that if needs be they may at once rejoin the others for the

cum aliis ad uersum, qui finito prandio uel cena dicitur.
Isti attente et reuerenter audiendi sunt in capitulo ;
auditis eis, qui sponte uenias petunt, istorum est primos
clamores facere.

CANTOR,[1] quamdiu abbas in monasterio est conuentum sequens, non scribatur in tabula ad lectionem, uel
ad responsorium, ut uidelicet si forte abbati commodum
non fuerit legere aut cantare, ipse sine mora pro eo
inueniatur paratus. Cum uero abbas extra monasterium est,* uel intra monasterium conuentum sequi non
potest, in locum ipsius scribatur cantor in tabula ad
lectionem et ad responsorium. Quicunque lecturus aut
cantaturus est aliquid in monasterio, si necesse habet,
ab eo priusquam incipiat debet auscultare. Ipsius est
omni hora sollicite prouidere, ne eueniat negligentia in
quocunque obsequio quod fit in monasterio. Si quis
obliuiosus non inceperit, cum incipere debet, responsorium, aut antiphonam, uel aliud huiusmodi, siue in
eodem iam bene incepto aliquo modo deuiauerit, ipse
debet esse prouisus atque paratus, ut sine mora, quod
incipiendum erat, incipiat, uel eum, qui fallendo deu-
iauerat, in uiam reducat. Ad ipsius arbitrium cantus
incipitur, eleuatur, remittitur ; nulli licet cantum leuare,
nisi ipse prius incipiat ; ipsius est omnes fratres in tabula
ad omnia officia annotare, non considerato conuersionis
ordine, aut uoluntate eorum, sed secundum quod ei
uisum fuerit, honestatem et aedificationem in hoc
uigilanter consideranti.

In festiuitatibus, quae fiunt in cappis, secretarius
debet eligere quot opus fuerit de melioribus cappis
earum, quae ipsa die habentur in choro, et ante initium

---

* *om.* A C
[1] Almost verbally from Bernard I iv 161 (of the Armarius)

versicle which is said at the end of dinner and supper. They shall be listened to in chapter with all care and reverence, and it is for them to make the first accusations after those who have asked pardon unbidden.

THE CANTOR [1] shall not be put down on the *tabula* for a lesson or a responsory so long as the abbot is in the monastery following the daily round, so that if haply it be inconvenient for the abbot to read or chant anything, the cantor may be prepared to take his place without any delay. If however the abbot is away, or is not following the daily round when at home, the cantor's name shall be put down for his in the *tabula* for lesson and responsory.

Whenever anyone has to read or chant anything in the church the cantor shall, if need be, hear him go over his task before he perform it in public. It is the cantor's business to watch carefully at all times, so that no negligence occurs in any service in the monastery. If through forgetfulness someone fails to begin a responsory or antiphon or suchlike when he should, or if, having begun it correctly, he goes astray in any way, the cantor should be quite ready to begin without delay what should have been begun, or to lead back into the right road one who has strayed. It is for him to decide when the chant is to be begun, and the note raised or lowered ; no one may raise the note unless he begin. It is his task to put down the brethren for all duties on the *tabula*, paying no attention to their seniority or their personal wishes, but according to his best judgment having regard only to good performance and edification.

On a feast celebrated in copes the sacrist is to choose the required number from among the best copes in use in choir that day, and should place them before Mass

missae ponere eas supra dextram formam chori. Cantor
148 uero distribuat / eas fratribus illis, quos secum in choro
habere uoluerit. Ipsa enim capparum distributio, eorum
est ad regendum chorum aduocatio. Nullusque eorum
ante finem missae de choro debet recedere sine eius
licentia. Cantor uero cuiuscunque ordinis, uel aetatis
sit, in medio eorum debet esse in choro. Quotiens-
cunque textus aut thuribulum affertur eis, utrunque
prius cantori offeratur, nisi aliquis episcopus, uel abbas,
seu maior prior, uel ille qui tenet ordinem, ibi sit inter
eos. Cantor in dextro choro semper sit, et dum tenet
chorum quicquid incipit, siue Kyrieleison, siue aliud
huiusmodi, dexter chorus prius suscipiat, quod ab eo
inceptum fuerit, et sequatur ipsum.

Omnes qui in choro sunt inclinati quidem cantent
Sanctus, sanctus, sanctus, nisi uersus interponantur ;
erecti uero Dominus Deus sabaoth, et caetera. Cantor
et illi qui cum eo sunt totum erecti canant. Ad collectas
omnes, et cum sacerdos dicit Orate fratres, et ad totum
Pater noster inclinentur, sed ad finem ipsius Pater noster,
responso Sed libera nos a malo, erigantur, quod aliis
non licet. Eodem modo fit cum in festis in albis solus,
uel cum aliis chorum tenet,* quod non licet ei, qui in
dominicis et huiusmodi festis ebdomadarius cantor
existit.

In omnibus praecipuis solennitatibus,† cum eueniunt
in dominicis diebus, scribatur in tabula ad officium
missae, et cum eo duo, quos ipse uoluerit. De thuribulo
post offerendam ei deferendo superius dictum est.

Cum fit opus manuum, ipsius est aut legere, aut

---

* tenet chorum C   † festiuitatibus C

begins on the right-hand desk of the choir, and the cantor shall distribute them to the brethren whom he wishes to have with him in choir. The distribution of copes is to be taken as the summons to join those who lead the choir, and none of those chosen is to leave the choir without the cantor's permission before the end of Mass.

Whatever the cantor's age or rank in orders he stands in the midst of the others in choir. As often as the gospel book or thurible is brought to them it is presented first to the cantor, unless a bishop or the abbot or great prior or superior for the time being be among them. The cantor shall always be on the right-hand side of the choir, and when he is leading the choir and begins anything such as *Kyrie eleison* or the like the right-hand choir should take up and follow what he begins.

The whole choir shall bow while singing *Sanctus, sanctus, sanctus,* unless a versicle is intercalated, and then stand erect to sing *Dominus Deus sabaoth* and the rest, but the cantor and those with him shall sing the whole standing erect. They shall bow at all the collects, and when the priest says *Orate fratres* and for the whole of the *Pater noster,* but at the end of the *Pater noster,* when the response *Sed libera nos a malo* is made, they alone shall stand erect. A similar procedure is followed when the cantor alone or with others leads the choir in feasts celebrated in albs, but this does not apply when the cantor of the week leads on Sundays or feasts of similar rank.

On all principal feasts occurring on Sundays the cantor and two others of his choice shall be put down in the *tabula* for duty at Mass. Mention has been made above of the thurible coming to him after the offertory.

When there is manual labour it is his duty either to

magistro infantum ostendere, quo in loco infans debeat
lectionem incipere.¹ In dominicis diebus, et huiusmodi
festis, incepta offerenda accedat qui chorum tenet ad
cantorem, faciatque signum incipiendi uersus offerendae.
Ad ipsum enim pertinet tunc incipere eos etiam si succentor chorum teneat. Cantor uiso signo inclinet ei, et
149 ebdomadarius cantor simi/liter ipsi. Incepto unoquoque
uersu, cantor ante et retro faciat, et omnes infantes
inclinent. Ipsius est notificare abbati omnes cantus,
quos ipse cantat, aut * incipit.

Cura breuium, qui foras mitti solent pro defunctis
fratribus² ; et cura numerandi tricenaria, et septenaria,
ad eum pertinet. De uniuersis monasterii libris curam
gerat, et eos in custodia sua habeat, si eius studii et
scientiae sit, ut eorum custodia ei commendari debeat.³

AD SECRETARII officium pertinet, omnia ornamenta
monasterii, et omnia instrumenta et supellectilem, quae
ad ipsum monasterium pertinent,† custodire ; horas
prouidere. In duodecim lectionibus, pronunciato euangelio in tertio nocturno, et in festiuis octauis altare
discooperire ; textum tunc in uestiarium portare, quem
sacerdos ferat cum incepto ‡ Per singulos dies processerit
ad altare.⁴ Sacerdoti ab altari ad analogium reuerso
absconsam cum candela ministrare, finitaque collecta
eamdem absconsam recipere, et postea textum ponere
super altare.

---

* uel A   † pertinet C   ‡ *sic codd. omn.* in cappa *Reyner et edd.*

¹ This is Lanfranc's only reference to manual labour, which fills such
a large place in the horarium of the Rule ; the casual mention here suggests
that it was not of frequent occurrence, and, if the work were to be accompanied by reading, it must have been a task accomplished by all together,
and indoors, such as, e.g. repairing clothes or cleaning precious objects.
But the records are silent in the matter.

² These are the *rouleaux des morts* or ' death-bills,' carried by a messenger
to houses linked in a union of prayers or, as later, to all the principal
religious houses and collegiate churches of the country.

³ The precentor for long remained the librarian, and hence the annalist
or chronicler, e.g. William of Malmesbury, Eadmer, and Symeon of Durham.

read himself or to indicate to the master of the children where the child who reads is to begin.[1]

On Sundays and feasts of like rank, when the offertory begins he who presides in choir should go up to the cantor and make him a sign to begin the offertory verse ; it is the cantor's office to begin this even if the succentor is leading the choir. The cantor on receiving the signal bows to him who gives it, and the cantor of the week in like manner bows to the cantor. When each verse is begun the cantor makes a double bow, and all the children bow. It is also the cantor's task to give the abbot notice of all chants that he sings or begins. It also pertains to his office to supervise the letters sent out to ask for prayers for the dead brethren,[2] and to keep count of the week's and month's mind. He takes care of all the books of the house, and has them in his keeping, if his interests and learning are such as to fit him for keeping them.[3]

THE SACRIST's office is to keep all the ornaments and utensils and furnishings of the church, and to see that the horarium is kept. On feasts of twelve lessons, after the gospel has been read in the third nocturn, and during festal octaves he shall uncover the altar, and then take to the vestry the gospel book for the priest to carry when at the words *per singulos dies* he proceeds to the altar.[4] When the priest returns from the altar to the lectern he waits upon him with a lantern and candle, and when the collect is done he receives the lantern from him and then places the gospel book upon the altar.

---

[4] The moment referred to is that at the end of Matins, when the priest of the week leaves the choir during the *Te Deum*, vests, and then carries the gospel-book to the altar, before reading the Gospel following the hymn in the office. The reading of the editions is explained by the failure of the editors to recognise the quotation from the *Te Deum*.

Ipsius est signa pulsare, uel qualiter pulsentur aliis indicare ; de nulla hora sonanda a quouis licentiam petit, nisi de sola prima et collatione, excepto de tercia et uesperis, cum loquentibus fratribus abbas in claustro sedet. Candelas per officinas distribuit, secundum quod opus fuerit, et abbas uel prior praeceperit. De sepulturis tam monachorum quam laicorum curam gerit, ut uidelicet fiant, et ubi fiant.

Sui officii est calices bis in ebdomada, aut sepius si opus fuerit * lauare.[1] Corporalia quoque ante pasca semper, et quoties reliquis anni partibus expedit, utrumque si diaconus aut presbiter sit ; si uero non sit, priori uel abbati indicare, et ipsius licentia alicui, qui huius 150 ordinis est, hanc / curam commendare ; lauandis corporalibus quanta possit diligentia adhibeatur ; uasa aenea ad nullos alios usus destinata ad hoc opus habeantur ; aqua, qua lauantur, sicut et calicum in sacrarium proiiciatur. Lotis, dum siccantur, ne aliquae sordes adhaereant, omnibus modis prouideatur.

Cura faciendi hostias super eum est, quae ut mundissime et honestissime fiant summopere studere debet. In primis, si fieri potest, frumentum cum magno studio granatim eligatur,[2] electum in saculo mundo, et de bono panno facto, et ad hoc opus tantum parato,† ponatur, et a famulo boni studii ad molendinum deferatur. Quo delato famulus aliud frumentum in ipso molendino moli prius faciat, ut illud, unde hostiae fieri debent, sine aliqua sorde moli postea ualeat. Reportata farina secretarius uas, et locum quo farina buletari debet, in circuitu

---

* si opus fuerit saepius A   † om. A
[1] Bernard of Cluny I liv 250
[2] Bernard of Cluny I liii 249 : ' colligitur deinde in saccum non qualemcumque, sed qui ad hoc solum de bono panno consutus est,' etc. There are many other verbal resemblances, but Lanfranc shortens his authority.

His task it is to ring the bells, or to instruct others how they are to be rung. He need ask permission to ring for the hours on no occasion, save only for Prime and the collation, and for Terce and Vespers, when the abbot is sitting and talking in the cloister with the brethren. He distributes candles throughout the household offices according to need, and as the abbot or prior may bid. He takes charge of the burial both of monks and laymen ; he sees to what is to be done, and decides the place of burial.

It is his task twice a week, or more often if need be, to wash the chalices,[1] and before Easter and as often as may be necessary at other times to wash the corporals— that is, if he be a priest or deacon. If he be not, he should tell the prior or abbot, and with his permission entrust the task to someone with the requisite order. All possible care shall be taken in washing the corporals ; vessels of bronze, used for no other purpose, shall be employed, and the water in which they are washed shall be thrown into a special place like that from the chalices. While they are drying, every care shall be taken to prevent any dirt lighting upon them.

It is his task to prepare the hosts, and he should take every care to ensure that they are perfectly pure and seemly. In the first place, if it be possible, the wheat is to be picked out grain by grain with great care,[2] and then put into a clean sack made of good cloth and reserved for the purpose ; a servant of good character shall carry it to the mill, and there shall see that other corn is ground first, so that that from which the hosts are to be made may be ground without any admixture of dirt. When the flour is brought back the sacrist shall

cortina paret, ipsemet uero, indutus alba, et uelato
amictu capite, hoc opus agat. Ea autem die, qua hostiae
fieri debent, secretarius, et fratres qui eum adiuuare
debent, antequam incipiant, manus et facies lauent,
albis induantur, capita amictibus uelent, praeter eum,
qui ferra tenturus, et inde seruiturus est. Horum unus
super tabulam mundissimam ipsam farinam aqua cons-
pergat, et manibus fortiter compingat, et maceret.
Frater, qui ferra, in quibus coquuntur, tenet, manus
cirothecis habeat inuolutas. Interim dum ipsae hostiae
fiunt et coquuntur, dicant idem fratres psalmos familiares
horarum, et horas canonicas, uel de psalterio ex ordine
quod tantumdem ualeat, si ita potius uoluerint. Silentium loquendi omnino teneant. Ille tamen qui ferra
tenet, si necesse sit, breuiter quod uult indicare potest
famulo, qui focum facit, et ligna portat, quae debent
esse ualde sicca, et ante multos dies de industria praeparata.

Eius sollicitudinis est ampullas uinarias et aquarias
bis in ebdomada, id est quarta feria et sabbato, lauare ;
omni die uinum et aquam ad missas celebrandas portare,
offerentibus ad utramque missam hostias ministrare ;
151 /candelas ad lectiones, et in matutinis laudibus, ad primam
collectam accendere.[1] Quae matutinae laudes, si ultra
modum et indecenter tardauerint, secretarius cui huius
rei cura tunc commissa erit, ante gradum satisfactionum
prosternatur, quousque ipsa collecta usque ad Benedicamus Domino finiatur ; quo incepto nulla expectata

---

[1] The bulk of the office was recited or chanted by heart with no lights
in choir, though the church would be illuminated, dimly or brilliantly
according to the rank of the feast, by lamps and tapers. Candles were
provided for the commemorations at Lauds, and a lantern (*v. supra*, p. 82)
for the reader of the lessons and the priest at the Gospel. Later, *c.* 1350,
it became usual to light the choir throughout. In Lanfranc's day the
memorising of psalmody and chant was a principal task of the noviciate,
and an examination preceded profession.

draw a curtain round the place and the vessel in which the flour is to be bolted, and he shall carry out this work in an alb, and with an amice over his head. On the day the hosts are to be made the sacrist and those who help him shall wash their hands and faces before they begin ; they shall wear albs and amices, save for the one who is to hold the irons and minister with them. One shall sprinkle the flour with water as it lies on an absolutely clean table, and shall knead it firmly and press it thin, while the brother who holds the irons in which the wafers are baked shall have his hands covered with gloves. Meanwhile while the hosts are being made and baked, these brethren shall recite the ' familiar ' psalms that go with the hours, and the canonical hours themselves, or, if they prefer, psalms of equal length taken in order from the psalter. Absolute silence shall be maintained, but he who holds the irons may, if need arises, give what instructions he will to the servant who tends the fire and carries the wood, which should be extremely dry and carefully prepared many days previously.

It is also the sacrist's task to wash the cruets of water and wine twice a week, that is, on Wednesday and Saturday ; he shall each day take wine and water for the Masses that are to be said, and shall provide hosts for those who make the offering at the Morrow and High Mass. He shall light the candles for the lessons, and at the first collect of Lauds.[1] If Lauds are notably late beyond what is permissible, the sacrist who was responsible at the time shall prostrate himself before the step in choir where penance is done until the collect with *Benedicamus Domino* is said ; when this is intoned he shall retire without awaiting permission and shall not make the double bow. In this manner shall the one responsible for negligence of this kind on any day do

licentia recedat, et ante et retro non faciat. Hoc modo satisfaciat, quacunque die huiusmodi neglegentia eueniat, et inde postea in capitulo aliam veniam non petat.

Et quia huius ministerii, et in his, quae scripta sunt, et in multis aliis, quae hic scripta non sunt, multiplex et ualde implicita cura est, non uni tantum, sed multis commendari, atque inter eos diuidi debet ; unus eorum sit magister aliorum, ad cuius dispositionem caeteri agant, maioribus causis seruatis arbitrio abbatis uel prioris.

CAMERARII [1] est procurare omnia uestimenta, et calciamenta, et lectos, et stramenta lectorum, quae fratribus sunt necessaria, et iuxta regulam habere concessa.[2] Rasoria quoque, et forpices, tersoria ad radendum ; tersoria in claustro pendentia ; tersoria et manutergia mandati, et omnia uasa eius. Uitreas dormitorii facit, et reficit cum opus est ; dat ferra quibus ferrantur equi abbatis et prioris et omnium hospitum, quibus ferra dari abbas uel prior praeceperit, fratribus quoque in iter profecturis cappas, fasciolas,[3] calcaria. Semel in anno renouari facit fenum in omnibus lectis fratrum, et tunc etiam mundari dormitorium.

AD CELERARII [4] ministerium pertinet, omnia quae in pane, et potu, et diuersis ciborum generibus fratribus sunt necessaria, secundum facultatem loci procurare, 152 omnia / uasa celarii et coquinae, et sciphos, et iustas,[5] et caetera uasa refectorii, et omnem horum trium necessariam suppellectilem ministrare. Pater totius congrega-

---

[1] The section on the Chamberlain is not taken from Bernard.

[2] *Regula* LV 31, where mattress, blanket, coverlet and pillow (*capitale*) are allowed.

[3] These were apparently the gaiters or outer leg-coverings of crossed bands of leather.

[4] The section on the cellarer is not as a whole taken from Bernard.

[5] The *justa* or *justitia* was the jug or flagon containing the day's measure of wine or beer. The *scyphus* was the tankard or cup.

penance, and he need not beg pardon at all in the subsequent chapter.

And since the sacrist's office, both in the matters mentioned and in many others which are not written here, is manifold and complicated, it should be entrusted not to one only but to many ; but one shall be in command over the rest, who shall act according to his direction, reserving important decisions to the abbot or prior.

THE CHAMBERLAIN [1] has the task of procuring all garments and shoes and beds and bedding which are needful for the brethren and allowed them by the Rule.[2] He also provides razors and scissors and towels for shaving ; also the towels hanging in the cloister, and the towels and handcloths and all the vessels for the maundy. He sees to the glazing and repairing of the dormitory windows ; he provides the horseshoes for the horses of abbot and prior and those guests to whom the abbot and prior shall order that horseshoes be given. To brethren about to go on a journey he shall give capes, gaiters [3] and spurs. Once a year he causes the straw to be renewed in all the beds, and at the same time cleans out the dormitory.

TO THE CELLARER's [4] office it belongs to procure all things necessary for the brethren in the way of bread and drink and all kinds of food according to the circumstances of the neighbourhood. He shall provide utensils for the cellar and kitchen, and flagons [5] and tankards and other vessels for the refectory, as well as all necessary furniture for these three places. He should be the father of the whole community, and should have a care both

tionis debet esse ; de sanis, et maxime infirmis fratribus sollicitudinem habere ; praeter consilium abbatis, uel prioris, de maioribus causis nichil facere.[1]

Rogandus est ab eo cantor,[2] ut ante aliquot dies praemuniat eum, et praenunciet ei diem quo sententia sua de regula legenda est in capitulo, ut uidelicet honestum et festiuum seruitium ipsa die possit facere fratribus in refectorio[3]; tabulae tamen refectorii non sint coopertae. Lecta vero in capitulo, et exposita praedicta sententia, cum dictum fuerit a priore, Loquamur de ordine nostro, statim prostratus in loco ubi mos est dicat : Istam obedientiam, quae mihi iniuncta est, mea culpa, negligenter et tepide et multo aliter quam oporteret * tracto ; et in ea in multis offendo Deum, et nostros seniores, mea culpa ; et requiro inde absolutionem uestram et seniorum. Quo dicto, absoluat eum, qui capitulum tenet, de his offensis, quas ibi enumerauit, et de omnibus reliquis, quae in eo sunt. Ad cuius absolutionis finem, responso ab omnibus cum omni devotionis affectu, ut mos est, Amen, uadat ad pedem eius, et deinde iubeatur ire sessum. Finito capitulo, et dicto Uerba mea, si ipsa die dici debet, in eodem capitulo dicant fratres pro eo quinquagesimum psalmum. Quo completo cum Gloria Patri, et Pater noster, dicat ebdomadarius Et ne nos inducas ; Saluum fac seruum tuum ; Dominus uobiscum ; Oremus † : Omnipotens sempiterne Deus, miserere famulo tuo,[4] et

---

* oportet A   † om. A C E
[1] *Regula* XXXI 5 : ‘cellararius omni congregationi sit sicut pater.’ 15 : ‘infirmorum . . . cum omni sollicitudine curam gerat.’ 6 : ‘sine jussione abbatis nihil gerat.’
[2] This paragraph is similar to Bernard of Cluny I vi 149
[3] This passage was cited by the Maurist, Dom Luc d’Achéry, in his preface to Lanfranc’s works (Paris, 1648), as a proof of his assertion that Lanfranc’s constitutions contained spurious and interpolated matter. Such a feast, he observed, ‘ Plane virum sanctum summae abstinentiae addictum . . . dedeceret.’ As noted above, Lanfranc takes the whole from Bernard of Cluny.

for the sound and still more for the sick. He shall do
nothing in important affairs without taking counsel of
the abbot or prior.[1]

He should ask the cantor [2] to give him several days'
warning and acquaint him of the day when the passage
in the rule referring to him is to be read in chapter,
so that he may on that day make the brethren a seemly
feast in the refectory [3] ; the tables of the refectory shall
not however be covered for the occasion. After the
aforementioned passage has been read in chapter and
expounded, and when the prior has said ' Let us now
speak of matters of discipline,' he shall at once prostrate
himself in the usual place and say : ' I confess that I
handle this office that has been laid upon me carelessly
and slackly and far otherwise than I should, and in the
course of it I offend God and our elders in many things,
I confess. And so for this I beg absolution of you and
of the elders.' When he has said this the president of
the chapter shall absolve him of these offences that he
has mentioned, and of all others that he has committed,
and when all have answered with all earnestness at the
end, as is the custom, ' Amen,' he shall go to the feet of
him who presides and then shall be bidden to go to his
seat. When the chapter is done, and the *Verba mea* has
been said, if it is to be said on that day, the brethren
shall say the fiftieth psalm for the cellarer ; that done,
with its *Gloria* and *Pater noster* the hebdomadarian shall
say *Et ne nos inducas* ; *Salvum fac servum tuum* ; *Dominus
vobiscum* ; *Oremus : Omnipotens sempiterne Deus, miserere
famulo tuo*,[4] and the rest. If they have received a death

---

[4] For some reason this prayer is written out at length in the Canterbury
MS (Brit. Mus. Cott. Claudius C. VI), copied by Baker's scribe ; it
therefore appeared in Reyner's edition at the end of the constitutions, and
was reprinted by d'Achéry, Giles and Migne. It occurs in no other MS.

reliqua. Quod si suscepto breui pro defuncto, ipsa die canentes Uerba mea in monasterium ituri sunt, priusquam eant praedictum psalmum cum capitulis et collecta dicant. Si autem praedictam sententiam contigerit tali die legi, qua non possit refectio honorabiliter fieri, sicut 153 est in / uigiliis quatuor temporum, et huiusmodi diebus, petat celerarius a priore et capitulo licentiam quo differri * possit refectionem in aliam diem, qua honestius et plenius fieri ualeat.

Frater qui ad suscipiendos hospites deputatus est, in ipsa hospitum domo haec praeparata habere debet : lectos, sedilia, mensas, manutergia, mappas, sciphos, scutellas, coclearia, baccilia, et si qua sunt huiusmodi ; ligna quoque. Panem uero et potum, et caetera cibaria, ad opus hospitum per famulos sibi deputatos in celario recipit.

Quicunque abbati, uel priori, seu alicui de claustro loqui uult,[1] legationem suam huic debet iniungere. Ipse uero nichil inde alicui aliquo modo indicans, ad abbatem uel priorem uoluntatem hospitis perferat, et postea quod ipse decreuerit fiat. Si autem fratri, qui in claustro est, loquendi cum hospite, uel propinquo, uel extraneo, concessa licentia fuerit, istius est ipsum fratrem de claustro ad hospitem ducere. Quod si abbati uel priori non placuerit ut simul loquantur, nec uerbum, nec signum, nec aliquem nutum ipsi fratri faciat, quo aliquid inde percipere quolibet modo ualeat.

Ipsius est prae omnibus sollicite obseruare de fratribus, qui in obedientiis sunt, cum ad monasterium redeunt, utrum famulos idoneos, et sellam regularem [2]

---

* differre C B   [1] Bernard of Cluny I ix 152
[2] i.e. ' regular ' for monks ; there is no mention of a saddle in the

notice on that day, and are going to the church chanting *Verba mea*, they say the forementioned psalm for the cellarer with its chapters and collect before they go. But if the passage in the Rule occur for reading on a day when a feast cannot be made, as on Ember Days and the like, the cellarer shall ask permission of the prior and chapter to put off the feast to another day when it may be kept more adequately in seemly wise.

THE BROTHER who is appointed to receive guests should have ready in the guest-house beds, chairs, tables, towels, cloths, tankards, plates, spoons, basins and such-like—firewood also. Bread and drink and other provisions he receives of the cellarer for his guests by means of the servants at his disposal.

Whosoever wishes to speak [1] with the abbot, prior or any monk of the cloister shall use the guestmaster as his ambassador, and he, without making a sign to anyone, shall tell the abbot or prior of the guest's wish, and then do what the superior may decide. If permission is granted to a monk of the cloister to speak with a guest, whether a relative or a stranger, it is the guest-master's business to take the monk from the cloister to the guest. If the abbot or prior is not willing that they should talk together, he must not say a word or make a sign or give the slightest nod to the brother concerned, so that he may not be able to gather at all what has happened.

It is his particular task to watch the brethren carefully when they return from obediences, to see whether they have servants of the right kind and the saddle as required by rule,[2] and if they behave with due restraint

---

Rule. Bernard (*loc. cit.* 153) adds : ' vel habeant in sellis suis pectoralia (ornament for the horse's breast) et postas (an ornament behind the saddle).'

habeant, et quomodo se in curia contineant, ut si extra ordinem aliquid fecerint, clamorem inde super eos in capitulo faciat. Si extranei clerici se dixerint in refectorio uelle comedere, istius est uoluntatem ipsorum abbati uel priori indicare ; quod si abbas uel prior petitioni eorum annuerit, iste eos quomodo in refectorio se habere debeant bene instruat, et ita instructos pulsato iam cimbalo in locutorium adducat, ibique abbas, uel prior, si abbas deest, manibus eorum aquam tribuat,[1] et postea praedictus frater eos ad mensam abbatis ducat. Com-
154 pleto autem prandio, atque exeunte / conuentu de refectorio, praefatus eorum ductor post abbatem uel priorem solus cum illis remaneat, et sequatur cum eis processionem, donec de hostio refectorii exeat, postea ducat eos extra claustrum mediocri uoce psallendo cum eis Miserere mei, Deus, et caetera quae secuntur.

Ipsius est extraneum monachum, qui ignarus loci sit, per claustrum in monasterium ad orationem ducere. Breues pro defunctis per manum illius magistro infantum dari, uel in capitulum deferri debent.[2] Ad eum pertinet seculares homines, qui societatem fratrum suscepturi sunt, adducere in capitulum. Ipsius est uolentibus uidere officinas, ipsas officinas ostendere, obseruato ut conuentus tunc in claustro non sedeat,[3] nec aliquem ocreatum,[4] uel calcaria habentem, nec aliquem qui nudis pedibus sit, uel solis femoralibus calciatus, in claustrum pro qualibet causa introducat. Suum praeterea est nouicios, qui de

---

[1] *Regula* LIII 25 : ' Aquam in manibus abbas hospitibus det ; pedes hospitibus omnibus tam abbas quam cuncta congregatio lavet.' As late as the end of the twelfth century Gerald of Wales notes that the washing of hands is for the Welsh the equivalent of an invitation to stay (*Descriptio Kambriae*, Rolls Series, p. 183).

[2] i.e. the incoming death-bills go to the chapter, the outgoing ones to the children, who wrote them out fairly and were often instructed to display their skill by adding a copy of verses in honour of the deceased ; *v.* many examples in L. Delisle, *Rouleaux des Morts* (Paris, 1866) and Knowles, *Monastic Order*, 501.

in the courtyard, so that if they do anything irregular he may accuse them of it in chapter.

If visiting clerks say they would like to dine in the refectory, it is his office to tell the abbot or prior of their desire, and if their request is granted he instructs them carefully how to behave in the refectory, and, after instructing them, when the gong is beaten he shall take them to the parlour, where the abbot, or the prior if the abbot is away, shall pour water over their hands [1] ; after this the aforesaid brother shall lead them to the abbot's table. When dinner is over and the community leaves the refectory, their guide remains alone with them after the abbot or prior has gone, and follows the procession with them until it goes out of the refectory, when he shall lead them out of the cloister saying with them in an ordinary tone of voice the psalm *Miserere*.

It is his duty also to lead strange monks who do not know the place through the cloister into the church for prayer. Death bills shall be given by him to the master of the children, and incoming ones shall be brought by him into chapter.[2] It is his duty also to introduce into chapter seculars who are to receive confraternity. His also it is to show the buildings to those who wish to see them, taking care that the community is not then sitting in the cloister [3] ; he shall not introduce into the cloister under any circumstances anyone wearing riding-boots [4] or spurs, nor anyone who goes barefoot or has only drawers on his legs. Finally it is his task to lead into

---

[3] The passage is an interesting instance, perhaps unique in this age, of arrangements being made for visitors and sightseers who wished to see round a monastery.

[4] Bernard of Cluny I ix 154: 'ne quis aliquando intret claustrum calcaria vel ocreas portans, vel in solis femoralibus.' *Ocreae*, originally 'leggings,' but also, as probably here, 'boots.' The regulations aim at excluding noise, dirt and slovenly dress.

saeculo ueniunt, in capitulum adducere, et docere eos priorem petitionem facere.

ELEMOSINARIUS[1] aut per se, si opportunum sibi est, perquirat, aut per ueraces et fideles homines cum multa sollicitudine perquiri faciat, ubi egri, et debiles iaceant, . qui non habent * unde se sustentare † ualeant. Si autem ipsemet ad perquirendum et uisitandum perrexerit, duos famulos secum habeat, et priusquam intret domum, ad quam iturus est, mulieres si aliquae in ea sunt exire faciat. Ingressus domum blande consoletur egrum, et offerat ei quod melius habet, et sibi intelligit esse necessarium. Quod si eger aliud requirit, et ipsum perquirat, si aliquo modo habere potuerit. In eas autem domos in quibus mulieres egrae uel debiles iacent nunquam introeat, sed per unum de famulis suis quod habere potest, et eis necessarium est, transmittat, prius tamen quam aliquid 155 de supradictis agat, abbati uel / priori indicet, et secundum eorum dispositionem elemosinam monasterii eis dispenset.

FRATER cui cura domus infirmorum committitur, et infirmis fratribus seruire deputatur, cocum suum habeat, et coquinam separatim, si loci situs et facultas talis sit, ut quod infirmis praeparari necessarium est, opportuno tempore parari possit. Omnia fercula apponenda infirmis ipse administret eis. Omni die post completorium spargat aquam benedictam per omnes eorum lectos ; factis tribus orationibus,[2] quae fiunt ante nocturna,

---

* habeant C   † sustinere C
[1] cf. Bernard of Cluny I xiii 159, but Lanfranc abbreviates. The function of the almoner as a district visitor seems to have ceased early in England, and alms were distributed at the gateway or in the almonry.
[2] i.e. the *trina oratio*

chapter novices coming from the world, and to teach them how to make their first petition.

THE ALMONER,[1] either himself if occasion serve, or by means of reliable and truthful servants, shall take great pains to discover where may lie those sick and weakly persons who are without means of sustenance. If he himself goes forth to seek and visit the indigent, he shall take two servants with him, and before he enters the house to which he is going he shall cause any women who may be there to leave it. Entering the house he shall speak kindly and comfort the sick man, and offer him the best of what he has that may be needful for him. If the sick man ask for something else he shall do what he can to obtain it. He shall never enter houses in which sick or infirm women are lying, but shall send to them all necessaries that he can by means of one of his servants. But before he gives any help of the kind mentioned above he shall tell the abbot or prior, and apportion the alms of the monastery according to their decision.

THE BROTHER to whom the care of the infirmary is given, and who is set to serve the sick, shall have his own cook and separate kitchen, if the plan of the buildings and the resources of the house allow, so that he may be able to prepare what is necessary for the sick at the right times. He himself shall place before the sick brethren all the dishes prepared for them.

Every day after Compline he shall sprinkle holy water over the beds of all the sick. When the three prayers[2] before nocturns have been said, he shall take a dark lantern and go round the beds of all the sick, seeing

circumeat cum absconsa lectos infirmorum omnium,
obseruans sollicite ne aliquis qui ualeret surgere in lecto
remanserit. Ipsius est praecipue manifestare, et clamare
in capitulo, negligentias omnium in praedicta domo
commorantium. Cum perceperit infirmum iam esse
prope finem suum, suum est praecipere famulis suis, ut
calefaciant aquam ad lauandum ipsum. Cura de feretro
custodiendo et administrando cum opus fuerit super eum
est, et super famulos suos, sicut et cura de administranda
tabula, quam ex more prior semel percutit, completa
ablutione ipsius defuncti. Defuncto fratre et in monasterium deportato, locum in quo iacuit mundari, et feno
uel iunco renouari faciat. Abbas uel prior omnibus
modis sollicitudinem gerat ne aliquid, quod ad hoc
ministerium necessarium est, in illa domo unquam
deficiat.

CUM DE CORPORE uel sanguine Domini tanta negligentia aliquo casu accidit, ut cadat deorsum, siue in alium
locum ubi plene percipi non possit quo ceciderit, et utrum /
ad terram inde aliquid uenerit, quam citius fieri possit,
indicetur res abbati uel priori, qui adiunctis sibi aliquibus
fratribus propere ueniat ad locum ubi hoc contigerit. Et
si corpus ceciderit, uel sanguis effusus fuerit super lapi-
dem, aut terram, aut lignum, aut mattam, aut tapetum,
aut aliquid huiusmodi, puluis terrae colligatur, pars illa
lapidis radatur, pars ligni, mattae, tapeti, et si quid aliud
est huiusmodi abscidatur, et in sacrarium proiiciatur.
Quod si locus ubi ceciderit manifeste deprehendi nequiuerit, et tamen deorsum cecidisse constiterit, in loco,
et circa locum in quem maxime cecidisse crediderint,
similiter colligatur, radatur, abscidatur, et in sacrario *

* sacrarium A

carefully that no-one who is capable of rising shall remain in bed. It is his special duty to disclose and accuse in chapter the negligences of all who abide in the forementioned infirmary.

When he perceives a sick man is now nearing his end, it is his duty to instruct his servants to heat water to wash the body. It is his business, and that of his servants, to keep the hearse and bring it out when necessary, and to provide the board which the prior strikes once, according to custom, when the washing of the body is done. When a brother has died and has been borne into the church, he shall wash the place in which he lay and spread fresh straw or rushes.

The abbot or prior shall take every care that nothing necessary for the infirmarian's office shall ever be lacking in the infirmary.

WHEN FOR ANY REASON there is such carelessness with regard to the body and blood of the Lord that it fall to the ground, or fall in such wise that it cannot be clearly seen where it has fallen, and whether any part of it has fallen to the ground, the matter shall be brought to the notice of abbot or prior as soon as possible, and he taking others with him shall go with speed to the place where the accident has happened. And if the body or blood of the Lord has fallen, or has been spilt, upon a stone or the earth or wood or mat or carpet or anything of that kind, the surface of the earth shall be taken up, that spot in the stone shall be scraped, and the part affected in the wood, matting, carpet or whatever it may be shall be cut out and thrown down the *sacrarium*. If the place where it fell cannot be accurately determined, and yet it is certain that it fell, a like procedure shall be accomplished in and around the spot where it is thought

recondatur. Hi vero quorum negligentia hoc euenerit, in proximo capitulo humiliter culpam suam dicant, iudicium nudi suscipiant,* et iniungatur eis penitentia, uel de ieiunio, uel iudiciis, uel psalmis, uel aliquid huiusmodi. Quibus de iudicio ad loca sua reuersis, omnes sacerdotes, qui tunc praesentes erunt, surgant, et ad iudicia suscipienda cum omni deuotione se offerant. Tunc ille qui capitulum tenet septem tantum quos uoluerit de ipsis ad suscipienda iudicia retineat, et caeteris ire sessum praecipiat. Finito capitulo omnes simul prostrati dicant septem psalmos in monasterio, incipientes eos psallere, cum exeunt de capitulo. Quos sequatur Pater noster cum his capitulis et collecta : Et ueniat super nos misericordia tua, Deus ; Ne memineris iniquitatum nostrarum antiquarum ; Dominus uobiscum, Oremus : Exaudi, Domine, preces nostras et confitentium tibi parce peccatis, ut quos conscientiae reatus accusat, indulgentia tuae miserationis absoluat ; aut illam collectam, Deus, cui proprium est misereri semper ; aut aliam pro peccatis.[1]

Si uero super corporale uel super aliquem honestum pannum sanguis ceciderit, certumque fuerit quo ceciderit, pars illa panni in aliquo calice abluatur, et prima ablutio a fratribus absumatur, reliquae duae in sacrarium 157 proii/ciantur. In primo autem capitulo dicta culpa, hi soli tantum, quorum negligentia hoc euenit, supradictam disciplinam sustineant ; fratres uero omnes septem psalmos cum capitulis et collecta, sicut superius dictum est, in monasterio dicant. Si ipsa die breuis pro defuncto in

---

* suscipiant nudi A
[1] The solemn severity of the penalty, which dislocates the horarium, was no doubt intended not only to emphasise the heinous carelessness, but also to act as a psychological deterrent.

most likely that the particle or drops fell. Those responsible for the carelessness shall humbly beg pardon in the chapter next following ; they shall be scourged on the bare flesh, and a penance, either of fasting or abstinence or corporal punishment or prayers or something of the kind shall be laid upon them. When they have returned to their places all the priests present shall rise and devoutly offer themselves for punishment. Then the president of the chapter shall keep seven of them, chosen at his discretion, for punishment, and order the others to be seated. When the chapter is over, all shall prostrate themselves and say the seven penitential psalms in the church, having begun to chant them on leaving the chapter-house ; the psalms shall be followed by the *Pater noster* with the following chapters and collect : *Et ueniat super nos misericordia tua, Deus ; Ne memineris iniquitatum nostrarum antiquarum ; Dominus uobiscum ; Oremus : Exaudi, Domine, preces nostras et confitentium tibi parce peccatis, ut quos conscientiae reatus accusat, indulgentia tuae miserationis absoluat,* or the collect *Deus, cui proprium est misereri semper,* or some other for the remission of sins.[1]

If the blood of the Lord shall have fallen upon the corporal or some other clean cloth, and it be quite certain where it fell, that part of the cloth shall be washed in a chalice and the water of the first washing shall be received by the brethren, and that of the two following washings shall be thrown down the *sacrarium.* In the chapter next following, when pardon has been asked, those only who are responsible for the accident shall undergo the punishment set out above, but the brethren shall say in the church all the seven psalms with the chapters and collect as set out. If a death bill has been read that day in chapter they shall first chant

capitulo lectus fuerit, prius canant Verba mea, pergentes in aecclesiam ; postea septem psalmos sicut superius dictum est. Si uero alio aliquo modo de hoc sacramento leuior negligentia euenerit, ex iudicio abbatis uel prioris leuiori uindicta frater, cuius culpa hoc contigerit, puniatur.

Qua die radendi sunt fratres [1] citius solito pulsetur signum ad primam, uel ad terciam, si ipsa tercia ante capitulum dici debet. In capitulo non diu sedeant, sed necessariis rebus explicitis surgentes, pulsata tabula, dictoque Benedicite, exeant in claustrum. Infantes ipsa die capitulum non teneant, sed statim post alios exeant, et in scolam suam pergant ; residentibus cunctis, et ad radendum paratis, incipiat abbas aut prior quinque psalmos, id est Verba mea pro defunctis. Sacerdos ebdomadarius sedens dicat collectas ; alter quoque ebdomadarius iuxta eum sedeat, et cum eo psalmos teneat ; post quinque psalmos dicant omnes canonicas horas, in quarum fine usque ad uesperas non dicat sacerdos Dominus uobiscum, nec Benedicamus Domino, sed post Per omnia saecula saeculorum statim incipiat Deus, in adiutorium meum ; post uesperas uero, dicto Benedicamus Domino, psallantur uesperae mortuorum, dehinc completorium ut canonici ; postea familiares psalmi horarum.

Nullus in cuculla radatur, sed prius cuculla exutus, et frocco indutus, cuculla plicata, et iuxta se posita, radatur. Ille qui radit frocco exutus sit. Iuuenes qui
158   sunt in custodia custodes suos radant, et / custodes ipsos

---

[1] There are many similarities between this and Bernard of Cluny I xxxi 215–16. Lanfranc does not state how often the communal shave took place, though the mention that the function coincided with the regular change of linen on the refectory tables suggests that the intervals left time for a notable growth. This alone would help to account for the considerable space of time allotted to it, and the head as well as the beard was shaved—hence the part taken by the children.

the *Verba mea* on their way to the church, and afterwards the seven psalms as aforesaid. If in any other way a less serious accident occur with respect to this Sacrament, the brother responsible shall be punished more lightly at the discretion of the abbot or prior.

ON THE DAY THE BRETHREN ARE TO BE SHAVED,[1] the bell for Prime (or for Terce, if Terce is to be said before chapter that day) shall be rung more rapidly than usual. They shall not sit long in chapter but when all necessary business has been done they shall rise, and when the board has been struck and *Benedicite* said they shall go out into the cloister. The children shall hold no chapter that day, but shall go into the cloister immediately after the monks and go to their school. When all are seated ready for shaving, the abbot or prior shall begin the five psalms, that is, the *Verba mea* and the rest, for the dead. The priest of the week shall say the collects seated, and the second hebdomadary shall sit by him saying the psalms with him. After the five psalms they shall say all the canonical hours ; at the end of each up to Vespers the priest shall not say *Dominus uobiscum* nor *Benedicamus Domino*, but after *Per omnia saecula saeculorum* shall begin at once *Deus in adjutorium meum* ; after Vespers, when *Benedicamus Domino* has been said, Vespers of the dead shall be recited, then Compline in the form used by canons, then the ' familiar ' psalms of the hours concerned.

No one shall be shaved in his cowl, but shall first take off his cowl and put on his tunic and be shaved with his cowl lying folded by him. He who shaves shall be without a tunic. The juniors under ward shall shave their guardians, and the guardians shall shave their juniors. If a guardian knows not how, or is physically unable to shave, he shall ask a brother of mature age to

iuuenes. Quod si custos nequiuerit, aut nescierit radere,
roget aliquem maturum fratrem, ut eum radat, ipse
tamen custodiens ipsum iuxta eum sedeat. Iuuenes
quoque, siue nutriti, siue de saeculo uenientes, utrique
tamen extra huiusmodi custodiam existentes, non prae-
sumant ut alter alterum radant, sed seniores ab illis, et
illi a senioribus radantur. Magistri pueros radant, et
ipsi a pueris radantur, si tamen huiusmodi scientiam
habent.

Hiemali tempore, quando pueri, et sanguine minuti,
atque infirmi, post capitulum accipiunt mixtum, refectorarii primi se radant, et post psalmos tam cito apparatum refectorii faciant, ut fratres accepturi mixtum omnia
parata inueniant. Quamdiu psalmi dicuntur nemo
tondeatur, uel caput abluat, uel ungues incidat, nec
extra claustrum sine licentia ire praesumat. Finitis
psalmis, dicat abbas, uel prior, Benedicite, et responso
Dominus, postea loquantur. Tunc lesciua in claustrum
deferatur, et qui uult caput lauet quisque sibi, nullus
alii, praeter magistros infantum, qui paruulis pueris,
qui id non possunt, capita lauare debent. Frater dum
raditur, si signum ad horam sonuerit, induat cucullam
super froccum, et pergat in chorum, si tamen omnino
barbam rasam aut omnino adhuc intactam habet.
Alioquin extra chorum maneat. Ipso die quo se radunt
fratres mappae in refectorio mutandae sunt. Aliis diebus
quando fratres in claustro locuntur, qui necesse habet
tonderi potest in claustro, sed per licentiam abbatis siue
prioris.

LICENTIA minuendi sanguinem[1] omni tempore statim
post capitulum petenda est, et celerario indicandum.

---

[1] See Appendix C, p. 151

shave his junior for him, but he himself shall sit by meanwhile. The juniors no longer under ward, whether alumni of the house or those who have come from the world shall not presume to shave one another, but shall shave, and be shaved by, senior monks. The masters shall shave their children and they shall be shaved by them, if they know how to do it.

In winter, when the children and those who have been bled and the sick receive the *mixtum* after chapter, those in charge of the refectory shall shave each other first, and shall then make things ready in the refectory with all speed, so that the brethren who are to receive the *mixtum* may find all ready. While the psalms are being said no one shall be shaved, or wash his head, or cut his nails, nor venture to leave the cloister without permission. When the psalms are done the abbot or prior shall say *Benedicite*, and when they have answered *Dominus* they shall be free to speak. Then soap shall be brought into the cloister and whoso wishes may wash his head. Everyone shall wash his own head, and none shall wash another's, save the masters of the children who must wash the heads of the little children who cannot do it for themselves. If the bell for one of the hours sound while a brother is being shaved, and his beard be either still untouched or wholly shaved, he shall put on his cowl over his tunic and go into choir ; otherwise he shall stay away. On the day of shaving the cloths are to be changed in the refectory. On other days when there is talking in the cloister, he who needs to be shaved may, by permission of the abbot or prior, be shaved in the cloister.

PERMISSION FOR BEING BLED [1] is at all seasons to be sought immediately after chapter, and the cellarer is to

Hora minuendi est : in hieme post euangelium maioris
159 missae ; in / aestate post nonam ante uesperas ; in
quadragesima post uesperas. Cum ii qui minuendi sunt,
calciati nocturnalibus suis ad locum qui huic operi
deputatus est uenerint, uersi ad orientem ante et retro
inclinent, deinde priore eorum incipiente uersum Deus
in adiutorium meum intende ter dicant, et caetera, sicut
in aestate post nonam in capitulo, quando fratres locuntur in claustro. Si unus tantum fuerit solus hoc faciat.
Postea exuant froccos, et parent se ad minuendum.
Silentium ibi omnino teneant nisi necessitas loqui cogat,
quae differri aut non possit, aut non debeat. Quod si
euenerit, breuiter et modeste et humillima uoce id fiat.

Chorum non cogantur intrare usque in crastinum
post orationem primae uel terciae, quo tempore ante
capitulum tercia dicitur ; si plus indigent petita licentia
diutius extra chorum remaneant. Crastina die nocturnales suos calcient, duobus diebus mixtum accipiant ; cum
ad ipsum mixtum uentum fuerit, si tempus sit quo fratres
semel reficiunt, simul omnes dicant uersum, et ante
mixtum et post mixtum, cum psalmo Miserere mei Deus
et reliquis, eo modo quo dicitur a conuentu, cum bis
reficiunt omnes fratres. Benedictio a priore sacerdote
detur ; lectio ab uno aliquo memoriter recitetur ; in
refectorio totum fiat. In crastino minutionis clamatus
aliquis minutorum surgat, et ad petendam ueniam se
offerat ; aliquis uero eorum, quibus minutio nota est,
priori dicere debet, quod frater ille minutus sit, et prior
ei praecipere ut stando loquatur, et maxime si de uena

be informed. The hour for blood-letting in winter is after the gospel of High Mass ; in summer after None and before Vespers ; in Lent after Vespers. When those to be bled have put on their night shoes and come to the place allotted for the purpose, they shall turn to the east and make a double obeisance ; then the senior among them shall begin the versicle *Deus in adjutorium meum intende*, which they shall say thrice with what follows, as is done in summer after None in the chapter-house when there is talking in the cloister. If only one monk is being bled he shall do all this by himself. Then they shall take off their tunics and make ready for being bled. They shall keep an absolute silence, unless it be necessary to speak on account of some matter which either cannot, or ought not, to be put off. When this happens speech shall be brief, and the words shall be seemly and spoken in a low tone of voice.

Those bled shall not be obliged to come to choir until the prayer at the end of Prime (or of Terce, when this is said before chapter) on the next day. If they need more indulgence they may, with permission, stay away for longer. On the day after they have been bled they shall wear their night shoes, and for two days they shall receive the *mixtum*. When they gather for this, if it be a season when the brethren have one meal only, all shall say the versicle together both before and after their refreshment, with the psalm *Miserere mei Deus* and the rest as said by the community when all are taking two meals. The blessing shall be given by the senior priest present, and the lesson shall be said by heart by one of them. All this shall take place in the refectory. If one of those who have been bled be accused in chapter the day following, he shall rise and make ready to do penance ; then one of those who know that he has been

brachii minutus sit.[1] Si culpa leuis est indulgeatur ei ; si autem talis fuerit, quae sine corporali disciplina dimitti non debeat, in aliud tempus differatur.

Haec sunt tempora quibus fratres minui non debent, nisi necessitas cogat : si in crastino festiuitas duodecim lectionum sit, exceptis sabbatis quadragesimae usque ad passionem Domini ; si crastina die festiuitas trium 160 lectionum sit, / in qua missa in cappis celebretur, sicut sunt tres dies post pasca, et tres post pentecosten ; quatuordecim dies ante pasca ; si ipsa die, uel in crastino, canonica ieiunia sint, quae uiolari non possint ; festiuitas omnium sanctorum, quia in crastino omnes sacerdotes pro defunctis missam celebrare, et reliqui psalmos pro missis ordinatos dicere debent.

CUM SACERDOTI maioris missae ebdomadario aliquid dormienti euenerit, propter quod ipsa die missam celebrare non debeat, si fuerit priuata dies non dimittat quicquam facere de suo officio, nisi missam et benedictionem in refectorio, et completorium, quia aqua benedicta post completorium fratres aspergere ad ipsum pertinet, qui completorium dixit et missam celebrauit. Quod si duodecim lectiones fuerint, dimittat etiam uesperas, matutinas quoque laudes, si ad ipsas reuestiri debeat sacerdos. Finita autem principali oratione, cum sacerdos reuestitus, qui pro eo facit officium, exierit de choro, sacerdos ebdomadarius de quacunque parte chori sit, nullo expectato signo, compleat reliqua omnia quae secuntur. Cum autem ipse ebdomadarius reuestitus

---

[1] This was the most common, though a vein in the foot was sometimes opened. The operation was at many houses performed by a skilled layman, who sometimes held a house or land in sergeanty for this purpose ; there is no suggestion in medieval English sources that it was regarded as at all dangerous.

bled should tell the prior that this brother has been bled and the prior shall tell him to stand while he speaks, particularly if a vein in his arm has been opened.[1] If the fault is light he shall go free ; if it be one that ought not to be dismissed without corporal punishment, this shall be put off to another time.

On the following occasions the brethren should not be bled unless strict necessity demand : if a feast of twelve lessons fall on the morrow, save for the Saturdays in Lent up to Passiontide ; if on the morrow there is a feast of three lessons when Mass is celebrated in copes, as is the case on the three days after Easter and Pentecost ; during the fortnight before Easter ; if on the day itself or the day following there is a canonical fast which cannot be broken ; and the feast of All Saints, because on the following day all the priests have to say Mass for the dead and the others have to say psalms instead of the Masses.

IF THE PRIEST OF THE WEEK who is due to celebrate the High Mass should be rendered unfit to celebrate by reason of anything occurring in his sleep, he shall omit none of his duties on an ordinary day save Mass and the blessing in the refectory and Compline, because it is the duty of the one who has celebrated the Mass and said Compline to sprinkle the brethren after Compline with holy water.

If it is a day of twelve lessons, he shall stand aside at Vespers and Lauds also, if the priest is to wear a vestment at these offices. But when the first prayer is done and the priest in a cope who is taking his place has gone out of choir, then the priest of the week, whatever be his position in choir, shall, without waiting for any sign, do all that remains to be done. When, however, the priest

cantat uesperas aut matutinas laudes, et completa principali oratione egreditur chorum ut exuatur, tunc uni de
suo choro cui voluerit signum faciat, ut agat pro eo
commemorationem sanctorum. Qua completa ebdomadarius reuersus in chorum compleat quae secuntur.

FRATER in aliquod iter profecturus, et in crastino
non reuersurus, accipiat benedictionem exeundi ; [1] si uero
161 conti/gerit ut altera die reuertatur, non accipiat benedictionem reuertendi ; si autem profecturus sperat se in
crastino rediturum, non accipiat benedictionem eundi.
Quod si euenerit ut ultra biduum moretur, reuersus
reuertendi benedictionem accipiat. Ille uero frater qui
accepta pergendi benedictione ultra biduum moratus
fuerit, si ipso die quo redierit in aliquem locum extra
monasterium perrexerit, et unius noctis moram fecerit,
in crastino reuersus omnes reuertendi benedictiones
accipiat, quia ex quo primum abiit non iacuit in monasterio ; si uero sine benedictione exeat sperans se in crastino rediturum, et ita eueniat, atque ipsa die qua rediit
extra monasterium, ubi una nocte moretur, in aliquem
locum pergat, reuersus ipsa die omnes reuertendi benedictiones accipiat. Hoc propterea fit, quia duabus con-
tinuis noctibus extra monasterium fuit. In exeundo
nullam benedictionem accipiat, nisi ultra biduum se
moraturum existimet.

Si frater quilibet de foris ueniens accipiat utramque
benedictionem, ueniendi scilicet atque exeundi, nec sit
ei opportunum statim, uel etiam per totam ipsam diem
exire, ad quotcunque horas in monasterio fuerit accipiat

---

[1] There are here echoes of Bernard of Cluny I lxxiv 268 (cf. Albers
I 143), but Lanfranc is more diffuse. These complicated regulations,
glossing the Rule, are a consequence of increased frequency of travel and
short absences on monastic business. The Rule, ch. lxvii, orders a single
blessing for all outgoers and a blessing at all the Hours for a returned
traveller.

of the week sings Vespers or Lauds in a cope, and goes out to unvest after the first prayer, then he shall make a sign to whomsoever he will on his side of choir that he may take his place for the commemoration of All Saints. When this is over the priest of the week having returned to choir shall do what remains to be done.

IF A BROTHER IS GOING ON A JOURNEY and is not to return the next day, he shall receive the blessing of one who is going forth.[1] If it so happens that he returns next day he does not receive the blessing of return, nor does one receive a blessing of departure if he hopes to return after a single night. But if it happen that he is away more than two days he receives a blessing on his return. The brother who, having received the blessing for departure, stays away for more than two days, and then goes away again to a place outside the monastery for a single night on the very day of his return, shall, when he returns next day, receive the full blessing of one who returns, since he has not spent a night in the monastery since his first departure. If, moreover, he depart without a blessing, hoping to return next day, and does so, but on the same day leaves the monastery again, to spend a single night outside, he shall on his return receive the full blessing. This is done because he spent two nights running outside the monastery. But he shall receive no blessing when he departs, unless he expects to be away for two nights.

If a brother returns from a journey and receives both blessings, that is, for returning and departing, but does not find it convenient to depart at once, or indeed during the whole day, he shall receive the blessing of one who has returned at every hour at which he is present, but not the blessing of one who departs, unless

benedictiones ueniendi, exeundi uero minime ; nisi forte
contigerit eum ipsa nocte in monasterio remanere, tunc
enim in crastino, si exire uoluerit, suscipiat eam. Ad
uesperas uel ad completorium nunquam debet dari
benedictio exeundi.

Frater accepta benedictione, si priusquam de claustro
exeat signum regularis horae sonuerit, cum caeteris in
chorum pergat, et dicta hora, in uiam suam uadat. Si
autem extra claustrum fuerit, et priusquam portam
curiae egressus sit, ad regularem horam signum pulsatum
fuerit, ad aecclesiam redeat, et regularem horam extra
chorum dicat, et postea uiam suam teneat. Fasciolatus,
aut cinctus, siue cum cappa, nunquam in claustrum
162 introeat./

Fratres in uiam directi cum horam regularem dicunt,
aut orationem faciunt, aut Deus in adiutorium * cum
Gloria Patri dicunt, si dies talis est, sicut in monasterio
genua flectant ; sed ante et retro nusquam faciant, nec
cum falluntur ueniam petant, nisi sint in ecclesia.[1] Diebus
quibus super formas orant dicturi aliquam horam, si
equitant de equis descendant, et inchoata hora, ac uenia
petita, a manibus cirothecas, et a capitibus capitia
auferant, et sic ascensis equis horam finiant. Quod si
inter psallendum necessitas loquendi eueniat, finita
locutione, iterum a capite horam incipiant. Dum hora
in hospitio canitur aut cum manducant froccis induti
sint aut solis cucullis. Cunctam psalmodiam quam in
nocte eis dicere commodum non est, equitantes per
uiam dicant, praeter eam, quam in die dicere solent ad
complendum ordinem, ad uitandam curiositatem, scur-
rilitatem, otiositatem. Antequam dormitum uadant

---

* + meum A E
[1] Bernard of Cluny I ii 140 ; cf. Albers I 144. Much of what follows
comes verbally from Bernard.

it so happen that he stay that night in the monastery, in which case he shall receive the blessing next day if he wish to depart. This blessing shall never be given at Vespers or Compline.

If, when a brother has received his blessing, the bell for one of the regular hours sounds before he has left the cloister, he shall go into choir with the others, and when the hour has been said shall go on his journey. If he be outside the cloister but not yet outside the gate of the courtyard when the bell rings, he shall return to the church and say the hour without going into choir, and afterwards go on his journey. He shall never enter the cloister gaitered or girded for the road, or wearing a cape.

When brethren on a journey say one of the regular hours, or pray, or say *Deus in adiutorium meum* with *Gloria Patri* if the order of the day require it, they bow the knee as they would in choir, but they never make the full obeisance, nor do they do penance when they make a mistake, unless they are in a church.[1] On such days as the brethren before an hour pray bowing down over their desks, they dismount if they are on horseback and, having begun the hour and bowed the knee, they take their gloves and hoods off, and so, remounting, finish the hour. If while they are saying the psalms it be necessary to speak, when they have finished what they had to say they shall begin the hour again. When they are saying an hour at an inn, and when they are eating, they shall wear their tunics or their cowls only. They shall say all the office which it is not convenient for them to say at night whilst they are on horseback on the road, as well as the regular psalmody of the day and the prayers they say to avoid idle talk and gossip and light words. They shall say Compline before they go

completorium dicant ; quo dicto, si grandis, quae uitari
non debeat, necessitas loquendi eueniat, dicto uersu quam
breuius fieri possit loquantur. Et si ante matutinas hoc
accidat, completorium iterum dicant, et postea silentium
teneant.¹ Ubicunque monachus sit, tota nocte ante eum
lumen ardeat.

De monachis in uiam directis hunc morem coenobia
illa tenent, quae nostro tempore nostri ordinis maiorem
auctoritatem habent.² Beatus tamen Benedictus moram
dierum non determinat, sed absolute imperat, ut de
itinere reuersus monachus per omnes canonicas horas
benedictionem accipiat.

Dum * regularis hora praeter completorium in monasterio canitur, nullus fratrum loquatur intra officinas
totius monasterii ; nec infra totam curiam ;³ nec etiam
163 in domo infir/morum, praeter illos infirmos,† quos tanta
infirmitas angustiat, ut eos interim silentium tenere non
sinat. Completorium uero dum canitur, licet priori, et
eis qui per licentiam de completorio remanent, de utilibus et necessariis rebus loqui.

Similiter dum regularem horam fratres in aecclesia
dicunt, nullus comedat in refectorio, excepto solo completorio ; tunc enim licet iis qui aliqua utilitate impediti
ante illam horam se expedire non possunt, et fratribus
qui de foris ueniunt, comedere in refectorio. Qui si
ante collationem incipientes comedere circa finem com-
pletorii cenam suam commode explere non ualent, licet

---

* Cum A E   † om. A C
¹ This was to comply with the ordinance of the Rule (ch. xlii) that
none should speak after Compline. Silence had in fact been broken ;
hence Compline must be said again.

to bed, and if, after Compline has been said, there arises a great and unavoidable necessity for speaking, they shall say the versicle and speak as briefly as may be. If this occur before the hour of Lauds, they shall say Compline again and afterwards keep silence.[1] Wheresoever a monk sleeps a light shall burn by his bed all night.

The above customs for monks sent on a journey hold in those monasteries which at the present time have the greatest reputation in our order.[2] The blessed Benedict, however, does not set any limit to the time of absence required, but simply orders that a monk who has returned from a journey shall receive a blessing at all the canonical hours.

WHILE ANY HOUR save Compline is being sung in the church no brother shall talk in any of the offices of the monastery, nor within the bounds of the courtyard,[3] nor even in the infirmary, save for those of the sick who are so straitened as to be unable to keep silence for that space. While Compline is being sung, however, the prior and those who have permission to stay out of Compline may speak of such matters as it may be advantageous or needful to despatch.

Likewise, while the brethren are saying a regular hour in the church none shall eat in the refectory, save only during Compline, when those who could not previously finish their business, and brethren who have arrived from a distance, take their meal in the refectory. These, if they began their meal before the collation, but have not been able to finish comfortably by the end of

[2] e.g. Cluny
[3] Bernard of Cluny I lxxiv 273

eis a mensa surgere, et in monasterium ad benedictionem ire,[1] et postea in refectorium ad complendam cenam redire.

AD LEUIS culpae satisfactionem adiudicatus[2] frater a communi mensa separetur, usurus cibo et potu quibus alii fratres, nisi ei nominatim fuerit interdictum, refecturus hora nona, si fratres sexta, uel ad uesperam, si fratres hora nona. In monasterio et in capitulo, in loco ubi solet esse sit, aut ultimus omnium, aut inter utrunque, secundum quod culpa fuerit, et abbas praeceperit. In aecclesia missam non celebret, epistolam uel euangelium uel lectionem non legat, responsorium non canat, antiphonam super psalmos non imponat, nec aliquid huiusmodi, nisi cum caeteris agat ; ad candelabrum uel ad thuribulum non se reuestiat ; ad offerendam uel ad pacem non accedat.

Circa finem regulariter instituti operis Dei, tam in nocte, quam in die, cum incipiunt Kyrieleison, prosternat se ante gradum ubi benedictiones accipiuntur, ibique tamdiu prostratus iaceat, usquequo dicatur Qui tecum uiuit ; si festiuitas duodecim lectionum eueniat, tamdiu 164 ab hac satis/factione quiescat, quousque priuati dies redeant ; dum fratres in refectorio comedunt, ipse sit in aecclesia. Cum abbati placuerit ab hac satisfactione absoluere eum,* si in monasterio in conuentu fuerit,†

---

* eum absoluere A   † fuerit in conuentu A

[1] i.e. the blessing at the end of Compline. The permission for absence from Compline was a consequence of the early hour for retiring, which cut what we now call the evening out of the horarium. Throughout the Middle Ages reformers were at odds with human frailty in an endeavour to prevent prolonged conversations and potations on the part of officials and returned travellers, reinforced by their friends.

[2] *Regula* XLIII ; Bernard of Cluny I xviii 174, and less nearly, Albers I 148–9. The monastic penal code has a long history, beginning in the desert and growing somewhat both in severity and in the detail of its tariff in its passage through Celtic lands ; in many orders it was retained, at least in its main lines, until the French Revolution. Lanfranc's code is distinctly more severe than that of the Rule, chs. xxiii–xxx, where no

Compline, may rise from table and go into the church for the blessing,[1] and afterwards return to the refectory to finish their supper.

WHEN THE PENALTY due for a light fault has been assigned to a brother,[2] he eats apart from the rest at the ninth hour, if the brethren dined at the sixth, and at Vespers, if the brethren dined at the ninth hour, but he may have the same meat and drink as they, unless it has been explicitly forbidden him.

In church and chapter he shall be either in his usual place, or last of all, or somewhere between the two, according to the measure of his fault and the command of the abbot. In church he shall not celebrate Mass, nor read Epistle, Gospel or lesson ; he shall not sing a responsory nor begin an antiphon, nor do anything of the kind save along with all the others ; he shall not carry a candle or thurible vested ; he shall not go up to make an offertory or receive the kiss of peace.

At the end of an office in choir, by day or by night, when *Kyrie eleison* is intoned, he shall prostrate himself before the step where the monks stand to receive blessings, and shall lie there until the words *Qui tecum vivit*. If a feast of twelve lessons occur, he shall cease from this penance until an ordinary day returns. While the brethren are eating in the refectory he shall be in the church.

When the abbot wishes to release him from this

---

daily chapter of faults is mentioned, and where reproof and excommunication precede corporal punishment save for the young and the uneducated. All penal codes, whether monastic or military, suggest to a reader unfamiliar with the life a régime of greater ferocity than that actually existing, and it is impossible to know how frequent flogging and confinement were at any given time or place. That confinement at least was not uncommon in the twelfth century, and was used for what may be called political offences, appears clearly from the most intimate chronicles, such as those of St Albans or Jocelin of Brakelond.

mittat ad illum, cum prostratus fuerit, unum de prioribus qui circa eum sunt, qui ex parte ipsius signum prostrato faciat ut surgat, qui statim surgens humiliter abbati inclinet,* et ad locum suum uadat. Porro si abbas in capitulo sederit, rogantibus fratribus, dicat ei Indulta sit uobis haec leuis culpae satisfactio, uel aliquid huiusmodi ; et ille frater statim surgat, et ad pedes abbatis uadat, et postea in locum suum reuertatur. Si abbas in itinere fuerit, licet priori, uel ei qui ordinem tenet, absente priore, hoc totum facere.[1]

Si frater aliquis, quod Deus auertat, culpam grauem commiserit, et ipsa culpa manifestata secreto emendari competenter nequiuerit, in capitulo ante abbatem in conuentu fratrum examinetur, et communi iudicio frater ille corporalem disciplinam acriter patiatur, et in grauis culpae satisfactione esse iubeatur. Qui accepta disciplina uestitus atque cinctus, cultellum suum ibi deponat, caput suum capitio cooperiat, et cum summo silentio ad locum huic negotio ordinatum pergat,[2] praecedente fratre illo, qui clauem ipsius loci seruat. Tunc abbas prouideat unum de senioribus, cui eum custodiendum secure possit committere, qui eum ad horas ducere, et post horas ad locum suum debeat eum reducere. Qui senior post capitulum secreto ab abbate inquirat quo ordine frater ille uiuat, et quid, aut qua hora comedere debeat ; loquatur ei frater ille, et alii quibus abbas praeceperit, caeterorum autem nemo illi societur, neque colloquatur.

---

* inclinet abbati A C

[1] Bernard of Cluny I lviii 252–4

[2] This was a place of confinement distinct from, and presumably more tolerable than, the prison proper, which was reserved for the contumacious, with whom physical force had been necessary and who were unwilling to accept regular punishment. Those familiar with the life of St John of the Cross will recognise in Lanfranc the broad outline of his régime at Toledo, though this was rendered harsher by gratuitious severity and climatic extremes.

penance and is himself in church with the community, he shall send one of the seniors about him to the brother as he lies prostrate, who shall give him a sign from the abbot to rise. Rising at once he shall bow humbly to the abbot and go to his place. If the abbot is in chapter and the brethren make intercession, he shall say to the brother ' You are released from your penance for a light fault,' or something of the kind, and the brother shall rise at once and go to the feet of the abbot, and then return to his place. If the abbot be on a journey, the prior, or whoever is superior at the time, may do all this.[1]

IF A BROTHER (which God forbid) commit a grave fault, and this become commonly known so that it cannot well be amended by private penance, the offence shall be examined before the abbot in chapter by the brethren, and the brother who is condemned by the judgment of all shall suffer severe corporal punishment, and be ordered to do penance as for a grave fault. When he has been scourged and has put on his clothing and girdle, he shall lay aside his knife, put up his hood and go in absolute silence to the place appointed,[2] led by the brother who keeps the key. Then the abbot shall appoint one of the seniors, to whom he may safely entrust the task of guarding him ; he shall lead him to the hours, and after the hours shall take him back again to his own place. After chapter this senior shall ask the abbot in private what shall be the condition of the brother's confinement, and what he shall have to eat, and when. The brother shall speak to his warden and to any others the abbot may appoint, but no-one else shall associate with the penitent or speak to him.

When the bell rings for office he shall come to the

Cum pulsatur signum ad horam, custode suo ducente, cooperto capite ante ostium monasterii ueniat ; et si conuentus adhuc monasterium non intrauit, quousque totus introeat ibi prostratus iaceat ; si uero iam intrauit, stet ibi, et inclinet, et genua flectat, sicut fratres qui in
165 choro / sunt, dum cantatur hora ; si aliqui fratres iuxta se transierint, humiliter inclinet eis. Transeunte tunc abbate prostratus ueniam petat, si frater ille iuxta se eum transire cognouerit. Finitis horis regularibus exeuntium ab aecclesia pedibus, cooperto capite, prosternatur quousque omnes pertranseant. Ingredientes uero et egredientes dicant ei sub silentio Misereatur tibi Deus. Egressis omnibus operto capite, custode suo eum praecedente, ad locum unde uenit reuertatur.

In capitulum, statutis ab abbate diebus, praedicto custode eum ducente, ueniat, et corporale iudicium humiliter et patienter sustineat ; de cibo et potu competens ei misericordia impendatur, ne forte nimiis angustiis oppressus immoderata tristicia absorbeatur[1] ; hoc modo tractetur quoadusque humilitate et patientia et emendationis promissione, adiunctis fratrum precibus, misericordiam consequatur. Qua uero die, precantibus fratribus, decreuerit abbas misericordiam ei impendere, eo modo, quo superius dictum est, in capitulum ueniat, prostratus culpam suam fateatur, et emendationem promittat, et misericordiam quaerat ; iussus surgere frequenter se prosternat, et eadem uerba et similia dicat, cessaturus cum abbas dixerit ei : Sufficiat. Postea iubeatur exuere, et corporalis disciplinae iudicium sustinere. Quo facto, dicat ei abbas : Motus fratrum nostrorum precibus, et patientia et humilitate uestra, et promissione emendationis uestrae, hanc misericordiam

---

[1] cf. *Regula* XXVII 8 : ‘ne abundantiori tristitia absorbeatur’ (a quotation from 2 Cor. ii.7).

church door, led by his warden and with his hood up, and if the community have not yet gone in he shall lie there prostrate until they have all entered ; if they have already entered he shall stand there, bowing and kneeling as do the brethren in choir while the office is chanted ; if any pass by him he shall bow humbly to them. If he see the abbot about to go by he shall prostrate himself while he passes. When the office is done he shall cover his head and prostrate himself at the feet of those who leave the church until all have passed. As they pass they shall say to him in a whisper, ' God have mercy upon thee.' When all are out he shall return to the place whence he came, led by his warden and with his head covered.

He shall come into chapter on days fixed by the abbot, led by the aforesaid warden, and undergo corporal punishment with humility and patience. A reasonable allowance of food and drink shall be made him, lest he be overcome by excessive hardship and fall into melancholy.[1] This shall be his treatment until he win pardon by his humility, patience and promise of amendment, added to the intercession of the brethren.

When the abbot has decided, at their prayer, to grant him pardon, he shall come into chapter as before, prostrate himself confessing his fault, promise amendment and ask for pardon. When bidden to rise he shall repeatedly prostrate himself, saying the same or similar words ; ceasing when the abbot says, ' That will do.' Then he shall be bidden to strip and undergo corporal punishment. After this the abbot shall say : ' I have been moved by the prayers of our brethren, and by your patience and humility and promise of amendment, and I grant you pardon, that henceforth you may be with the brethren ; you shall eat in the refectory, sitting in

uobis impendo, ut dehinc cum fratribus sitis ; in refectorio in loco, quem uobis designabimus, comedatis ;
disciplinam corporalem pro hac culpa ulterius non
suscipiatis. De caeteris ad comprobandam * adhuc
humilitatem et patientiam uestram, ita uos habete sicut
frater, qui in leuis culpae penitentia esse iubetur, excepto
quod incepto Kyrieleison ad gradum uos non prostre-
netis, sed expleta regulari hora, in loco in quo stabitis,
sicut beatus Benedictus [1] praecipit, flexis ad terram
166 genibus, sicut qui / in psalmo fallitur, humiliter satis-
facietis. Hoc audito frater ille ad pedes abbatis uadat,
et rediens in locum, in quo stabat, tres genuum flexiones,
ante scilicet et ad dexteram et ad sinistram, cum omni
deuotione faciat, gratias referens fratribus, quia pro se
rogauerint, et humiliter supplicans quatenus adhuc
rogare dignentur. Postea designet abbas ei locum, ubi
esse debet, et eo praecipiente sessum uadat.

Haec quidem culpa ad abbatem proprie pertinet
corrigenda ; qui tamen si desit a patria, nec ad praesens
ut ueniat expectatur, a priore corrigi potest totius congregationis assensu.

SI FRATER peccans peccatum suum defendere potius
quam cognoscere et emendare uoluerit, proclamatus
etiam abbati uel priori contumaciter respondere prae-
sumpserit ; admonitus quoque ut resipiscat, in sua
pertinacia permanere decreuerit ; hunc talem surgentes
fratres, quot et quibus iussum fuerit, uiolenter arripiant,
et in carcerem huiusmodi arrogantibus deputatum
trahant uel ferant, ibique depositus tamdiu seruata
discretione affligatur, quousque superbiam deponat,
culpam cognoscat, humiliter emendationem promittat.
Quod si, inspirante Deo, euenerit, res prius in capitulo

* comprobandum A   [1] *Regula* XLIV 15

the place to be allotted you ; and you shall receive no further corporal punishment for your fault.   In all other respects, in order to prove your humility and patience still further, you shall do as a brother who is in penance for a light fault, save that you shall not prostrate yourself at the step when *Kyrie eleison* is intoned, but when the office is done you shall kneel in your place as blessed Benedict orders [1] and humbly do penance like those who make a mistake in psalmody.'   At this the brother shall go to the feet of the abbot, and then, returning to his place, shall reverently bow the knee thrice, to those facing him, that is, and to right and left, giving thanks to the brethren who have interceded for him, and humbly begging them to continue their intercession. Then the abbot shall appoint him a place to take, and shall bid him be seated.

Grave faults are of themselves reserved to the abbot for correction, but if he be out of the country and not expected to return for some time, they may be corrected by the prior, with the assent of the community.

IF A BROTHER AT FAULT tries to defend his wrongdoing rather than to admit and amend it, and when accused of this ventures to answer the abbot or prior rebelliously ; if when warned to think better of it he persist in his obstinacy, then a certain number of the brethren shall be told to rise and lay violent hands upon him, and drag or carry him into the prison appointed for rebels such as he.   There confined he shall be punished with all due measure until he lay aside his pride, admit his fault and humbly promise amendment. When this happens, through divine inspiration, the matter shall first be reported in chapter, and then the culprit shall be brought into chapter by the brother

ostendatur, dehinc a fratre, cui huiusmodi cura iniuncta sit, in capitulum deducatur. Introeat autem uel nudus sicut fugitiuus monachus, uel indutus, prout res poposcerit, considerata qualitate et quantitate uel praecedentis culpae, uel subsequentis arrogantiae ; postea tractetur sicut superius dictum est, hoc est, uel grauiter, si graui, uel leuiter, si leui culpae fuerit deputatus. Quod si spiritu diabolico plenus superbire magis quam promittere emendationem elegerit, adhibeantur ei de toto conuentu orationum suffragia.[1] Si uero abbas nec sic suam industriam praeualere conspexerit, prudenter tractet cum consilio omnium fratrum, utrum expediat eum uel 167 diutius detineri, uel de monasterio expelli./

FUGITIUUS de monasterio monachus, si reuersum ad monasterium suscipiendum eum abbas iudicauerit, hoc modo suscipiatur.[2] In hospitali domo aliquantis diebus primum maneat, ad claustrum, uel ad officinas claustri, uel ad monasterium nisi iussus nullatenus accedat, ut interim penitudinis suae, et humilitatis, et patientiae aliquod documentum ostendat ; nullus frater * secum conuersetur, nullus ei in aliquo consortio uel colloquio coniungatur, nisi ei ab abbate uel a priore, uel ab eo qui seruat ordinem, iubeatur.

Ea uero die, qua in capitulum intraturus est, in locutorio uestimentis suis se exuat, staminia,[3] si habitum non reliquit, circumposito cingulo se circingat, sinistro brachio cucullam plicatam, et in dextera manu uirgas sumat, et sic nudis pedibus, et nudo desuper corpore, ducente eum fratre, cui iniunctum fuerit, in capitulo ueniat. Quo ingressus, in loco, ubi prosterni solet,

---

* fratrum B *om.* C

[1] *Regula* XXVIII 13 : 'Adhibeat abbas . . . omnium fratrum pro eo orationem' ; ibid. 12 : 'si viderit nihil suam praevalere industriam, etc.'

[2] Bernard of Cluny I lviii 252–3 ; contrast the simple brevity of the Rule, ch. xxix.   [3] *Staminia*—a long woollen shirt or shift

entrusted with the task. He shall come in either un-
clothed, like a fugitive monk, or in his habit, according
to circumstances and the degree and kind of his previous
offence and his subsequent obstinacy. Then he shall be
treated as set out above ; that is, he shall receive grave
punishment if his fault was grave, light if the fault was
light. But if he be full of diabolical pride instead of
being willing to promise amendment, the prayers of the
whole community shall be enlisted for him.[1] If the abbot
perceives that his care is not even then of any avail he
shall treat of the matter prudently with the whole community, whether it behoves to keep him in confinement
still longer or to expel him from the monastery.

IF A FUGITIVE MONK apply for readmission and the
abbot judges that he should be received, it shall be in
this wise.[2] He shall first remain in the guest-house for
some days and, unless bidden, shall never come to the
cloister or the domestic offices or the church, but shall
give some proof of his penitence and humility and
patience. No brother shall associate with him, or have
any intercourse or conversation with him, unless so
bidden by the abbot or prior or superior for the time
being.

On the day that he is to come to chapter, he shall
take off his clothes in the parlour and gather his shift[3]
about him with his girdle, if he has not abandoned his
habit, and shall carry his cowl folded over his left arm,
while in his right hand he shall bear a bundle of rods.
In this fashion, with bare feet and body bare from the
waist up, he shall be led to chapter by the brother in
charge of him. Having entered he shall at once prostrate
in the usual place, and when asked in the usual form he
shall confess his fault. Then seated he shall receive

statim se prosternat ; interrogatus more solito culpam
dicat ; dehinc sedens corporalem disciplinam ad im-
perium abbatis suscipiat. Qua suscepta, cuculla tantum
ibi * induta, sicut uenit, sed non ferens uirgas, in locutorium redeat, ibi se calciet, et regulariter induat, et in
capitulum rediens, tamdiu se prosternat, donec ab
abbate dicatur ei † : Sufficiat. Iniungatur ei satisfactio
grauis culpae, et in ipsa satisfactione habeat se sicut
superius dictum est, cum de graui culpa ageretur. Si
abiectis monachicis uestimentis in seculari habitu ad
monasterium redit, seruatis circa eum ‡ caeteris, quae
superius dicta sunt, saeculari ueste in qua reuersus est
circumcinctus, sicut supra de staminia dictum est, et
non portans cucullam, capitulum ingrediatur, et post
susceptam disciplinam, cuculla a camerario ante ipsum
168 posita, ab eo suscipiatur, et ibi statim induatur./

VENIENS aliquis ad conuersionem[1] de saeculo, in primis
sicut alii hospites suscipiatur in hospitio ; cuius uoluntate
cognita, frater, qui cellae hospitum procurator est, abbati,
uel absente abbate, ei qui ordinem tenet, rem nuntiet.
Loquatur cum eo abbas, uel prior, uel aliquis spiritualis
frater, cui iniunctum fuerit. Qui § si desiderium petentis
ex Deo esse cognouerit, ostendatur res fratribus in
capitulo, quorum audito consilio, si suscipiendum eum
esse abbas decreuerit, statuta die, ducente eum praedicto
hospitum susceptore, et doctus ab eodem qualiter petitionem facere debeat, in capitulum ueniat, in loco, ubi
prosterni solet, se prosternat ; interrogatus quid dicat,
quam humiliter poterit, in his, uel in similibus uerbis

---

* ibi tantum A   † ei dicatur C ei *om.* B   ‡ circa eum] cum cura C
§ Qui *supra rasuram* Quod (*ut uidetur*) D.   Quod *Reyner et edd.*
[1] There are many resemblances with Bernard I xv 164–7, and this
section follows fairly closely in broad outline the corresponding chapter
(lviii) of the Rule.

corporal punishment at the discretion of the abbot ;
after this, putting on his cowl only, he shall return to
the parlour as he came, but without the rods. There
he shall put on his shoes and the regular habit, and
returning to chapter shall prostrate himself until the
abbot says ‘ That will suffice.’ Penance for a grave
fault shall be given him, and the penance shall be
carried out as described above when we were treating
of grave faults.

If he return to the monastery in secular clothes,
having thrown off the monastic habit, all shall be done
as above, save that he shall gird up the secular clothes
in which he came back instead of the shift, and shall
enter chapter bearing no cowl. After he has been
scourged he shall take up a cowl laid before him by the
chamberlain, and shall put it on at once.

WHEN ANYONE TURNS FROM THE WORLD to the mon-
astic life [1] he shall first be received like other guests in the
guest-house, and when his desire is known the brother
in charge of the guest-room shall report the matter to
the abbot or, in the abbot’s absence, to the superior for
the time being. Then the abbot or prior or some
spiritual brother chosen for the purpose shall speak with
him, and if he see that the newcomer’s desire is from
God, the matter shall be made known to the brethren
in chapter, and, when their counsel has been given, if
the abbot deems that he should be received, he shall
come into chapter on a day fixed, led by the aforesaid
guest-master, who shall have instructed him in the form
of the petition he is to make. Prostrating in the usual
place, when he is asked what he would say, he shall
answer in the most humble wise, and make petition in
these or similar words : ‘ I ask for the mercy of God,

petitionem suam faciat : Dei misericordiam, et uestram
societatem, et fraternitatem huius loci requiro, et * in
hoc monasterio monachus fieri, et Deo seruire desidero.
Respondeat ei abbas, vel qui loco abbatis ordini praeest :
Societatem et consortium electorum suorum concedat
uobis omnipotens Dominus ; et responso a toto conuentu
Amen, iussus surgere surgat, pronuntientur ei dura et
aspera,[1] quae in hoc ordine perferunt, qui pie et regulariter
uiuere uolunt ; item duriora et asperiora quae, si in-
disciplinate se habeat, sibi poterunt euenire. Quibus
auditis, si adhuc in proposito suo perstiterit, et duriora
et asperiora se paratum perferre promiserit, respondeatur
ei ab eo qui capitulum tenet : Dominus Iesus Christus
sic perficiat in uobis quod pro eius amore promittitis, ut
eius gratiam et uitam aeternam habere possitis. Et
respondentibus omnibus Amen, subiungat : Et nos pro
eius amore hoc tenore concedimus uobis, quod tam
humiliter et tam constanter requiritis. Hoc audito
nouitius uadat, et humiliter osculetur pedes ipsius. Tunc
ipso praecipiente ducat eum magister nouitiorum in
aecclesiam, ibique coram quolibet altari extra chorum
169 sedens praestoletur, donec capitulum finiatur./

Quo finito ducat eum praedictus magister suus in
cellam camerarii, uel in aliam domum, ubi id quod
agendum est opportunius fieri possit, benedicta sibi prius
corona,[2] si laicus sit, cum antiphonis et psalmis et collectis
ad hoc officium ordinatis, uel in aecclesia ante introitum
missae ad gradum ubi benedictiones fratres accipiunt,
uel in capella infirmorum, aut in capella abbatis, secundum quod ipsi abbati placuerit : ductus itaque nouitius

---

* om. C B E
[1] *Regula* LVIII 16 : ' Praedicentur ei omnia dura et aspera per quae
itur ad Deum ' (cf. Vergil *Aeneid* V 730 : ' gens dura et aspera ').
[2] The monastic tonsure or ' circle.' Bernard of Cluny I lix 255-6.

and to be of your company and to be accounted a
brother of this house, and I desire to become a monk of
this monastery, and to serve God here.' The abbot, or
he who presides in his stead, shall answer : ' May
almighty God grant you the fellowship and company of
his chosen ones,' and the whole community shall answer
' Amen.' Then he shall be bidden to rise, and shall be
told of all things hard and harsh [1] which those who wish
to live a devout and regular life endure in this estate, as
well as the things harder and harsher which may befall
them if they bear themselves disorderly. If, when he
has heard this, he still stands fast in his intent, and
promises that he will be ready to endure still harder
and harsher things, he who presides at chapter shall
answer him : ' May the Lord Jesus Christ so make
perfect in you what you promise for His love, that you
may win His grace and life eternal.' To this all shall
answer ' Amen,' and he shall continue : ' And we for
the sake of His love grant you on such conditions what
you ask with such humility and constancy.' On this
the novice shall go and humbly kiss his feet. Then at
his command the novice-master shall lead him into the
church, and there he shall sit by an altar outside the
choir and wait till the chapter is done.

After that his aforesaid master shall lead him into
the chamberlain's cell, or some other room more convenient for what is to be done. Before this, however,
he shall receive the tonsure,[2] if he is a layman, with its
accompaniment of blessings with antiphons and psalms
and collects as ordained. This shall be done either in
church before the introit of the Mass on the step where
the brethren ordinarily receive blessings, or in the chapel
of the infirmary, or in the abbot's chapel, according as
the abbot think fit. Then the novice, whether clerk or

siue laicus, siue clericus, in praedictum locum tondeatur,
et radatur more monachorum ; dehinc uestibus saecularibus exuatur et rebus monasterii regularibus, praeter
cucullam, capitio assuto tunicae induatur. Dum haec
aguntur, a fratribus quibus iniunctum fuerit septem
penitentiales psalmi indirectum dicantur. Sic paratus
ducatur in conuentum fratrum ; in choro, si clericus est,
ultimus sit in ordine clericorum ; si laicus, laicorum ;
et ad processionem similiter. In capitulo et refectorio,
sicut est ordo conuersionis eius.

In cella nouitiorum dormiat, aut in dormitorio, si
cenobium huiusmodi cellam non habet. In conuentu
non legat, solus non cantet, ad missam non offerat, pacem
non sumat, in claustro separatim sedeat cum magistro
suo in loco nouitiis deputato ; nullus ei loquatur aut
signum faciat absque magistri sui licentia ; magister talis
sit, qui exemplo uitae et uerbo doctrinae possit eum de
anima sua monere et ordinem docere. Loquentibus in
claustro fratribus si quis amore Dei et zelo iustitiae ad
eum uenire, eumque uel arguere uel monere uoluerit,[1]
licet ut ueniat, et accepta a magistro licentia, quod dicere
uoluerit, dicat ; facto autem clamore, statim surgens
coram magistro suo, sicut fratres in capitulo, ueniam
petat, non sessurus donec, emendatione promissa, idem
magister praecipiat. Et de leuibus quidem culpis hoc
modo agatur : pro maioribus autem culpis, aut in capitulo pro quantitate culpae corripiatur, aut si ibi
cella nouitiorum est, in ea quemadmodum in capitulo
170 in/crepetur et uerberetur. De capitulo, facto sermone,
cotidie exeat, et interim in monasterio maneat, nisi pro

---

[1] Bernard of Cluny I xv 165

layman, shall be led to the place aforesaid and there shall be shorn and shaved in monastic fashion ; then he shall put off his secular clothes and put on the regular monastic habit, save for the cowl, including the hood sewn to the tunic. While this is being done, the seven penitential psalms shall be said in monotone by brethren who have been appointed to do this. Thus dressed, he shall be taken to the community : if he is a clerk, he shall sit last among the clerks ; if a layman, last among the lay monks ; and in processions likewise. In chapter and refectory he shall take his place according to the time of his conversion.

He shall sleep in the cell of the novices, or, if the monastery have no such special cell, in the dormitory. He shall not read in public, nor sing anything alone, nor make offering at Mass, nor receive the kiss of peace. In the cloister he shall sit apart with his master, in a place appointed for the novices, and none shall speak to him or make a sign to him without leave of his master ; this master shall be such a one as may by the example of his life and by the words of his teaching give him good advice for his soul and teach him our way of life.

If, when the brethren are talking in the cloister, anyone from a love of God and zeal for justice wish to reprove or warn him,[1] he may approach, and on receiving permission from his master may say what he has to say. When a charge is made he shall at once rise before his master and prostrate like the brethren in chapter, and he shall not be seated until, after he has promised amendment, his master bid him sit. This shall be the way for light faults ; for greater ones he shall either be reproved in chapter according to the degree of the fault or, if there is a novices' cell, he shall be there rebuked and scourged as in chapter. He shall leave the chapter-

maiori culpa, ut dictum est, castigandus remaneat ; de his culpis, quas in saeculo gessit, et quae in hoc ordine sibi euenerunt uel eueniunt, frequentes confessiones faciat abbati, priori, spiritualibus fratribus quibus haec cura iniuncta est.

Transactis plerisque diebus,[1] si uita eius fratribus, et fratrum conuersatio sibi placuerit, monendus est a magistro suo quatenus roget priorem, et aliquos maiores fratres, ut et ipsi pro eo intercedant apud abbatem pro benedictione tribuenda et professione suscipienda. Quod si eum benedicere abbati* placuerit, statuta die in capitulo finito sermone, in loco ubi solet se prosternat, prostratusque pro impetranda benedictione petitionem faciat. Iusso eo surgere, narrentur ei iterum dura et grauia, quae in nostro ordine a sanctis patribus sunt instituta. Qui si haec omnia, et adhuc grauiora, si necesse fuerit, humiliter et patienter se ferre paratum esse responderit, interroget abbas considentes fratres, quid inde sentiant, et utrum precibus eius annuendum esse concedant. Quibus respondentibus se libenter concedere, adiungat Et nos concedimus in nomine Domini. Quo dicto, uadat ad pedes abbatis, uel eius qui ordini praeest, si abbas deest ; dehinc reuersus in locum in quo stabat, flexis ad terram genibus, humiliter inclinet ante et ad dexteram et ad sinistram, gratias referens fratribus pro misericordia eorum precibus sibi impensa. Postea praecipiente abbate cum magistro suo exeat, finitoque capitulo, si scribendi scientiam habet, professionem suam scribat, aut si nescit scribere alium roget, qui pro se scribat [2]; ipse tamen in

---

* + non A

[1] The novitiate of a year, one of the notable regulations of the Rule (ch. lviii 19–29) had been abandoned in favour of a shorter indeterminate period of probation, partly, no doubt, because the number of adult vocations was small. Cluny, in particular, had become extremely lax. The reintroduction of the year's probation was one of the features of the Cistercian reform, and when, around the middle of the twelfth century,

house each day after the sermon, and remain in the church, unless, as has been said, he stay behind to be punished for a grave fault. As to the faults committed in the world, or occurring in the monastic life, he shall make frequent confession to the abbot, prior and spiritual brethren appointed for this purpose.

When many days have passed,[1] if the brethren approve of his behaviour and he of their way of life, he is to be told by his master to ask the prior and some of the elders to intercede for him with the abbot that he may be blessed and make profession. If the abbot is willing to bless him, on the day fixed, when the sermon in chapter is done, he shall prostrate in the usual place and, thus lying, shall make petition to be blessed. After he has been bidden to rise, he shall again be told of all the hard and difficult things in our way of life that have been appointed by the holy fathers. If he answer that he is ready to endure all these things, and harder still if need be, the abbot shall ask the brethren who sit with him what they think, and whether they grant that his prayers should be heard. When they reply that they grant this willingly, he shall say 'And I too grant it in the name of the Lord.' Then the novice shall go to the feet of the abbot, or of him who is superior at the time if the abbot is away ; then returning to where he stood, and kneeling, he shall humbly bow in front and to right and left, giving thanks to the brethren for their kind prayers on his behalf. Then at the abbot's bidding he shall retire with his master, and, when the chapter is over, if he know how to write he shall write his profession, if not, he shall ask another to write it for him[2] ;

---

the practice of the oblation of children became rare and the new orders multiplied, the noviciate of a year became general, and was ultimately imposed by Rome, whence it passed into canon law. cf. Pantin, *Chapters of the Black Monks* I 99 (1278).   [2] *Regula* LVIII

fine ipsius professionis signum crucis faciat ; deinde,
ablato a tunica capitio, usque ad horam benedictionis
suae extra chorum maneat.

Cantor uero procurare sibi debet membranam, et
171 in/caustum, et scriptorem si nescit scribere. Hora bene-
dicendi in arbitrio abbatis est, uidelicet aut ante introitum missae, si missam non celebrat, aut post euangelium,
siue missam celebret siue non. Ipse tamen in consecra-
tione monachi si ei commodum est missam celebrare
debet, sicut canones praecipiunt.

Lecto igitur euangelio,[1] intrante chorum nouitio,
praecedente eum magistro suo, incipiente dextero choro,
dicat conuentus psalmum Miserere mei Deus ; nouitius
ante altare ueniens super gradum se prosternat. Dictoque psalmo surgens professionem suam legat, et super
altare ponat. Quod si ignarus litterarum est, magister
suus debet eam pro eo legere, et ipse nouitius super altare
ponere. Quo facto, flexis coram altari genibus, ueniam
petat, et postea ad locum ubi se prostrauit rediens uersum
Suscipe me Domine, ter dicat,[2] ibique inter dicendum ter
genua flectat ; quem uersum ter repetens conuentus,
adiungat ad ultimum Gloria Patri ; Kyrieleison ; Christe
eleison ; Kyrieleison ; Pater noster. Conuentu incipiente
Gloria Patri, nouitius inclinatus peruoluat se in circuitu,
et statim prosternat se. Abbas, dicto Et ne nos inducas
in tentationem, et responso Sed libera nos a malo,
incipiat psalmum De profundis,[3] quo finito a conuentu
cum Gloria Patri, adiungat Saluum fac seruum tuum ;
Mitte ei, Domine, auxilium de sancto ; Nihil proficiat

---

[1] Bernard of Cluny I xx 180. For this ceremony and the prayers
v. *Missale Westmon.* II 1187ff., and *Officium Abbatum secundum usum Eveshamensis Monasterii*, col. 29ff.

[2] The threefold intoning or reciting of the *Suscipe*, together with the
reading of the vows, forms the profession ceremony of the Rule (lviii 51) ;
it has been embodied in all subsequent monastic rituals. Much of the
ceremonial that follows in Lanfranc is common to a number of medieval

in this case he shall himself make the sign of the cross at the end of his profession. Then, having removed the hood from his tunic, he shall stay out of choir till the blessing of his habit.

It is for the cantor to supply him with parchment and ink and a scribe if he cannot write. The abbot shall choose the hour of his blessing : either before the introit of the Mass, if the abbot be not celebrating, or after the gospel, whether he be celebrating or not. If possible, the abbot should celebrate Mass when a monk is blessed, for so the canons ordain.

When therefore the gospel has been read,[1] the novice, following his master, comes into choir, and the right-hand side begins the *Miserere* which is said by the community. The novice goes to the step before the altar and prostrates himself ; when the psalm is finished he shall rise and read his profession and lay it on the altar. If he knows no letters his master shall read it for him, and the novice himself shall lay it on the altar. After this, kneeling before the altar, he bows profoundly, and then, returning to the place where he lay prostrate he shall say the verse *Suscipe me Domine* thrice,[2] genuflecting thrice as he says it. The community repeat the verse thrice, and add after the third time *Gloria Patri, Kyrie eleison, Christe eleison, Kyrie eleison, Pater noster.* When the community begins *Gloria Patri* the novice bows and turns right round, and then at once prostrates himself. The abbot then says *Et ne nos inducas in tentationem*, and when the response *Sed libera nos a malo* has been made he begins the psalm *De profundis*[3] ; when the community have finished this and its *Gloria* he shall continue *Saluum fac seruum tuum* ; *Mitte ei, Domine*,

---

and modern customaries, including that of the English Benedictine Congregation.   [3] Ps. 129 (130)

inimicus in eo ; Esto ei, Domine, turris fortitudinis ;
Domine, exaudi orationem meam ; Dominus uobiscum ;
deinde collectam, Deus indulgentiae pater ; item aliam,
Deus, qui per coaeternum filium * : item aliam, Domine
Iesu Christe, qui es uia. Dictis his tribus collectis
singulis cum integro Per Dominum nostrum, incipiat
abbas ymnum Veni creator Spiritus.[1] Quo a conuentu
deuote et solenniter decantato, dicat collectam, Sancte
Spiritus, qui te Deum ac Dominum ; qua dicta surgat
172 nouitius, et spargat super eum abbas aquam benedictam,/
eoque stante benedicatur cuculla, et aspergatur aqua
benedicta. Qua benedicta accedat nouitius ad abbatem,
et flexis genibus stet ante eum, quem tunica exuens
abbas dicat ; Exuat te Dominus ueterem hominem cum
actibus suis. Et induens eum cuculla subiungat, Induat
te Dominus nouum hominem, qui secundum Deum
creatus est in iusticia et sanctitate ueritatis. Ad
utrumque respondeant audientes fratres Amen. Subse-
quatur super eum flexis genibus inclinatum oratio, Deus
misericors, Deus clemens. Qua dicta osculetur eum
abbas, induens caput eius capitio : dehinc ducatur per
chorum ad osculandum omnes fratres ; ultimus col-
locetur.[2]

Tribus diebus communionem corporis et sanguinis
Christi accipiat. Tercia die ad pacem missae auferat ei
capitium de capite abbas, uel cui abbas praeceperit, si
ipse id faciendi opportunitatem non habet. Ante hanc
horam, ex quo benedictus est, summum silentium teneat[3] ;
de capitulo, facto sermone, exeat, ad processionem non

---

* *om.* A C
[1] The hymn of ?Rabanus Maurus (ob. 856) ; for text, see any breviary
or *Oxford Book of Medieval Latin Verse*, no. 31.
[2] It will be noted that the modern rite of prostration upon a funeral
pall, signifying the death of the newly professed to the world, does not form
part of Lanfranc's ceremony, or of those at Westminster and Evesham.

auxilium de sancto ; *Nihil proficiat inimicus in eo* ; *Esto ei,
Domine, turris fortitudinis* ; *Domine, exaudi orationem meam* ;
Dominus uobiscum. There follow the collects *Deus indulgentiae pater* ; *Deus qui per coaeternum filium* ; and *Domine
Jesu Christe, qui es uia*. When these three collects have
been said, each with the full *Per Dominum nostrum*, the
abbot shall begin the hymn *Veni creator Spiritus*.[1] When
this has been solemnly and devoutly sung by the community he shall say the collect *Sancte Spiritus, qui te Deum
ac Dominum*. When this is ended the novice shall rise,
and the abbot shall sprinkle holy water over him, and
then he shall stand while his cowl is blessed and sprinkled.
When this is done the novice shall approach the abbot
and after genuflecting shall stand before him ; the abbot
shall remove his tunic, saying, ' May the Lord strip thee
of the old man with all his acts.' Then clothing him
with his cowl he shall continue : ' May the Lord clothe
thee with the new man, who is created according to God
in justice and the sanctity of truth.' To both these
prayers the brethren who are listening shall say ' Amen.'
Then, as the brother kneels before the abbot, the prayer
' God of mercy, God of pity ' shall be said over him.
Then the abbot shall kiss him, and set the hood upon his
head, after which he shall be taken through the choir to
kiss all the brethren, being set finally in the lowest place.[2]

For three days he shall receive the Communion of
the body and blood of Christ. On the third day when
the kiss of peace is given at Mass the abbot or his deputy,
if the abbot be unable to be present, shall let down his
hood from his head. Until this moment the newly
professed shall keep absolute silence from the moment
of his blessing ;[3] he shall leave chapter after the sermon,

---

[3] This rite is still commonly practised ; cf. Bernard of Cluny I xx 180.

uadat, cuculla indutus cucullato capite dormiat. In
primo autem capitulo, quo ei licet loqui, debet magister
eius de eo memoriam habere coram abbate dicens :
Domine, si placeret uobis praecipere, posset iste frater
ab hac die in antea legere et cantare in conuentu, sicut
alii fratres. Respondente abbate : Faciat cum benedictione Dei,* inclinet ipse nouitius ad abbatem de loco
in quo sedet. Ex illa die cuiuscunque ordinis sit habet †
licentiam exequendi omnia, quae sui ordinis sunt, nisi
sit sacerdos ; ipsi enim infra primum conuersionis suae
annum missam celebrare non licet, nisi in saeculo pro-
batae castitatis fuerit, et abbas pro hac re specialem ei
licentiam dederit.

OFFERENDUS puer,¹ facta sibi prius corona, manibus
portans hostiam, et calicem cum uino, sicut mos est,
post euangelium sacerdoti, qui missam celebrat, a paren-
tibus offeratur. Qua oblatione a sacerdote suscepta,
inuoluant praedicti parentes manus pueri in palla, qua
173 altare coopertum est, et / cuius pars anterius pendet, et
tunc suscipiat eum abbas. Quo facto praefati parentes
coram Deo et sanctis eius statim promittant, quod per
se, uel ‡ per suppositam personam susceptum ordinem
puer nunquam reliquat ; neque ei se † aliquid scienter
daturos, unde puer, quod absit, perire possit² ; hanc

---

* Dei benedictione A C   † habeat C B E
‡ aut A C B   § se ei A C B se] si E

¹ The practice of oblation, by which parents offered their small children
to God, was already common in the age of St Benedict (*Regula* LIX, where
sources show it also in Basilian monachism) and continued for some six
centuries to be a common and often the principal source of recruitment.
However alien to modern sentiment, its advantages were numerous under
the social conditions of the early Middle Ages, and almost at the very
moment of Lanfranc's writing two children, the one of feudal family, the
other of obscure parentage, Ordericus Vitalis and Suger of St Denis, born
respectively *c.* 1070 and 1081, were entering upon the round of life as
children of the cloister. The Cistercians—here deliberately departing from
the Rule—refused to accept oblates, and by the middle of the twelfth
century the practice, under the influence of changing social and educational
conditions, was on the wane in north-western Europe.

he shall not join the procession and shall sleep in cowl and hood. At the first chapter at which he can speak his master should make mention of him to the abbot, saying : ' My Lord, if it please you so to order, this brother would be able henceforward to read and sing in community like the other brethren.' Upon the abbot answering, ' Let him do so, with God's blessing,' the novice shall bow to the abbot from his seat. From that day forward he shall have leave to do all that pertains to any Order he may have, save in the case of a priest, who shall not be allowed to celebrate Mass within a year of his conversion, unless he were a man of approved chastity in the world, and the abbot have given him special permission to this effect.

IF A CHILD is to be offered to the monastery [1] he shall be tonsured, and then, bearing in his hands a host and chalice with wine in it, as is the custom, he shall be offered by his parents after the Gospel to the priest celebrating Mass. When his offering has been received by the priest, his parents shall wrap the child's hands in the cloth which covers the altar and which hangs down in front, and then the abbot shall accept him. When this is done the parents shall straightway promise before God and his saints that the child shall never abandon the monastic life through their agency or that of anyone representing them, and that they will never knowingly give him anything that might lead to his ruin.[2] This promise shall have been previously written down and

---

[2] *Regula* LIX 7 : ' Parentes . . . promittant . . . quia numquam per se, numquam per suffectam personam . . . ei aliquando dent . . . per quam rem deceptus perire possit, quod absit.'

promissionem prius scriptam coram testibus uerbis ibi
prius edicant, et postea super altare ponant. His expletis,
benedicat abbas cucullam, et exuens puerum cappa, uel
pellibus, uel aliqua huiusmodi clamide dicat : Exuat te
Dominus ueterem hominem, ut supra ; et induens eum
cuculla, subiungat : Induat te Dominus nouum hominem, et caetera. Dehinc ducatur ad radendum et
uestiendum, sicut nostri ordinis consuetudo est. Cum
uero adulta aetate facturus professionem fuerit, fiant ei
caetera quae superius debere fieri conuerso iam diximus.
Hoc autem quod modo factum est, iterari non oportet.

OMNI DIE minimi signi ad designandum capitulum
incipiente sono,[1] fratres omnes, qui sedent in choro,
statim surgere, et uersi ad orientem interim debent
stare ; fratres quoque, qui alicubi in monasterio sunt,
chorum intrare. Nullus eorum librum teneat ; nullus
in libro aliquid legat aut inspiciat ; nullus in claustro
pro qualibet occasione tunc sedeat ; praedicti signi
cessante sonitu, praecedentem priorem sequantur alii,
sicut est ordo conuersionis eorum. Considentibus fratribus in capitulo, ad nutum ordinem tenentis, petita
benedictione, lectis et pronunciatis, quae legi et pronunciari consuetudo est,[2] facto sermone,[3] dicto Loquamur
de ordine nostro, si clamatur aliquis, qui commune cum
uno aut pluribus nomen habeat, nisi clamans ita discernat
et determinet, ut nulla dubitatio possit esse, omnes qui
eiusdem nominis sunt, cuius est ille qui clamatur, statim
174 debent surgere, et ad uenias humiliter se / praesentare,

---

[1] For the daily prayers in chapter, now the latter part of Prime in the
monastic breviary, v. HB V 451.
[2] Bernard of Cluny I lxxiv 275. Lanfranc enlarges on Bernard in
what follows.
[3] Many of the Sermones of monastic saints, e.g. those of Bernard of
Clairvaux, were delivered at this point of the daily chapter. Later, the

witnessed, and now they shall make it verbally and then place it on the altar.

When this is done the abbot shall bless a cowl and, taking off the child's cloak or tippet of fur or any other kind of smock he may be wearing, shall say, ' May the Lord strip thee of the old man,' as above, and, clothing him with the cowl, shall continue, ' May the Lord clothe thee with the new man,' and the rest. Then the child shall be taken to be shaven and clad in the monastic fashion. When he has grown up and is to make his profession, all is done as described previously for the case of one coming into the monastery from the world, save that the part which has been done already should not be repeated.

WHEN EACH DAY the smallest bell begins to ring for chapter,[1] all the brethren sitting in choir shall at once rise and stand facing the east and waiting, while the brethren elsewhere in the monastery shall enter the choir. No one at that time shall hold a book, nor read nor look at a book ; no one shall for any reason whatever remain seated in the cloister ; but when the bell ceases to ring all in order shall follow their leader out of church.

When the brethren are seated in chapter the superior gives a sign, and the reader, after asking a blessing, reads and gives out the customary lesson and notices.[2] Then, after the sermon,[3] the superior says, ' Let us now speak of matters of discipline.' If anyone is accused who bears a name common to one or more others, and the accuser does not make it absolutely definite beyond doubt, then all of that name shall at once arise and humbly offer themselves for penance, until the accuser

---

sermon of the president was formalised, abbreviated and finally abandoned altogether.

donec clamator determinate eligat de quo dicat. Ipsa
autem determinatio ab ordinibus, uel officiis, si possit
fieri, debet esse, hoc modo : domnus Eduuardus * [1]
presbiter, diaconus, subdiaconus, secretarius, magister
infantum uel iuuenum, uel aliquid huiusmodi, non
archidiaconus,[2] non Lundonensis,† non aliquid cogno-
minatum de saeculo.

Clamator ei super quem clamorem facit in ipso
capitulo iudicium non faciat.[3] Interrogatus more solito
qui prosternitur, ad omnes uenias Mea culpa dicat,
excepto cum societatem postulat, aut obedientiae absolutionem, aut cum aliquis frater misericordiam petit pro
suo propinquo nouiter, et postquam ad ordinem uenit,
defuncto, patre scilicet, matre, fratre, sorore, uel cum
unus aut plures pro eo, qui in grauis culpae satisfactione
positus est, misericordiam petunt, uel cum aliquis frater
in longum iter profecturus est, aut cum aliquid magnum,
et arduum, et suis uiribus impar fratri iniungitur.[4] In
his et huiusmodi hoc modo respondetur : Dei misericordiam et uestram requiro, et obsecro, et caetera, sicut
ratio rei, pro qua petitur, postulat.

Suscepturus iudicium aut sola grossiori uirga super
staminiam uerberetur, et prostratus iaceat, aut pluribus
gracilioribus uirgis, et nudus sedeat, utrumque ad
arbitrium eius qui praeest ordini, considerata qualitate
et quantitate culpae.   Dum corporalis disciplina infertur
fratri, ‡ omnes inclinato capite debent esse, et pio et §

* Aeduardus A   Rotbertus B
† Ludoniensis A   Lunduniensis C
‡ fratres B E   fratri] + et C   § om. C
[1] Lanfranc would seem to have taken as his typical name the English
Edward ; the Norman Robert is the reading of a single MS (of Dover
priory).
[2] The monastic archdeacon in certain monasteries held the ecclesiastical
courts and supervised discipline in territories of greater or smaller extent,
either exempt from the bishop's jurisdiction (as at Evesham, St Albans
and elsewhere), or relinquished to the monks by custom, as at Worcester,
Durham and Canterbury. The reason for avoiding the title in chapter was

says clearly whom he means to accuse. This he shall do by specifying, if possible, the dignity in order or office, as follows : ' Dom Edward [1] the priest,' or ' deacon,' or ' subdeacon,' or ' sacristan,' or ' master of the children or juniors,' or something of the sort ; he shall not say ' Dom Edward the archdeacon,' [2] or ' of London,' or any surname that he bore in the world.

The accuser shall not, during the chapter in question, inflict punishment on him he accuses.[3] The brother who is lying prostrate shall, when questioned in the usual way, answer *mea culpa*, save when he is asking for confraternity, or is resigning office, or when one is asking prayers for a relative, father, mother, brother or sister, who has died recently, and since he entered the monastery, or when one or more intercede for a brother doing penance for a grave fault, or when a brother is departing for a long journey, or when something great and difficult and beyond his powers is put upon a brother.[4] In this, and similar cases, he should answer, ' I ask the mercy of God, and your mercy, and I beseech etc.,' as circumstances require.

He who is to undergo punishment shall be scourged either with a single stout rod while he lies in his shift on the ground, or with a bundle of finer rods while he sits with his back bare. In each case he is punished at the discretion of the superior, who should consider the degree and the magnitude of the fault. While he is

presumably that it was not a strictly monastic one, just as, at the present day, the headmaster of a lay school is never given that title in monastic documents. There is an interesting parallel from Westminster in *Consuetudines Monasterii S. Petri Westmonasteriensis*, ed. E. M. Thompson (Henry Bradshaw Society, XXVIII. 1904), II 95 : ' Archidiaconus vero, quia nomen habet seculare, non consuevit antiquitus in claustro, et maxime in capitulo, ab aliquo ita vocitari . . . sed puro nomine semper in congregacione rite appellabatur.' As these customs show many resemblances to Lanfranc, this particular passage may well be a reflection of the text above.

[3] Bernard of Cluny I lxxiv 275–6 almost verbally   [4] cf. *Regula* LXVIII

fraterno affectu compassionem super eum habere. Interim nemo in capitulo debet loqui, nemo ad illum
aspicere exceptis grauibus personis, quibus licet pro eum
intercedere. Clamato super eum a quo clamatus est,
in ipso capitulo clamorem facere non licet. Disciplinam
corporalem inferat quicunque ille sit cui ab abbate uel
priore iniungitur, hoc obseruato, ne infantibus uel
iuuenibus aut nouitiis id facere iniungatur. Nemo ibi
cum uno aut pluribus secreto loquatur ; quicquid
loquitur a rectore ordinis et a toto conuentu audiatur.
175 /Sermo tantum sit de utilibus, et de his quae ad ordinem
pertinent ; loquente uno taceant alii ; uerba loquentis
nemo interrumpat praeter eum qui rector est ordinis,
cui licet loquenti praecipere ut sileat, si forte ei sermo
illius superfluus et inutilis uideatur. Rectore ordinis
incipiente loqui, etiam si aliquis loquebatur taceat, et
ab omnibus summum silentium fiat.

Si placet abbati aliquem fratrem pro suis meritis
honorare, et considerata personae eius honestate, in
superiori loco statuere,[1] audito frater ille ab abbate sedente
in capitulo, Ite superius sedere iuxta illum fratrem, statim
surgens ad pedes abbatis uadat, et postea ad locum ubi
ei praecipitur sessum pergat, et ex illa die in monasterio,
et processione, et refectorio ipsum locum habeat. Laicum
conuersum beatus Benedictus non praecipit taliter pro-
moueri[2] ; si tamen abbati promouere eum * placuerit,
locum, quem in capitulo suscipit, in refectorio etiam
tenebit, in monasterio uero, et processione, super eos

---

* non E
[1] Bernard of Cluny I lxxiv 276
[2] *Regula* LXI 25–31. The Rule, however, does not consider the case
of a promotion within the existing community, but of the advancement
of a newcomer—priest, cleric or strange monk. Among the last-named
some would have been laymen, but the term *laicus* is never used in the Rule.

being scourged all the brethren should bow down with a kindly and brotherly compassion for him. No-one should speak, and no-one look at him save for the seniors who may make intercession for him. No-one who is accused may in the same chapter accuse his previous accuser. The abbot or prior shall appoint him who is to administer punishment, taking care that neither child, nor junior, nor novice is bidden.

No-one shall speak privately in chapter with another, or with several. Whatever is said shall be heard by the superior and the whole community. Only matters of utility and pertaining to the religious life shall be discussed ; while one is speaking the rest shall keep silence ; no-one shall interrupt a speaker save the president, who may bid a speaker have done if it seem to him that his words are too many or to no purpose. When the president begins to speak, even if one is already speaking he shall cease, and absolute silence shall be preserved by all present.

IF THE ABBOT should wish to do honour to one of the brethren on account of his deserts, and to advance his place in the community in consideration of his excellent character,[1] when that brother shall hear the abbot in chapter say ' Go up higher and sit next to such-and-such a brother,' he shall at once rise and go to the feet of the abbot, and afterwards seek his seat as bidden, and thenceforward in church and procession and refectory he shall take his new place. The blessed Benedict gives no command regarding a lay converse in such matters [2] ; nevertheless, if the abbot think fit to promote him he shall take in the refectory the place assigned him in chapter ; in the church, however, and in the procession he shall be told to go before those converses who sit

conuersos esse iubebitur,* quibus frater ille iuxta quem locum habet prior esse dinoscitur.

Euenire potest cum huiusmodi promotio ordinatur, ut absentes sint aliqui fratres honesti, et bonis actibus praediti, quibus prior sit frater ille, iuxta quem promotus sedere iubetur, et ideo determinate oportet ei in capitulo dici, utrum super ipsos etiam absentes, cum redierint, esse debeat.

Ingrediens frater capitulum loquentibus aliis Benedicite dicat. Egrediens uero si est reuersurus nec ante et retro faciat, nec Benedicite dicat ; si non est reuer-
176 surus utrumque agat./

MONACHUS petiturus concedi sibi societatem et beneficium monasterii,[1] introductus in capitulum Benedicite dicat ; deinde † prostratus ad gradum ubi consuetudo est, interrogatus quid dicat, humili et deuoto corde in his uerbis respondeat : Peto per misericordiam Dei, et uestram, et omnium istorum seniorum, societatem et beneficium huius monasterii. Quo dicto, respondeat abbas, Omnipotens Dominus concedat uobis quod quaeritis, et ipse praestet uobis consortium electorum suorum. Postea iussus ut surgat,‡ accedat ad abbatem, et ab eo per librum regulae sumat monasterii societatem. Qua sumpta, acceptoque ab eo osculo, inclinet se ad pedes abbatis, deinde osculetur omnes fratres in circuitu. Quo facto reuertatur ad locum ubi se prostrauit, ibique tres genuum flexiones solito more faciat ; fratres uero inclinent ei. Dehinc praecipiente abbate sessum uadat,

---

* uidebitur C   † dehinc A   ‡ ut surgat] surgere A
[1] For unions and confraternities between houses and of individuals, *v.* Knowles, *Monastic Order,* 473–9. Several records of the kind are contained in the Canterbury MS (now B.M. Cott. Claudius C. VI), from which Reyner printed. The most elaborate collection of names now extant in England is probably that of the Durham *Liber Vitae* (ed. Surtees Society, 1923). What follows is not taken from Bernard of Cluny.

below the brother whose neighbour in chapter he has become.

It may happen that when a promotion of this kind is given out a number of estimable brethren are absent, who have served the monastery well, and who sit next in order beneath the brother named by the abbot as neighbour to him who is to be promoted. To meet such a case, the abbot should tell him explicitly in chapter whether he is to be above those also who are absent, when they return.

When a brother enter the chapter when others are speaking he shall say *Benedicite*. When he leaves, if he intends to return he shall not make a double bow nor shall he say *Benedicite*; if he is not to return he shall do both.

WHEN A MONK proposes to ask that he may be allowed to enjoy confraternity [1] and all common privileges of the house, he shall be brought into chapter and shall say *Benedicite* ; then, lying prostrate on the step in the usual place, when he is asked what he wishes to say he shall answer with a humble and devout heart in these words, ' I ask through God's mercy and yours, and that of all these elders, confraternity and all common privileges of this house.' This said, the abbot shall reply, ' May the almighty Lord grant you what you ask, and may He admit you to the company of His elect.' Then, being bidden to rise, he shall approach the abbot and receive from him, by taking into his hand the Rule, the confraternity of the house. After this, and after the kiss of peace from the abbot, he shall bow at the abbot's feet and then be kissed by all the brethren round the chapter-house. This done he shall return to the place where he lay, and there make three genuflections in the customary manner. The brethren shall bow to him in return, and

designato ei prius loco ubi sedere debet.* Porro si abbas fuerit, ingrediente eo in capitulum totus conuentus ei assurgat, et tamdiu stet, quousque humo prostratus, sicut superius, petitionem faciat, et erectus cum monachis suis societatem suscipiat, eaque suscepta iuxta abbatem consideat. Monachi uero eius societate suscepta, reuersi ad locum ubi se prostrauerunt, tres genuum flexiones, sicut superius dictum est, faciant. Egredientes fratres de capitulo osculentur abbas et monachi eius. Si maior congregatio fuerit ab osculo cessari potest, quod in multis iam cenobiis fieri consueuit. Si secularis persona fuerit, ante abbatem uel iuxta abbatem, si honorabilis persona sit, sedeat ; postea ostensa eius petitione fratribus, per textum euangelii societatem suscipiat ; dehinc ad osculandum fratres, si mulier non sit,[1] in circuitu pergat.

TALI HORA prior mane ad excitandos fratres sonitum debet facere, ut pueri [2] factis solitis orationibus, in claustro
177 ua/leant legere ; qui cum legere inchoant, alte aliquandiu legant. Separati ab inuicem ita sedeant, ut alter alterum nec manibus, nec uestibus contingere possit. Infans infanti non signo innuere, non uerbo aliquid dicere, nisi uidente atque audiente magistro, praesumat ; non de loco in quo sedet sine praecepto uel licentia surgat.

---

* debeat A

[1] This would seem to imply that women admitted to confraternity might make their petition in chapter in person ; cf. *Monastic Order*, 412 n. 2.

[2] The *pueri* and *infantes*, if the practice of the Rule still obtained (*Regula* LXX 7), were all those under fifteen years of age. They were of course *oblati*, not boys boarded for education—there is no trace in Lanfranc, nor indeed in contemporary English monastic records, of the ' external ' monastic schools common a little earlier on the Continent—but their presence in choir and at all liturgical duties, and the employment of a number of monks as their teachers and guardians, must have affected the life of the house at many points, as these regulations imply. In the Rule no special masters are assigned to them, and their correction is summary and promiscuous, thus : ' pueris per omnia ab omnibus disciplina conservata ' (*Regula* LXIII 21) and : ' infantum . . . disciplinae diligentia ab omnibus et custodia est ' (ibid. LXX 8). Here, as in many other respects, the discipline

then at the abbot's word he shall be seated, having previously received an indication where he is to sit.

Moreover, if an abbot be the petitioner, when he enters the chapter all shall rise in his honour and shall stand while he makes his petition prostrate, as above, and rising receives confraternity with all his monks, and then takes his seat by the abbot. Meanwhile his monks, when they have received confraternity, shall return to the place where they lay and shall make three genuflections as noted above. As the brethren leave the chapter they shall receive the kiss of peace from the abbot and his monks.

If the community is a large one the kiss of peace may be omitted, as is customary at the present day in many houses. If the applicant be a secular, and a distinguished person, he shall sit before or by the abbot, and when his request has been made known to the brethren he shall receive fellowship by taking into his hand a book of the gospels. Then he shall go round receiving the kiss of peace, which is not given when the applicant is a woman.[1]

IN THE EARLY MORNING the prior shall make a sound to waken the brethren at an hour when it is possible for the children,[2] after their usual prayers, to see to read in the cloister. When they begin to read they shall for a space read in a loud tone of voice. They shall sit apart from one another, in such a way that no-one can touch his neighbour either with his hands or his clothes. No child shall make a sign to another, nor say a word to him, save with leave from his master and within earshot of him, nor shall a child rise from his place save under orders, or with permission.

---

of the Rule is simpler and relies more frankly and hopefully upon honest good will than do many of the later codes.

Quocunque pergunt infantes unus magister inter duos infantes sit. Transeuntes ante fratres inclinent fratribus, et fratres eis sedentes tantum. Duobus una laterna sufficiat ; si tres fuerint tertius alteram portet ; si plures fuerint, hoc ordine disponantur. In nullius manum aliquid dent[1] ; de nullius manu aliquid accipiant nisi abbatis, prioris maioris, magistri eorum, et hoc non ubique, sed in congruis locis, ubi aliter esse non possit aut non debeat. Cantor quoque, cum in scholis eorum est, potest librum in quo cantari aut legi debet dare eis et accipere ab eis. Ad altare si seruiunt, dant etiam ibi et accipiunt, sicut ordines eorum exposcunt. In capitulo suo uapulent, sicut maiores in maiori capitulo.

Confessuri ad abbatem, uel ad priorem uadant, uel ad eos, quos specialiter in capitulo designauerit abbas ; dum confitetur unus, sedeat alter in suppedaneo, magistro eorum extra capitulum sedente in proximo.[2] Si post uersum, qui ante cibum dicitur, ingrediuntur refectorium, uel post Gloria primi psalmi ad horas intrant chorum, ipsi quidem ad loca sua uadant, solito more inclinent ; magister uero eorum ad loca, quae tardantibus instituta sint, eat. Puero, qui ante mensam abbatis seruit, abstinentia cibi uel potus sine eius praecepto minime iniungatur. Quod si praecipiente eo iniungitur, aut ei indulgeatur, aut interim a mensa abbatis remoueatur.[3] In choro praesente abbate nisi praecepto eius nullus eos percutiat, nullus exuere faciat. Absente eo cantor de

---

[1] cf. Bernard of Cluny I xxviil 201, 204 ; but there are not many similarities that suggest actual derivation.

[2] The confessor would be seated, with the penitent kneeling by him on the step, and the next in order sitting at some distance on the same step. cf. Albers I 166, where the confessing child stands, and the next in order sits on one of the seats at a distance ; the master waits outside the door.

[3] Presumably this was intended to leave the abbot free to give his server a special morsel or draught.

Whithersoever the children go a master shall be
between every two. When they pass before the brethren
they shall bow to them, and the brethren in return shall
bow without rising. One lantern shall suffice for two ;
if they be three the third shall carry a second lantern,
and so on if they be more. They shall not hand anything to anyone,[1] nor receive anything save from the
abbot, great prior and their masters ; such giving or
receiving shall only be allowable in suitable places and
when fitness or necessity demands. The cantor likewise,
when he is in their school, may give or receive from
them the book from which they are to read or sing.
Also when they are serving at the altar they give and
receive whatever is necessary in the service they perform.
They are flogged in their chapter, as their elders are in
theirs.

They shall make their confessions to the abbot or
prior or those whom the abbot has specially appointed
in chapter. While one is confessing, the next shall sit
on the footpace ; their master meanwhile shall sit
nearby outside the chapter-house.[2]

If they enter the refectory after the verse that is said
before meals, or enter choir after the *Gloria* of the first
psalm, they shall go to their places with the customary
bows, while their master shall go to the place appointed
for those who come late.

Abstinence from food or drink shall not be imposed
as penance on the child who serves at the abbot's table
unless the abbot so bid ; should the abbot order a
penance, this shall either be remitted or he shall for the
time being be taken away from the table of the abbot.[3]
When the abbot is present in choir no-one shall strike a
child, or cause him to strip for flogging, unless the abbot
so order. When the abbot is away the cantor may

iis, quae sui officii sunt, eos castiget. Prior uero de caeteris, in quibus se leuiter habent. Ubicunque sint, 178 praeter personas su/perius designatas, nullus eis signum faciat, nullus arrideat. In scolam eorum nullus ingrediatur, nullus cum eis alicubi loquatur, nisi sibi ab abbate uel priore ingrediendi, uel loquendi, licentia concedatur.

Meridianis horis in lectis suis nunquam legant, nihil aliud ibi agant, sed cooperti tantum quiescant ; unus, super alios magistros, sit magister eorum maturus et discretus, qui auditis clamoribus culpas delinquentium moderata discretione sciat uel punire uel indulgere. Collocatis in lectis suis assistant magistri dum sint cooperti ; in nocte cum accensis candelis.

IUVENES,[1] tam nutriti quam de saeculo uenientes, qui magistris custodiendi commendantur, in multis sicut infantes, de quibus superius dictum est, custodiantur. Remoti, ut supra, a se inuicem sedeant ; extra locum custodiae suae sine custode nusquam procedant ; duo et duo laternas ferant ; abbati uel priori, et nulli alii, nisi specialiter designatum sit, confessiones suas faciant. Meridianis horis in lectis suis non debent legere, non scribere, non quippiam operis facere, sed cooperti tantum quiescere ; lectos suos ante, uel inter, lectos magistrorum habere.[2] Si necesse habent surgere, prius magistros excitent, et postea accensa laterna, si nox est, ad necessitates suas explendas cum magistris ambulent. Praeter abbatem, priorem, magistrosque eorum, nulli liberum

---

[1] These were the young monks, either ' old boys ' of the house or new-comers, who for a longer or shorter term of years (sometimes till 21) were kept more strictly and allowed more indulgences in food and sleep than were the monks of the cloister.

[2] cf. *Regula* XXII 15 : ' Adulescentiores fratres juxta se non habeant lectos, sed permixti cum senioribus.'

beat them for faults in performance that fall under his jurisdiction ; in all other small matters the prior shall punish them.

Wherever they may be, no-one save the persons mentioned above shall make a sign to them, or smile to them. No-one shall enter their school or speak to them anywhere unless permission has been granted to enter or to speak by the abbot or prior.

In the afternoon they shall never read or occupy themselves when in bed, but shall merely take their rest with the bed-clothes over them. A monk of mature age and known discretion shall be their head master ; he shall be skilled to punish or remit their faults when they are accused as a discreet moderation may suggest. When they go to bed their masters shall be present, with candles if it be night, until they have the bed-clothes over them.

THE OLDER BOYS,[1] whether brought up in the monastery or coming from the world, are put under the charge of masters, and shall be kept in many ways like the children who have just been dealt with. They shall sit apart from one another as has been described ; they shall never leave their ward-room without one of their guardians ; they shall carry lanterns two by two ; they shall confess to the abbot or prior or one specially appointed. In the afternoon they shall not read or write or do any work in bed, but shall simply rest under the clothes ; their beds shall be between, or at the foot of, those of their masters.[2] If necessity causes them to rise, they shall first rouse their masters, and then, lighting a lantern if it is night, they shall go with them to relieve themselves.

Save for abbot, prior and their masters no-one may

sit in loco custodiae eorum deputato sedere, nec uerbo
nec signo aliquid eis innotescere, nisi accepta licentia ab
abbate uel priore.   Quae licentia cum conceditur,
magister sedere debet inter iuuenem et eum, qui iuueni
loquitur.   Iuuenis cum iuuene non loquatur, nisi audiente
et intelligente magistro quid utrimque dicatur.   Magistri
inter eos sedeant uel ante eos sic ut eos cum uolunt con-
spicere ualeant.   Cum dormitum uadunt tamdiu stent
ante ipsos magistri usque dum ipsi iuuenes in lectis suis
iaceant cooperti.   Si nox est, cum candelis accensis
179 assistant ; in monasterio, capi/tulo, refectorio, processione mixti sint senioribus, non obseruato, si necesse sit,
ordine conuersionis eorum.   Si ad mensam legunt, uel
de coquina seruiunt, surgentibus a mensa fratribus cum
eis ad monasterium uadant, et dicto Et ne nos, cum
custodibus ad refectorium reuertantur ; duo simul aut
plures, si fieri possit, de conuentu non remaneant.   Quod
si paucitas maiorum, et pluralitas iuuenum aliter
agendum coegerit, sufficientes eis custodes deputentur.[1]

Porro si custodia illa iuuenum, quae in nonnullis
cenobiis tenetur, magis placet, ut uidelicet in diuersis
ac separatis ab inuicem locis per claustrum sedeant,
singuli singulos, aut plures, si tanta copia est, custodes
habeant ; singuli singulas 'laternas in nocte ferant.
Custos iuuenem non relinquat nisi commendatum alicui
fratri, in quo et de quo bene confidat.   Omnis denique
custodia ei adhibeatur quae superius descripta est.

FRATER aliqua sui corporis incommoditate detentus,

---

[1] The translation gives what would appear to be the sense of a somewhat
obscure passage.

sit in the place set aside as their ward-room, nor may anyone give them a message by word or sign save with permission of abbot or prior. When such permission is granted, the master should sit between the boy and the monk who speaks with him. One of the boys shall not speak with another unless a master is present to hear what is being said by both. The masters shall sit between them or before them so that they may oversee them whenever they wish.

When they go to bed their masters shall stand over them until the boys lie covered up in bed. If it is night they shall stand by with candles. In church, chapter, refectory and processions they shall be dispersed among the seniors without necessarily having regard to their order of priority. If they read at table or serve in the kitchen they shall go with the brethren after the meal to church, and when *Et ne nos* is said they shall return to the refectory with their wardens. If possible, two or more shall never be away from the community at the same time. If the elders are so few and the boys so many as to make some other arrangement necessary, a sufficient number of guardians shall be appointed for them.[1]

However, the manner of looking after the boys that prevails in some monasteries may be preferred, viz., that they sit separate from each other in different parts of the cloister, that they have each one or more guardians, if this is practicable, and that each one carries a lantern by night. A guardian shall not leave a boy without entrusting him to another brother in whom he has full confidence. In a word, exactly the same care shall be taken of them as has been set out above for the children.

IF A BROTHER so suffer from bodily indisposition as

si conuentum * sequi non potest,[1] humiliter prius in
capitulo petita uenia, iussus surgere stans fateatur se
non posse conuentibus † interesse propter infirmitatem
suam. Cui respondeat abbas, uel qui loco abbatis ordini
praesidet : Omnipotens Dominus concedat uobis utilem
sanitatem, sicut uobis expedire cognoscit. Amodo
tractate uos secundum infirmitatem uestram, et remanete
de conuentibus,‡ sicut uobis melius uisum fuerit.

Si egritudo adeo inualuerit, ut in conuentu remanere
non possit, praecipiat abbas fratri, cui huiusmodi cura
imposita est, ut ducat egrum in cellam infirmorum, in
qua domo seruiatur ei secundum possibilitatem loci, tam
de communibus cibis, quam de esu carnis,[2] ut nullius rei,
si fieri possit, indigentiam patiatur. Ex quo carnem
180 comedere / incipiet, quocunque perget caput opertus
capitio, et baculo se sustentans incedere debet.

Qua uero die sanitate recepta ad conuentum redire
uoluerit, si carnem comedit, prius rasus ad horam quae
ante capitulum canitur chorum introeat, et si post
ipsam horam in conuentu missa dicitur ad ipsam non
offerat. Ingressus capitulum, cum indictum fuerit de
ordine loqui, primus surgat, et in loco ubi consuetudo
est prostratus ueniam petat. Interrogatus, et respondens
ut fieri solet, iussus surgere haec uel similia uerba dicat :
Domine, infirmitate mea grauatus in domo infirmorum
diu fui ; in cibo et potu et aliis multis offendi, et contra
ordinem nostrum feci, et inde peto absolutionem uestram.
Hoc dicto absoluat eum abbas dicens : Omnipotens
Dominus absoluat uos ab his, et ab omnibus aliis uestris

---

* conuentus B E   † conuentui A C   ‡ conuentu A C
[1] Bernard of Cluny I xxiii 186, for what follows throughout the rest
of the section.
[2] *Regula* XXXVI 17 : ' Sed et carnium esus infirmis omnino debilibus
pro reparatione concedatur.' Strict as the Rule is on the point of meat-
eating, it has none of the sentiment of ritual pollution of later codes.

to be unable to follow the daily round,[1] he shall first humbly prostrate in chapter, and when he is bidden to rise he shall confess his inability to carry out the daily round owing to sickness. Then the abbot or superior for the time being shall answer, ' May the almighty Lord grant you such good health as He knows to be expedient for you. Meanwhile treat yourself as your sickness demands, and stay away from conventual duties at your discretion.'

If his sickness increase so that he cannot remain with the community, the abbot shall tell the brother who has charge of such to take the sick man into the infirmary ; there he shall be given as circumstances allow both of ordinary fare and of fleshmeat,[2] so that he suffer the lack of nothing, if this be possible. So soon as he begins to eat meat he shall wear his hood up wherever he goes, and should walk leaning upon a staff.

When he has recovered and wishes to return to the community, if he has eaten meat he shall be shaved and enter choir for the hour before chapter : and if Mass is said before the community after that office he shall not make an offering. When he is in chapter, and the command has been given to speak of matters of discipline, he shall be the first to rise, and shall beg pardon prostrate in the usual place. When the usual question and answer have been made and he has been bidden to rise, he shall say the following or similar words : ' My Lord, I have been long in the infirmary borne down by sickness ; I have offended in matters of food and drink and much else, and I have acted against our established discipline, and for this I beg of you absolution.' When he has finished the abbot shall absolve him, saying, ' May the almighty Lord absolve you from these and all other faults.' When the brethren have answered ' Amen '

delictis.   Conuentu respondente Amen, offerat se frater
ille ad pedem abbatis ; postea reuersus ad locum ubi
se prostrauit gratias referens abbati et toti conuentui,
quia ministrata sunt ei quae infirmitati suae fuerant
necessaria, tres genuum flexiones solito more faciat.   Ipsa
die, et deinceps quantum opus fuerit, iubeatur mixtum
accipere.   Si uero carnem non comederit, in dispositione
abbatis sit qua hora in conuentum petita licentia redire,
et quomodo se de caetero habere debeat.

SI INFIRMUS magis ad mortem, quam ad salutem ten-
dere uideatur,[1] et se petat inungui, frater qui domui
infirmorum praeest rem fratribus in capitulo narret ;
tunc iubente abbate, uel qui loco abbatis in capitulo
sedet, exeant sacerdos ebdomadarius, secretarius, quat-
tuor conuersi, et parent quae ad huiusmodi negotium
parari oportet.   Quibus paratis, expletisque quae in
capitulo agi ordo requirit, exeuntes de monasterio
181 transeant ante capitulum, / hoc ordine procedentes :
primus ex conuersis unus cum situla aquae benedictae,
dehinc alius cum cruce, post hos duo cum candelabris,
extremi secretarius cum oleo, et sacerdos, alba indutus
et stola cum manipulo, portans librum.

Istis transeuntibus surgens conuentus, percussaque
tabula, si dies talis est, egrediens de capitulo iungatur
eis, et psallentes septem psalmos [2] ad egrum ueniant ; et

---

[1] cf. Bernard of Cluny I xxiv 190 ; but the similarities are not striking.
The monastic customaries vie with each other in regulating the last moments
and burial of the monk.   Here again the simplicity of St Benedict is noteworthy.   Though his monk is to have death daily before his eyes (*Regula*
IV 54), and to consider himself every moment as about to appear before
the bar of judgment, there is no chapter on the death and burial of the
monk, and indeed the two words do not occur in Abbot Butler's *index
verborum*.   Nevertheless, the solemnity of Lanfranc's directions will not
escape the reader, and there is something very impressive in the concern
of the whole family shown by its assistance at the last moments and its
urgent prayers for the departed soul of one of its members.   cf. also
Dom Gougaud's Chapter VII [' La mort du moine '] in *Anciennes Costumes*

the brother shall present himself before the abbot's feet, and then returning to the place where he lay, and thanking the abbot and all the community for doing all that was needful for him in his sickness, he shall make the three usual genuflections. He shall be told to take the *mixtum* on that day, and for so long as shall be necessary. If however he did not eat meat, it shall be for the abbot to decide at what hour he shall return with permission to the community, and whether special disposition shall be made for him in the future.

IF THE SICK MAN should seem to be tending towards death rather than towards recovery,[1] and should ask to be anointed, the brother in charge of the infirmary shall tell the brethren in chapter. Then at the bidding of the abbot or his representative in chapter, the priest of the week, together with the sacrist and four converses, shall go out to prepare what is necessary.

When they are ready, and all regular business has been accomplished in chapter, they shall leave the church and pass before the chapter-house, going in the following order : first, one of the converses with a vat of holy water, then another bearing the cross, then two with the candlesticks, and finally the sacrist with the holy oil and the priest wearing alb, stole and maniple and carrying the book.

As they go by the community rises and, when the board is struck (if it be a day for this), leaves the chapter-house and joins them, chanting the seven psalms [2]

Claustrales, where reference is given to much kindred literature, ancient and modern. For a contemporary account of a saintly monk's death, see the death-bill of Lanzo of Lewes in William of Malmesbury, *Gesta Regum*, 414, and Knowles, *Monastic Order*, 152. For the medieval rite of administering Extreme Unction and the Commendation of a departing soul, *v. Missale Westmon.* III 1266ff.

[2] i.e. the seven Penitential Psalms (for list, *v. supra*, p. 3)

ordinate circumstent, sicut locus in quo iacet fieri
permittit. Primum spargatur aqua benedicta, dehinc
finitis psalmis sequatur Kyrieleison et capitula et collectae
quae ordinatae sunt, usque ad confessionem ; facta
confessione absoluatur ab omnibus, et ipse absoluat
omnes. Dehinc osculetur ab omnibus. Interim dicantur
aliae collectae usque ad unctionem ; facta unctione,
lauet sacerdos manus, et proiiciatur aqua in ignem, uel
in sacrarium deferatur.[1] Quo facto, dictis collectis quae
sequuntur, uadat sacerdos, praecedentibus duobus conuersis cum candelabris, uadat et tertius ad thuribulum
deferendum. Quibus reuertentibus flexis genibus adorent
omnes corpus Domini quod a sacerdote affertur. Quo
allato, abluto prius ore eius, communicetur infirmus,
nisi forte ipsa die communicatus sit.

Si fratres ipsa die post capitulum psallentes Verba
mea in monasterium ituri sunt, expletis in choro psalmis,
dictaque collecta, paratis ante maius altare quae supra
dicta sunt, exeant, et sequantur eo ordine quo superius
indicatum est. Quod etiam finitis quibuslibet horis a
prima usque ad completorium obseruandum est, si
necessitas urgeat non expectare capitulum. Porro si
nec ipsa hora,* qua percantata id fieri debeat, expectari
potest, disponat abbas uel prior sicut melius possit, quia
necessitas lege non tenetur. His expletis, reuertatur
conuentus in claustrum. Sed infantes minime ingrediantur ad tenendum suum capitulum.

Ab hac die nisi melioretur infirmus carnem non
comedat. Cotidie istud pro eo seruitium impendatur :
182 ad missam / matutinalem collecta Omnipotens sempiterne

---

* hora ipsa A
[1] The drain in church or sacristy, leading into the ground, into which
water from the chalice etc. was thrown

till they come where the sick man lies. They then stand round him in order so far as the place where he lies may permit. First he is sprinkled with holy water, then when the psalms are finished there follows *Kyrie eleison* and the chapters and the collects appointed before the *Confiteor* ; when he has said this he is absolved by all, and himself absolves all present. Then he shall be kissed by all. Meanwhile the other collects preceding the anointing are said. When the anointing is done the priest shall wash his hands and the water shall be thrown on the fire, or into the *sacrarium*.¹ When this has been done, and the prayers that follow have been said, the priest goes out, preceded by two converses with candlesticks, while a third goes to carry the thurible. When they return, all kneel to adore the body of the Lord which is brought by the priest. When it is brought, the sick man, after washing his mouth, receives Communion, unless he shall by chance have already received Communion that day.

If, however, it is a day when the brethren are to go into the church after the chapter singing the *Verba mea*, when the psalms in choir are done and the collect has been said, all is prepared as above before the high altar, and they leave the church and do all as has been set out above. The same order is observed at the end of any of the hours from Prime to Compline, if the case is so urgent as to forbid delay till the next chapter. But if it is impossible even to delay till after an hour has been chanted, then the abbot or prior is to arrange things as seems best to him, for necessity knows no law. When all is done the community shall return to the cloister, but the children shall not go in to hold their chapter.

As for the sick man, henceforward he shall not eat fleshmeat unless he makes a recovery. Prayers shall be said for him daily as follows : at the Morrow Mass the

Deus, salus aeterna credentium, cum caeteris duabus.[1] Aliquando si dies vacuus fuerit ipsa matutinalis missa pro eo cantatur ; ad maiorem missam post Sanctus psalmus primus, Domine, ne in furore tuo, ab unoquoque sub silentio dicatur ; Kyrieleison ; Pater noster ; Saluum fac seruum tuum ; Mitte ei, Domine, auxilium de sancto ; collecta * : Omnipotens sempiterne Deus, salus aeterna.† Et hoc tamdiu agatur quousque ad sanitatem redire uideatur.

Porro si ad sanitatem minime redire, mortique potius appropinquare dignoscitur, ex quo certa in eo mortis signa apparere inceperint, sine duobus fratribus esse non debet, qui diebus et noctibus quamdiu intellectum tenet legant coram eo passiones Domini et euangelia ; et cum intellectu priuatus fuerit, quamdiu superuixerit, psalterium ex ordine decantare non cessent. Et sic ordinetur ut discedentibus duobus succedant duo alii ; horas uero regulares ibi dicant. Egro autem in agonia posito, et iam iam ‡ si ita uisum fuerit morituro, famulus, qui ad hoc deputatus est, cilicium expandat, et supra illud, ad mensuram longitudinis et latitudinis quam ipsum cilicium habet, signum crucis de cineribus faciat, morientemque fratrem desuper ponat. Cui postea indesinenter assidens studiose consideret qua hora exitum eius conuentui debeat indicare.

Cumque eum iam in exeundo uiderit laborare,[2] gestans manu tabulam ad hostium claustri currat, ictuque creberrimo acriter eam ibi percutiat, quousque in conuentu auditum esse cognoscat. Quo percepto sonitu si ad maiorem, uel minorem missam, uel ad regularem horam fuerint, remanentibus in choro infantibus cum

---

* *om.* A C B E   † + credentium A C B E   ‡ *om.* C E
[1] This is the collect for the sick in the Roman Missal.
[2] cf. Bernard of Cluny I xxiv 192 for not very exact similarities

collect ' Almighty everlasting God, the eternal salvation of those who believe in Thee,' [1] with the Secret and Postcommunion. From time to time, if there is a free day, the Morrow Mass shall be sung for him. At the High Mass after the *Sanctus* the first psalm *Domine ne in furore tuo* shall be said in silence by all, with *Kyrie eleison, Pater noster* ; *Salvum fac servum tuum* ; *Mitte ei Domine auxilium de sancto*, and the prayer as above. And this shall be continued until he be convalescent.

But if he seem not to be recovering, but rather to be coming nigh to death, as soon as sure indications of this make their appearance he shall never be left without two of the brethren who shall read to him day and night, while his senses remain, the narratives of the Passion and other parts of the gospels. When his senses fail, they shall recite the psalter without ceasing so long as he remains alive. And it shall be so arranged that when two go another pair shall replace them, and they shall say the regular hours there. When the sick man is in his agony and at the very point of death, if God so wills, then the servant in charge shall unfold a sackcloth and lay on it ashes in the form of a cross from edge to edge of the sackcloth, and set the dying brother thereon. And then he shall sit by him, never leaving him, and watching carefully for the moment to come when he shall let the community know that he is passing.

When he sees him now in the agony of passing,[2] he shall take the board in his hand and run to the door of the cloister and beat the board there with sharp and rapid blows until he is sure the community have heard. When they hear the sound, if they are at the High or Low Mass or a regular hour, a few brethren shall be

magistris suis, et aliquibus fratribus, quibus iussum fuerit,
reliqui omnes ad egrum currant, et mediocri uoce canentes Credo in unum Deum, ad eum ueniant. Fratres uero
qui remanserunt, expleto quod coeperant, eodem modo
currentes et canentes ad morientem properent. Ubi-
183 cunque uero alias, uel quocun/que alio negotio occupatos
praedictus sonus inuenerit, sine aliqua excusatione uel
mora similiter currentes, et Credo in unum Deum
canentes, ad egrum ueniant. Quo peruenientes, et
Credo in unum Deum communiter explentes, canant
septem psalmos penitentiales sine Gloria, quibus expletis
subiungat sacerdos capitulum Parce Domine, parce
famulo tuo, quem redimere dignatus es pretioso sanguine
tuo, ne in aeternum irascaris ei. Hoc tertio a sacerdote
dicatur, et per singulas uices a toto conuentu repetatur ;
deinde sequatur letania quae solet, quam protrahi uel
breuiari oportet, secundum quod fratris exitus uisus
fuerit admonere. Si autem, ut aliquando fit, letania
expleta nondum migrauerit, conuentus discedat, aliquibus fratribus, quibus iussum fuerit, ibi remanentibus, qui
psalterium ex ordine psallere incipiant. Cum autem
uenerit hora, ut iterum uocari debeant fratres, supra
dicto modo uocentur et ueniant.

Egressa iam de corpore anima, tribus uicibus, cum
paruis interuallis, pulsentur signa, cantor incipiat responsorium Subuenite sancti Dei. Quo cum uersu et
regressu expleto, subiungat sacerdos, Proficiscere anima
christiana.[1] Quo dicto incipiant commendationem animae, dictaque prima collecta Tibi, Domine, commendamus, sacerdote et conuentu prosequente caetera,

---

[1] The *Subvenite* and *Proficiscere* are both in current use in the Roman
Ritual, but the latter—' the most noble and inspiring of all liturgical forms,'
familiar to many from its introduction into the *Dream of Gerontius*—is there
recited, as the sense of the words demands, before the moment of death.
For the order as here, *v. Officium Abbatum Eveshamensis Monasterii*, col. 123ff.

told to remain in choir with the children and their masters, while all the rest run to the sick man, reciting the *Credo* in an ordinary tone of voice as they go. The brethren who remain, when they have finished the office, shall run in like manner, chanting the *Credo*, to the dying man. Wheresoever else they may be, and whatsoever they are doing when the sound of the alarm reaches them, they shall make no pretext for delay but run to the sick man, chanting the *Credo*. When they get there they shall complete the *Credo* together, and then chant the seven penitential psalms without the *Gloria* ; then the priest shall add the chapter, ' Spare, O Lord, spare Thy servant, whom Thou didst deign to redeem with Thy precious blood ; be not wroth with him for ever.' This shall be said thrice by the priest, and repeated each time by the whole community ; then follows the ordinary litany, which should be prolonged or shortened as the brother's time of passing may demand. If, as sometimes happens, when the litany is finished he be not yet gone, the community shall depart, leaving a few brethren, as ordered, to recite the psalter from the beginning. When the time comes for the community to be recalled, they shall be called and shall come as above.

When the soul has left the body the bells shall be tolled thrice at short intervals, and the cantor shall begin the responsory *Subvenite sancti Dei*. When it is done, with its verse and the repeat, the priest shall add the prayer ' Set forth, O Christian soul.' [1] When that is said they shall begin the commendation of the soul, and when the first collect *Tibi Domine commendamus* has been said the priest and community shall continue with what remains. Meanwhile the corpse shall be taken for washing by those of the same order as the dead man ; that is, priests for a priest, deacons for a deacon and so forth,

portetur corpus ad lauandum ab iis de quorum ordine
fuit, id est, sacerdos a sacerdotibus, diaconus a diaconis,
et sic in reliquis ordinibus, conuersus a conuersis ; infans
tamen non ab infantibus, sed a conuersis. Hi uero sunt
qui lauare non debent corpus defuncti [1] : sacerdos ebdomadarius, et reliqui ministri qui circa altare seruiunt, et
uasa sacrata contrectant ; ebdomadarii coquinae, celerarii, refectorarii. Dum lauatur corpus, camerarius
praesto esse debet, habens uestimenta idonea, et fila, et
acus ad consuendum, et caetera quae sui officii sunt, et
huic * operi necessaria. Inter lauandum circumcinctus
184 sit / staminia, qua indutus antea erat, circa pudendas sui
corporis partes.

Lotus autem uestiatur staminia noua, uel nouiter
lota, et cuculla, et in capite eius ponatur sudarium in
modum capitii de staminia factum ; huic superducatur
capitium cucullae, et cum filo in tribus locis annectatur.
Calcietur caligis de supra dicto panno factis, usque ad
genua attingentibus, et nocturnalibus. Manus cuculla
sint coopertae. Cuculla hinc et inde consuatur, et circa
crura similiter ; nocturnales alter alteri filo connectatur.[2]
Taliter paratum corpus feretro imponatur, et pallio
cooperiatur.

Quo expleto, expletisque quae in conuentu dici
coeperant, percutiat prior tabulam uno ictu. Quo
audito inclinati fratres dicant Pater noster. Sacerdos
circa corpus aquam benedictam spargat, et incenset.
Dehinc dicat, Et ne nos inducas ; A porta inferi ; postea
collectam. His ita gestis pulsentur signa ; cantor incipiat
responsorium, Subuenite sancti Dei, et praecedentibus

---

* suo C
[1] Bernard of Cluny I. xxiv. 194 is very similar to this.
[2] The practical purpose of all this sewing was to prevent disarray before
and during burial, as no coffin was used—as none is used among the
Carthusians and Trappists of today.

converses for a converse. A child's corpse shall however not be washed by children but by converses.

The following shall not wash a corpse [1] : the priest of the week and the other ministers who serve at the altar and handle the sacred vessels ; the brethren of the week in kitchen, cellar and refectory. While the corpse is being washed the chamberlain should be present with grave-clothes of the right kind and thread and a needle for sewing, and all else that pertains to his office and the task in hand. While the corpse is being washed it shall have about its waist the shift previously worn.

When washed it shall be clad in a new shift, or one newly washed, and a cowl ; a headcloth of linsey-wolsey in the shape of a hood shall be on its head ; the hood belonging to the cowl shall be brought over this and attached in three places with thread. Gaiters of the same material reaching to the knees shall be put on the legs, and night shoes on the feet. The hands shall be covered by the sleeves of the cowl. The cowl shall be sewn together from arm to arm, and round the legs likewise. The night shoes also shall be joined together with thread.[2] So dressed, the corpse shall be set on the hearse and covered with a pall.

When all this is done, and the prayers finished by the community, the prior shall strike the board once ; when they hear this the brethren shall bow down and say the *Pater noster*, while the priest goes round the hearse sprinkling holy water and incensing the body. Then he shall say *Et ne nos* ; *A porta inferi* ; and then the collect. After this the bells shall be tolled, and the cantor shall begin the responsory *Subvenite sancti Dei*. All shall then proceed to the church ; those who bear the vat of holy water, the cross, the candlesticks and incense shall go first, then the children and the rest of the community ;

his, qui situlam cum aqua, crucem, candelabra, thuribulum portant, sequentibus infantibus et reliquo conuentu, extremis eis qui corpus lauerant et portant,
ueniant in aecclesiam ; positoque corpore in loco ubi
poni solet, cessent signa ; figatur crux ad caput eius ;
ponantur duo candelabra, unum ad caput, et alterum
ad pedes, cum cereis desuper accensis, qui continue ibi
ardeant usquequo ad sepulturam deferatur.   Finito
cantu, inclinati dicant Pater noster ; sacerdos, Et ne
nos ; A porta inferi ; collectam sicut superius dictum
est.   His peractis, si sonitus tabulae de refectorio fratres
adduxerat, ablutis manibus ad refectorium reuertantur,
perficiantque quod imperfectum remanserat, remanentibus cum corpore aliquibus fratribus, quot et quibus
iniunctum fuerit, qui psalmos ibi interim canant ; nunquam enim sine psalmodia corpus esse debet, excepto
quando in choro aliquid communis officii celebratur.

Conuentus in die circa corpus semper debet esse, nisi
185 /quando canunt horas uel missas, uel processionem circa
claustrum uel extra claustrum, si ita contingat, faciunt,
uel in capitulo sunt, aut in refectorio, aut in dormitorio meridianis horis, et tunc tantum deputentur aliqui
fratres qui ibi remaneant.   Psalterium ex ordine psallant,
commendationem animae agant, uesperas, uigilias cum
laudibus, Uerba mea, et haec eadem frequenter.   Nocte
uero post completorium, incipiens primam uigiliam
dexter chorus faciat, secundam sinister,[1] persoluentes
utrique supra dicta obsequia, prout quantitas noctium
fieri permiserit, hoc obseruato diligenter, ne utrique
priores in una uigilia deputentur.   Circa primae finem *
uigiliae exeat prior ferens absconsam, et uadat in

----

* finem primae A C B E
[1] At Cluny, where the community was very large, the night was divided
into three watches.

last of all, those who have washed the body and now carry it. When the corpse is placed in the usual position in church the bells cease to toll ; the cross is set up at the feet of the dead man, and the two candlesticks are placed one at his head and the other at his feet, with tapers burning without cease till the body is taken out for burial. When the chant is done they shall bow and say the *Pater noster* ; then the priest shall say *Et ne nos* ; *A porta inferi*, and the collect as above. When this is done, if the brethren were in the refectory when the board was sounded, they wash their hands and return thither to resume the unfinished meal. Meanwhile orders shall be given for a certain number of brethren to remain with the corpse and chant psalms, for the corpse should never be left without psalmody, save when a common office is being celebrated in choir.

During the day the community should be always about the body, save when they are singing the Hours or Masses, or making procession within or, if it so chance, without the cloister, or are in chapter or refectory, or dormitory during the afternoon ; on such occasions certain of the brethren shall be deputed to remain by the hearse. They shall recite the psalter in order, with the prayers for the commendation of a soul, Vespers, Vigils and Lauds of the dead with *Verba mea*. All these they shall frequently repeat.

In the evening, after Compline, the right-hand choir shall make the first watch, and the left-hand choir shall follow with the second watch [1] ; each choir shall carry out the service just mentioned above, so far as the length of the night allows ; they shall take care that the two priors together shall not be deputed for the same watch. Towards the end of the first watch the prior shall leave the choir with a dark lantern, and shall go to the

dormitorium, excitetque fratres qui secundam uigiliam facturi sunt. Post matutinas laudes, dictis in choro quae dici ordo exposcit,* quicquid superest noctis infantes cum magistris canendo expendant ; intersint quoque infirmi illi, qui in domo infirmorum assidue conuersantur, et facultatem hoc faciendi habere uidentur. Caeteri uero fratres in lectis suis quiescant usquequo facto mane surgentes, calciati, loti et pexi, factisque orationibus aggregentur et ipsi ad corpus. Quibus aggregatis pergant infantes se calciare, lauare et pectere, solitasque orationes facere, et post accedant et ipsi, et hoc fit si dies talis sit ut post matutinas laudes ad lectos redire fratribus licitum sit. In hieme uero quando interualla fiunt, si post letaniam aliquid superest noctis, licet praedictis reliquis fratribus in lectis suis usque ad diem quiescere ; uestiti tamen et calciati quiescant.

Infantes sicut superius dictum est, cum magistris et infirmis suam circa corpus agant uigiliam, ea autem hora. Postea omnes calcient se, et lauent et pectinent, solitasque orationes faciant, quas ordo illius temporis poscit. Sedentes psallant nisi ad Magnificat, et ad 186 Benedictus ; / tunc enim stare debent ; ad Pater noster, et ad collectas quas sacerdos dicit, inclinati sint super genua sua. Si ante nocturnas uigilias frater obierit, tanta iam noctis parte transacta, ut duas uigilias facere commodum non sit, locato in aecclesia corpore, fratres omnes uigilantes et psallentes ibi remaneant ; infantes cum magistris suis dormitum in dormitorium redeant.

---

* deposcit A

dormitory to wake the brethren who are to keep the second watch. After Lauds and the regular prayers, the children and their masters shall take over the psalmody for the remaining space of night ; they shall be accompanied by such ailing brethren as are permanently in the infirmary and are therefore able to be free at this time.

The rest of the community shall remain in bed until they rise at daybreak, put on their shoes, wash and comb themselves and, having said the usual prayers, join the others round the hearse. When they arrive the children shall go to put on their shoes, wash their hands, and comb their hair and say the usual prayers ; then they too shall rejoin the others. This is the order to be kept on days when the brethren are allowed to return to bed after Lauds. In winter, however, when there is an interval between the offices and the night is not yet spent when the litany is ended, the community may rest in bed until the day break, but in this case wearing their clothes and shoes.

As has been said above, the children with their masters shall keep vigil about the body at that time. Later, all shall put on their shoes, wash and comb their hair, and say the usual prayers appointed for the season. They shall recite the psalms seated, save during the *Magnificat* and *Benedictus*, during which they shall stand ; during the *Pater noster* and collects said by the priest they shall be on their knees and bow.

If a brother die before the night vigils, when so much of the night is already spent as to make it impracticable to recite two nocturns for him, the whole community shall remain in church when the body has been set there, keeping vigil and chanting psalms. The children and their masters shall return to sleep in the dormitory.

Quamdiu corpus super terram est, nullus in claustro
loquatur ; tabula tamen si dies talis sit, in capitulo
pulsetur, et Benedicite dicatur, sicut aliis diebus.   Si
tamen ipsa die post capitulum sepeliri debet, priusquam
sepeliatur nulli liceat extra claustra * monasterii exire,
nisi tam prope sit locus ut ad sepeliendum fratrem possit
redire.   Omnes, qui possunt, ipso die pro eo missam
celebrent.   Missa matutinalis pro eo festiue agatur,
etiamsi dies praecipuae festiuitatis sit.   Ad quam missam
quotiens diaconus incenset † altare, ad corpus quoque
incensandum cum thuribulo debet accedere.   Facto in
capitulo sermone absoluat eum abbas, uel qui ordini
praeest.   Deinde praecipiat celebrari pro eo triginta
diebus triginta missas, singulis uidelicet diebus singulas
missas, praeter eas quae in conuentu celebrandae sunt,
ita ut nullus praetereat dies quo missa pro eo non
celebretur, nisi parasceue sit aut sabbatum sanctum ; et
qui inchoat non ipsa die qua sepelitur, sed in crastino
inchoare debet.   Celebratis quisque sibi iniunctis missis
ipso die id in capitulo dicat, quatinus alii, qui subsequi
debeat, ibidem abbas aut ‡ prior idem iniungat.   Ipso
die infantes suum capitulum non teneant.

Quacunque hora per totam diem post sonitum, quem
prior ad excitandos fratres mane facere solet, frater
moriatur, sepultura eius usque post crastinum capitulum
differatur, nisi rationabilis causa existat, quae uel post
maiorem missam, uel post nonam sepeliri eum suadeat,
et maxime si ante horam quae uel aestate uel hieme

---

* claustrum A   † incensat A C B E   ‡ uel A

So long as the corpse remains unburied no-one shall speak in the cloister ; nevertheless, the board shall be struck in chapter, if it is a day for this to be done, and *Benedicite* shall be said, as on other days. If however the burial is to be that very day after chapter, no-one shall be permitted to leave the cloister before it is over, unless he go so short a distance as to be able to return for the funeral.

All who can shall celebrate Mass for the dead brother that day. The Morrow Mass shall be said with festal rite for him, even though it be a principal feast, and during that Mass the deacon shall approach with the thurible to incense the corpse whenever he incenses the altar.

After the sermon in chapter the abbot or his representative shall absolve the dead man. Then he shall give command that thirty Masses shall be celebrated for him for thirty days, that is, every day a Mass, in addition to the public Masses offered for him ; in this way not a day shall pass without Mass being said for him, unless it be Good Friday or Holy Saturday. The first Mass of the series shall not be said on the day of the funeral but on the morrow.

When each has said the Mass allotted him he shall report it that day in chapter, so that the abbot or prior may there issue orders to the one who is to follow him. On the day of the funeral the children shall not hold their chapter.

At whatever time of the day a brother die, if it be after the alarum made by the prior at break of day to call the brethren, the funeral shall be put off till after chapter on the morrow, unless a reasonable cause exist for burying the dead man after High Mass or after None ; this may well be so if he happen to die before the part

187 ante ca/pitulum dicitur, mori eum contingat. Quod cum accidit, praeter seruitium quod pro mortuo fratre facere solent fratres, integrum psalterium, cum integra mortuorum psalmodia, pro eo singulis est fratribus iniungendum. Si ante nocturnas uigilias moritur, subsequente similiter die post capitulum sepeliatur. Si inter ipsas uigilias, uel postea ante praedictum sonitum de hoc saeculo migret, post maiorem missam tradi eum sepulturae oportet. Si festiuitas duodecim lectionum aut trium, in qua in claustro minime loquantur fratres, ipsa die fuerit, post capitulum celebretur pro eo missa matutinalis festiuo more, sicut superius dictum est. Dehinc dicta tercia missaque maiore, pergant ad sepeliendum fratrem. Ad quem accedentes siue de capitulo, siue de choro exeant, canendo Verba mea ad corpus ueniant; interim pulsetur tribus uicibus unum de maioribus signis, ut si qui forte absunt ad hunc sonum sine mora conueniant. Secretarius abbati et priori et sacerdoti, qui obsequium facturus est, cereos distribuat, candelas reliquis fratribus, magister infantibus. Sacerdos indutus sit alba, cum stola et manipulo; albis duo fratres ex iis, qui antea lauerant mortuum. Albae uero sint ad huiusmodi negotium specialiter deputatae. Ii qui portant situlam cum aqua benedicta, crucem, candelabra, thuribulum, stent hinc et inde ad caput defuncti, reliquus conuentus ad dexteram et ad sinistram, sicut est ordo eorum.

Sacerdos adueniens prius aspergat corpus aqua benedicta,[1] dehinc accedens ad caput defuncti, stet ita ut praedictos portitores ad dexteram suam et sinistram

---

[1] For all these rites and prayers v. *Officium Eveshamensis Monasterii*, 133–7, and *Missale Westmon.* III 1287–1302. Many of the formulae, of which only a few are in the modern rite, are singularly felicitous in expression.

of the office which either in summer or winter is said before chapter. When this happens, the brethren are all to be charged with the duty of saying each one a whole psalter for him together with the office of the dead, in addition to the customary office which is said for a dead brother.

If he die before the night vigils the funeral shall be on the morrow after chapter. If he die during the vigils, or after them, but before the aforesaid morning alarum, he should be buried after the High Mass. If it be a feast of twelve lessons, or three, on which the brethren do not talk in the cloister, the Morrow Mass shall be celebrated for him after chapter with festal rite, as described above.

When Terce has been said and the High Mass celebrated, they shall proceed with the funeral. Whether they go from chapter or choir, they shall go to the body singing *Verba mea* ; meanwhile one of the great bells shall be tolled thrice, so that any who may be absent may come without delay when they hear it.

The sacrist shall distribute tapers to the abbot, prior and celebrant, and small candles to the rest of the brethren. A master shall give candles to the children. The priest shall be vested in alb, stole and maniple, and the two brethren who previously washed the corpse shall be in albs. There shall be albs specially set aside for this purpose. Those who bear the vat of holy water, the cross, candlesticks and thurible shall stand on right and left at the head of the body ; the rest in order on either side of it.

When the priest arrives he shall first sprinkle the body with holy water,[1] then going to the head of the corpse shall stand with the aforementioned bearers on his right and left. Two cantors shall approach ; they

habeat. Accedant duo cantores, et stantes inter altare,
quod ibi situm est, et corpus, dicant Kyrieleison ; Christe
eleison ; Kyrieleison ; conuentu duo priora repetente, et
188 ultimum Kyrieleison cum eis dicente. Postea sacerdos, /
humiliter inclinatis omnibus, dicat collectam : Oremus :
Non intres in iudicium. Qua dicta, praedictis cantoribus
incipientibus, canatur responsorium cum uersu Qui
Lazarum ; quod dum canitur, incenset sacerdos altare,
quod ibi est, et corpus. Hoc agatur secundo et tertio,
excepto quod aliae collectae et alia responsoria dici
debent, sicut in libris, ubi actio huius officii ordinata
est, continetur. Finitis uersibus tertii responsorii, quot
cantor praecepit, repetatur a capite responsorium ; quo
percantato roget sacerdos pro eo orari, ita dicendo :
Pater noster ; Et ne nos ; Non intres ; A porta inferi ;
Dominus uobiscum ; Oremus : Inclina, Domine, aurem
tuam, et reliqua.

His ita peractis, cantore incipiente antiphonam In
paradisum,[1] exeant canentes psalmum In exitu Israel.[2]
Praecedant praedicti portitores aquae, crucis, cande-
labrorum, et thuribuli ; sequantur sacerdos et cantor,
cuius officii specialiter interest omni sollicitudine prouidere, ne in hoc obsequio aliqua possit negligentia euenire.
Post hos procedant infantes cum magistris suis, dehinc
reliqui fratres, extremis prioribus, praecedentibus iunioribus, sicut est ordo conuersionis eorum. Post omnes
ueniant qui corpus portant. Hi uero sint, si commode
fieri possit, qui lauerant illud, adiuuantibus eos, si opus
fuerit, aliis fratribus, quibus abbas aut prior praeceperit.
Cum exire incipiunt, pulsentur signa usquequo corpus
collocatum sit in sepulchro.

---

[1] Bernard of Cluny I xxiv 197. This magnificent antiphon is set to
a plain-song melody of exceptional purity.

CONSTITUTIONS OF LANFRANC

shall stand between the altar and the body and intone
Kyrie eleison, Christe eleison, Kyrie eleison. The rest shall
repeat the two first and shall say the third with the
cantors. Then the priest, while all bow low, shall say
the collect *Oremus : Non intres in judicium.* After that the
aforesaid cantors shall intone the responsory and verse
Qui Lazarum ; while this is being sung by all, the priest
shall incense the altar and the corpse. This shall be
done a second and third time, save that different collects
and responsories should be said, as is prescribed in the
books containing this office.

When as many verses of the third responsory as shall
be directed by the cantor are done, the whole responsory
is repeated from the beginning ; when this has been
done the cantor shall ask prayers for the dead man,
thus : *Pater noster* ; *Et ne nos* ; *Non intres* ; *A porta inferi* ;
Dominus uobiscum ; *Oremus* ; *Inclina, Domine, aurem tuam*
and the rest.

After this, when the cantor has intoned the antiphon
In paradisum [1] they shall leave the church, singing *In exitu
Israel.* [2] The aforesaid bearers of holy water, cross, candlesticks and thurible shall go first ; then the priest and
the cantor, whose particular task it is to take every
possible care that no negligence occur in this office.
After them come the children with their masters, then
the rest of the brethren in conventual order, with the
seniors last following the juniors. Last of all come those
who bear the body ; these, if it can conveniently be
done, shall be those who washed the body, with others
to help them, if need be, at the command of the abbot or
prior. When the procession begins to leave the church
the bells shall be tolled until the body is in the grave.
When they come to the grave they shall stand in

---

[2] Ps. 113 (114–15)

Cum uero ad sepulturam peruenerint stent ordinate
hinc et inde, sicut in choro stare solent. Sacerdos stet
inter duos choros, non longe a sepultura ; ad dexteram
eius et ad sinistram, qui portant aquam et crucem, et
caetera de quibus dictum est superius.* Dicta collecta
Piae recordationis affectu, accedat sacerdos, et aspergat
sepulchrum aqua benedicta, et imposito thure tribuat
thuribulum uni eorum, qui albis induti illuc descenderant,
et incensetur sepulchrum. Dehinc dicta collecta Obsecramus misericordiam tuam, duo ex fratribus qui foris
189 sunt pallium desuper / extendant, alii duo, corpus de
feretro accipientes, illis tribuant, qui in tumulum descenderant. Illi diligenter illud in sepulchro componant, et
absolutionem scriptam, et a fratribus lectam, super
pectus eius ponant ; et operiant, et statim exeuntes, et
ad monasterium reuertentes, exuti albis, et induti uestibus suis, ad conuentum redeant. Corpore in sepultura posito, protinus extinguantur candelae, et cessent
signa.

Expletis reliquis, sicut in codice, in quo hoc officium
ordinatum est, reperitur, reuertantur canentes septem
psalmos penitentiales ; sacerdos praecedens infantes,
cum ad monasterium uenerit, diuertat in uestiarium et
deposita alba et manipulo, atque indutus uestibus suis,
reuertatur in chorum, et prostratus cum caeteris pros-
tratis, quod reliquum est de psalmis dicat. Quibus
dictis subiungant Requiem aeternam dona ei Domine ;
Pater noster ; Et ne nos ; A porta inferi ; Dominus
uobiscum ; collecta : Satisfaciat tibi, Domine Deus
noster. Post haec reuertantur in claustrum, et dicto
ab infante Benedicite, loquantur in claustro, si dies talis,

----

* superius dictum est A C B E

order on each side, as they stand in the choir. The priest shall stand between the two sides of the choir near the grave, with the bearers of holy water and the cross and the rest on his right and left, as has been said above. When the collect *Piae recordationis affectu* has been said, the priest shall draw near and sprinkle the grave with holy water, and having put incense in the thurible shall hand it to one of those in albs who have gone down into the grave, who shall incense the place. Then when the collect *Obsecramus misericordiam tuam* has been said, two of the brethren who are without the grave shall hold the pall stretched over it, while two others, taking the body from the hearse, shall give it into the hands of those who have gone down into the tomb. These shall lay it out carefully in the grave, and put upon its breast the scroll of the words of absolution read by the brethren. Then, having covered the body, they shall at once come forth from the tomb, and returning to the church, taking off their albs and putting on their ordinary clothes, shall rejoin the community. When the body is laid in the tomb the candles shall straightway be extinguished, and the bells shall be silent.

When all is done as written in the book containing this office, all shall return singing the seven penitential psalms ; the priest shall lead, followed by the children, and when he reaches the church shall go to the vestry ; when he has put off his alb and maniple and has put on his ordinary clothes he shall return to choir where, lying prostrate with the others, he shall recite what remains of the psalms. When these are done they shall add : *Requiem aeternam dona ei Domine ; Pater noster ; Et ne nos ; A porta inferi ; Dominus uobiscum*, with the collect *Satisfaciat tibi, Domine Deus noster*. After this they shall return to the cloister, and when one of the children has

et hora sit. Septem plena officia pro eo in conuentu
agant, triginta diebus Verba mea, et ad omnes horas
Voce mea[1] pro eo dicant. Singulariter unusquisque
quantum abbas praeceperit pro anima eius faciat ;
triginta quoque diebus, aut pluribus, si abbas ordinauerit, panem unum cum potu et regularibus cibis
elemosinarius accipiat.

SI FRATER extra monasterium de hac uita migrauerit,
nec fratres secum fuerint, qui eum abluant, caeteraque
quae superius dicta sunt circa eum adimpleant, deportatus ad monasterium in feretro, quod sibi praemitti
debet, cum pallio per portas curiae ingrediatur, et
cooperante fratre, cui infirmorum cura commissa est, in
190 domo infirmorum depona/tur. Quo deposito famulus,
ut solet, ad hostium claustri ueniat, tabulam percutiat,
conuentus adueniat, fiantque caetera, ac si de hac uita
migrasset in eadem infirmorum cella, excepto quod non
dicitur Proficiscere anima christiana.

Porro si fratres secum fuerint unus aut plures, factaque
sunt * ei † quae in tali negotio fieri oportet, procedat ei
conuentus obuiam per maiores monasterii portas, psallendo hos psalmos : Miserere mei, Deus, secundum ;
Deus, in nomine tuo ; Miserere mei Deus, miserere mei ;
Ad Dominum cum tribularer[2] ; et qui sequuntur, donec
ad corpus perueniant ; at ‡ ubi peruenerint, faciant
stationem uersi ad alterutrum ; sacerdos alba indutus
et stola accedat et aspergat corpus aqua benedicta et
incenset ; deinde moneat, ut orent pro eo, dicendo, Pater
noster : Et ne nos : Non intres in iudicium : Requiem

---

* + fratri C   † ea A   ‡ ac A C B E
[1] Ps. 5 and Ps. 141 (142)
[2] Ps. 53 (54), 56 (57), 119 (120)

said *Benedicite* they shall talk, if it be a day and hour when this is allowed.

Seven complete offices of the dead shall be said in choir for a dead brother, and for thirty days they shall say for him the *Verba mea* and after every hour the psalm *Voce mea*.[1] Each one shall say prayers for his soul as ordered by the abbot, and for thirty days or more, if the abbot so order it, the almoner shall receive a loaf with a measure of drink and regular food.

IF A BROTHER pass from this life outside the monastery, and there were no brethren with him to wash him and do all for him as above, then he shall be brought back to the monastery on a hearse, which shall be sent for him, together with a pall. The body shall enter by the gate of the courtyard, and with the assistance of the brother in charge of the sick shall be set down in the infirmary. Then the servant shall go to the door of the cloister in the usual way and strike the board. The community shall assemble, and the remaining ceremonies shall take place as if the brother had died in the infirmary, save that ' Go forth, O Christian soul ' is not said.

But if one or more of the brethren were with him, and all had been done that could be done in such circumstances, the community shall go to meet the body through the main door of the church, chanting the psalms *Miserere mei Deus, secundum* ; *Deus, in nomine tuo* ; *Miserere mei, Deus, miserere mei* ; *Ad Dominum, cum tribularer*,[2] and those which follow, till they reach the body ; then they form ranks facing one another, and the priest wearing alb and stole approaches, sprinkles the corpse with holy water and incenses it. Then he admonishes all to pray for him, saying, *Pater noster* ; *Et ne nos* ; *Non intres in judicium* ; *Requiem aeternam* ; *A porta inferi* ;

aeternam : A porta inferi : Dominus uobiscum ; Oremus ; collecta : Suscipe, Domine, animam serui tui ;
aliam : Suscipe, Domine, seruum tuum. Inde reuertantur cantore incipiente responsorium Subuenite. Dum
intrant in aecclesiam, pulsentur omnia signa, et deponatur in loco in quo caeteri fratres deponi solent, et agantur
caetera quae agerentur si in domo infirmorum mortuus,
et de illa domo illuc deportatus fuisset.

QUACUNQUE hora, ex quo infantes mane incipiunt
legere usque ad collationem, de monacho congregationis
alibi defuncto, atque sepulto, uel sepeliendo, certus
nuntius aut breuis ad monasterium uenerit ; si fratres
non sint in capitulo, aut in refectorio, aut in dormitorio
meridianis horis, aut si in monasterio, uel extra monasterium non intersint alicui obsequio, quod deseri et
imperfectum relinqui commodum non sit, statim prior
tabulam percutiat, et residentibus in capitulo fratribus,
fratris obitum nunciet, et subiungat : Eamus, et faciamus
ei quod iustum est, et nostri ordinis consuetudo habet.
Et surgentes, et Uerba mea canentes, sonantibus signis
191 in chorum ueniant, expletisque / inceptis psalmis cum
collecta, uesperas mortuorum, et officium cum nouem
lectionibus et laudibus dicant, accensis ante altare
duobus luminaribus ; missa matutinalis pro eo festiue
dicatur, nisi dies dominicus aut magna solennitas sit.
Quod si euenerit, in alium diem differatur. Post haec
in primo capitulo absoluatur.

Continuatio triginta missarum, si in eo loco, ubi
mortuus est, non fit, pro eo iniungatur, fiantque caetera,
quae pro fratre congregationis in congregatione defuncto
fieri solent.

Dominus uobiscum ; *Oremus*, with the collect *Suscipe, Domine, animam servi tui*, and the other, *Suscipe, Domine, servum tuum.* Then they return to the church, the cantor intoning the antiphon *Subvenite*. While they are entering the church all the bells are tolled, and the body is set down in the usual place, and all is done which would be done if he had died in the infirmary and had been brought thence into the church.

AT WHATEVER HOUR OF THE DAY, from the time when the children begin to read in the cloister till the evening collation, that sure tidings or letters are received that a monk of the community has died elsewhere, and has there been buried or is to be buried, then if the brethren are not in chapter or refectory or dormitory in the afternoon, and if whether in the church or not they are not engaged in any duty which cannot well be abandoned and left unfinished, then the prior shall at once strike the board, and when all the brethren are seated in chapter he shall announce the brother's death, adding, ' Let us go and accomplish what is his due and what is customary in our order.' Then rising and chanting *Verba mea* while the bells toll they shall go into choir, and when the psalms are done with the collect they shall say Vespers of the dead and the office with nine lessons, and Lauds, with two lights burning before the altar. The Morrow Mass shall be said for him with festal rite, unless it be a Sunday or great solemnity ; in that case it shall be put off to another day. After this the absolutions shall be given in the next chapter.

The series of thirty Masses shall be ordered for him, if it be not done in the place where he died, and all else shall be done that is done for a monk of the house who dies at home.

INSTRUCTIO NOVICIORUM
SECUNDUM CONSUETUDINEM
ECCLESIE CANTUARIENSIS

THE INSTRUCTION OF NOVICES
ACCORDING TO THE CUSTOM OF
THE CHURCH OF CANTERBURY

What follows is taken from a code of instructions for the novices of Christ Church, Canterbury. These instructions, based upon a directory derived from Lanfranc's Constitutions, show the daily practice so clearly, especially in some features which are scarcely mentioned by Lanfranc, that it seemed worth while to print part of the document as an illustration of what has gone before.

The manuscript in which they occur is MS 441 of Corpus Christi College, Cambridge, written perhaps at the end of the thirteenth century. The hand is not good, and the Latin is often awkward and sometimes apparently faulty, either through bad copying or original solecisms. I owe my acquaintance with this treatise to the kindness of Mr W. A. Pantin, of Oriel College, Oxford, who drew my attention to it some years ago, and kindly lent me his photostats of the manuscript. The excerpt begins at the foot of the *verso* of fol. 359 of the manuscript.

INSTRUCTIO NOVICIORUM
SECUNDUM CONSUETUDINEM
ECCLESIE CANTUARIENSIS

F.360*a* CUM longeui usus et antique consuetudinis non uilis sit autoritas, illis sine nature offensa derogare facile posse non videtur, cum ipsa consuetudo altera dicatur natura. Unde uolentibus claustralis uite ingredi militiam, sub cuius conflictu constat non tantum consuetudinem et uite usum preterite sed etiam reuera ipsam oportere naturam alterare, quedam preambula et quasi introductoria in regulam beati patris Benedicti scire et actu et habitu expedit necessario. Que si fuerint sepius in mente sicut erunt in exercitio reuoluta quicquid * in predicta regula uidetur durum [1] et amarum quasi medicamento Elysei [2] dulcorabitur et que aspera in uiam rectam conuertentur et dura leuia si diligenter hec regule misceantur ; incognita apparebunt, ac sterilitas mentis uage fructifera † reddetur et ad uitam eternam fructifera.

Quomodo radi debent monachi

Et quoniam principia artis in initio debent proficisci, ut notis primis ad artem facilior sit processus, ab exordio dicte uite claustralis militie incipiatur. Cum ergo in capitulo alicui societas instanter petenti fuerit concessa, et dura ac leuia, et labor ac premium laboris proposita,

---

* quicquid *scripsi* ; sicut MS   † *sic* MS ; ? *legendum* fertilis
[1] cf. *Regula S Benedicti*, lviii. 17 : *Dura et aspera per quae itur ad Deum*
[2] 2 Kings ii. 20–2

THE INSTRUCTION OF NOVICES
ACCORDING TO THE CUSTOM OF
THE CHURCH OF CANTERBURY

WHEREAS long use and ancient custom are of no small authority, it would seem hard to depart from them without offence to nature, since custom is itself called second nature. Hence it is well for those who wish to enter upon the warfare of life in the cloister—in which, as is well known, not only the habits and customs of a man's past life, but nature herself must undergo a change—to know both by practice and by the force of habit certain ways of behaviour which form as it were an introduction and preface to the Rule of our holy father Benedict. If these are allowed often to recur to the memory as they will often recur in practice, whatever appears hard [1] and bitter in the Rule itself will be sweetened as by Elisha's medicine [2] ; rough places will be changed into a high way and hard things will become easy if these rules are carefully mingled with them ; things hitherto unknown will be plain, and the barren soil of the errant mind will be made fruitful even unto eternal life.

How monks are to be shaven

And since the principles of an art should start from the beginning, that when the first steps are known progress may be the easier, let a beginning be made at the very outset of the life of cloistered warfare. When therefore the fellowship of the house has been given in chapter to one who sought it earnestly, one before whose eyes things hard and easy, the toil and its reward, have been

ad locum quo placuerit honestum et secretum ducetur,
ibique tonsus et rasus secundum legem non tantum
nouam sed et mosaycam, qua precipitur quod leuitis,
F.360b antequam sacra ingrediantur, pilis depositis, / laventur,
et sic mundi ingrediantur.   Deinde exuant habitum
ueterem et utinam hominem ueterem cum actibus suis,[1]
et habitu nouo induto, nichil penes se, quod in seculo
habuerint, remaneat sine sui licentia magistri.

Assignatio stationis et sessionis *

Postea ad ecclesiam ducatur et locus assignetur quo tunc
statio sua firmetur.   Tunc dico, quoniam in sequentibus
dicetur quod secundum diuersas horas et diuersa tempora
diuersa loca sortientur nouitii.

De ecclesia in dormitorium ducetur, ei locus quo
pausare debeat ostendatur, et etiam ad loca ulteriora
ducetur, et celle ostendentur, ad quas secretis nature
exigentibus diuertere debeat, et instruatur quod ibidem
honeste residendo et recedendo se habeat et uerecunde
expleat quod natura deposcit.   Hoc in dormitorio statim
recipiat documentum ac preceptum, quod capite semper
bene uelato, capucio ultra frontem dependente, in
dormitorio incedat, neminem cognoscat, nec uerbo nec
signo uel nutu quolibet alloquatur.   Omnia cum summo
silentio in dormitorio que ibi fieri debent fiant.   Die
illa sequatur nouitius, in refectorio sedes sibi assignetur.

Doceatur induere habitum

Sequenti die a magistro in suum ductus capitulum, in
primo addiscat quod habitum suum honeste sciat induere

---

* *scripsi pro lectione* MS *post* stat *corrupta.*
[1] cf. the prayer recited at the monastic clothing, *v. supra*, p. 109

set, he shall be led to an appointed seemly and private place, and there shall he be shaven and shorn according to the new law as well as the Mosaic law, which bids that levites, before they enter the sanctuary, shall be shorn and washed, and so enter clean. Then they shall put off their old raiment, and, we pray, the old man with all his acts,[1] and putting on a new garment shall retain nothing which they had in the world save with the permission of their master.

The allotment of places and seats

After this he shall be taken into the church and a place assigned to him where he shall then take up his station. I say ' then,' because it shall be told in the sequel how at different hours and times the novices shall occupy different places. From the church he shall be taken to the dormitory, and the place shown him where he is to rest, and he shall be taken beyond the dormitory, and the cells shown him to which he is to repair when nature's ways demand it, and he shall be told how to bear himself seemly there in sitting and departing, and how to satisfy the demands of nature with modesty. In the dormitory he shall be taught forthwith ever to walk there with his head covered and his hood veiling the forehead ; he shall show no sign of recognition there and shall address no-one either by word or sign or nod. All that is to be done in the dormitory shall be done in absolute silence. On that day the novice shall follow, and a seat in the refectory shall be assigned to him.

Let him be taught how to put on the habit

The next day he shall be taken by his master into his chapter, and first shall learn how to put on and off his

et exuere. Dicatur illi quod manus suas in manicis frocci
F.361a sui / quociens sederit, honeste habeat super genua sua
cancellatas, semper habens in memoria, quod mundo
crucifixus sit et mundus illi. Item quod caputium suum
competenter capiti suo coaptet, ita quod neutra parte
dependeat, et omni loco extra dormitorium frontem
habeat discoopertam, nisi intemperies yemis uel solis
calor aliud inducat, et etiam aliqua pars corone discooperta appareat. Honeste et maturis passibus incedat,
ut maturitas morum in omni gestu suo merito possit
commendari.[1]

*   *   *

F.376a *Quomodo surgendum sit secundum diversa tempora*
Hiis ita locis distinctis quomodo nouicius habere se
debeat in quolibet illorum et quibus uti obseruantiis
oporteat dicendum.

In primis igitur cum propheta media nocte[2] surgendum, honeste sumatur habitus qui sero ante lectum
super pedale fuerat positus, et deinde ad ecclesiam simul
cum fratribus proficiscatur, et secundum tempus et diem
ingressus ecclesiam primo ante crucem inclinato capite
facta breui oratione procedat usque ad chorum. Sed
hoc notandum quod secundum uarietatem temporum et
dierum uariantur gestus et obseruantie in ecclesia et
etiam locis. A festo uero sancti Remigii[3] usque ad capud
quadragesime uno modo hore in ecclesia et secundum
horas uariantur et alia quedam et gestus. Tunc enim
uenit uigilia prima,[4] que uigilia dicitur eo quod summo

---

[1] This section is followed in the manuscript by others of less direct
interest, including some not connected with the daily life, which have
therefore been omitted.

[2] cf. *Regula S. Benedicti* xvi. 9, quoting Ps. cxviii (A.V. cxix), 62

[3] i.e. 1 October, when the time-table underwent several changes

[4] The ' first vigil ' should denote the first nocturn of the office of the dead,
which in winter was said by night and in summer by day. But this change

habit in seemly wise. He shall be told to have his hands crossed upon his knees and in the sleeves of his frock whenever he is seated, always remembering that he is crucified to the world and the world to him. Also he shall adjust his hood aright upon his head, so that it does not hang down on either side, and everywhere outside the dormitory he shall have his forehead uncovered unless the cold of winter or the heat of summer move him otherwise ; part of his tonsure also shall be uncovered and visible. He shall walk with dignity and steady gait, that steadiness of character may duly be approved in every movement.[1]

How they are to rise at different times

Now that these places have been described, we must now say how the novice is to bear himself in each of them, and what observances he is to use. First of all, therefore, he is to rise with the prophet at midnight,[2] and modestly take the habit which was laid in the evening over the foot of his bed. Then let him go with the brethren to the church and having entered in the manner suited to the season and the day let him first bow before the crucifix and make a short prayer, and then proceed into choir. But it is to be noted that according to the difference of seasons and days postures and observances in church and other places are varied. From the feast of St Remigius [3] till the beginning of Lent the hours in church are performed in a uniform way, and postures and other things are varied according to the hour.

Then comes the first vigil,[4] which is called vigil

---

was usually made on 1 November. I owe the substance of this note to Mr J. B. L. Tolhurst.

mane quasi sub obscuritate noctis magis quam claritate diei cantatur. Sunt etiam tunc ieiunia que a festo exaltationis sancte crucis [1] incipiunt, ita quod illa die nisi die dominica eueniat erit ieiunandum, et sic continire * usque ad pascha nisi festum in cappis euenerit, et tunc propter laborem cena indulgetur a prelatis et sanctorum reuerentiam. Die uero eodem finientur sompni post nonam, ita quod die sancte crucis nisi dominica euenerit non dormient fratres, nec aliqua die ulterius, nisi diebus dominicis usque ad festum sancti Ieronimi. [2]

F.376b *De doctrina primi temporis*

In crastino igitur sancti Ieronimi principium sumat temporis traditionis huius doctrina. In chorum ingressus, si solus fuerit ante gradus prostratus ante magnum altare ibi incuruatur in curta uenia [3] quamdiu primus sonitus pulsatur, et loquatur cum Deo et proponat illi quod ipse eidem in mente dederit in oratione. Finito sonitu sic iacens in curta uenia humiliter dicat Beati immaculati [4] usque In quo corriget cum gloria et kyrieleison, Pater noster. Statim audito signo a priore erigat se et procedat modicum uersus sinistrum ante altare sancti Alphegi, [5] et ibi inclinatus sicut prius dicat In quo corriget usque Retribue cum gloria et kyrieleison et Pater noster, et signo iterum audito a priore facto, id est modica percussione, erigat se et erectus signet se crucis signo et procedat ad dextram, et ante magnum altare facta devote inclinatione ueniat ante altare sancti Dunstani [6] ubi sicut prius incuruatus dicat Retribue usque Adhesit et si uoluerit

---

* *sic* MS ? *pro* continue
[1] i.e. 14 September [2] i.e. 30 September
[3] *Curta uenia*, i.e. the profound bow as opposed to the complete prostration.
[4] Ps. cxviii (A.V. cxix). The divisions of the psalm that follow are of eight verses each.
[5] The chapel of St Alphege [6] The chapel of St Dunstan

because it is said at earliest dawn, rather in the darkness of night than in the brilliance of day. During this period also occur the fasts which begin on the feast of the Exaltation of the Holy Cross [1] ; that is, the fast begins on that day if it be not a Sunday and continues till Easter unless a feast in copes occur, when on account of the exertion and the reverence due to the saints supper is allowed by superiors. On the same day the afternoon siesta ceases, so that on the feast of the Holy Cross, unless it be a Sunday, the monks take no siesta, nor on any day thereafter save Sundays up to the feast of St Jerome.[2]

What is taught for the first season of the year

Therefore on the morrow of St Jerome let the traditional teaching begin. Having entered choir the brother, if he be alone, shall first prostrate himself before the steps of the high altar, remaining profoundly bowing [3] there until the first bell rings, and shall speak with God and shall say to Him what He himself shall have given him to say. When the bell ceases he shall humbly say, still bowing, the psalm *Beati immaculati* [4] down to the verse *In quo corrigit*, with *Gloria*, *Kyrie eleison* and *Pater noster*. When the superior gives the signal he shall straightway stand erect and go a little to the left and there, before the altar of St Alphege,[5] bowing as before shall say *In quo corrigit* as far as *Retribue*, with *Gloria*, *Kyrie eleison* and *Pater noster*, and when he again hears the signal given by the superior, that is, a light rap, he shall sign himself with the cross and proceed to the right, and having bowed devoutly before the high altar shall go before the altar of St Dunstan,[6] and there, bowing as before, he shall say *Retribue* as far as *Adhaesit*, and if he so will and time permits as far as *Legem pone* with *Kyrie eleison*

et spacium hore sustinuerit usque Legem pone cum kyrieleison et Pater noster. Statim signo audito signet se et cum
aliis incipiat Ad Dominum cum tribularer [1] ; procedet
ad sedem suam et sedens pro facie [2] super scampnum [3]
dicat primos v psalmos sine gloria sed cum Pater noster.
In fine quinti statim incumbat super formam ; sic
super illam incuruetur quamdiu dicitur collecta pro
fidelibus. Quociens dicuntur preces in feriis hoc tempore
uel etiam Pater noster sine precibus ut fit post psalmos de
F.377a mortuis / et Exultabunt et Dirige [4] quando dicitur scilicet
ante collectas ultimas uel post Verba super formas est
iacendum. Qua dicta iterum sedeat super scampnum
stalli sui dum dicuntur alii quinque psalmi cum gloria
quilibet et cum Pater noster extremus. Et tunc iterum
incuruentur super formam dum dicitur collecta a
sacerdote. Qua dicta sedeat in stallo suo dum dicuntur
extremi quinque quilibet cum gloria et extremus cum
Pater noster et tunc ut prius incuruentur super formam
dum dicitur collecta. Qua dicta statim dicetur Deus in
adiutorium, [5] Domine labia mea et continue sequatur
Domine quid multiplicati sunt. Statim dum dicitur
gloria super formas iacent et hoc in omni gloria scilicet
in principio cuiuslibet hore et laudum. Quo dicto
sequatur inuitatorium et Venite. Hic memorandum
quod quociens dicitur Venite stabunt fronte uersus altare
uersa, et in omni neupmate et omni capitulo et uersiculis
et omnibus suffragiis et memoriis. In omni psalmodia
stabunt omnes in utroque choro frontibus uersis quilibet

---

[1] This is the first, cxix (A.V. cxx), of the fifteen Gradual Psalms to be
said before Matins.
[2] This is presumably the meaning of the unusual phrase *pro facie*, which
appears to be the reading of the manuscript.
[3] *scamnus* usually means stool or bench, but here it appears to mean
the seat of the stall, mentioned below, as opposed to the misericord.
[4] The first words of the first antiphons of Lauds and Matins of the
Dead respectively.
[5] i.e. the beginning of the Office of Matins

and *Pater noster*. When he hears the signal he shall straightway stand erect and begin with the rest *Ad Dominum cum tribularer* [1] and proceed to his stall, and sitting facing the opposite choir [2] in his stall [3] shall say the first five psalms without a *Gloria* but with a *Pater noster*. At the end of the fifth he shall straightway kneel at his desk and remain bowed over it while the collect for all the faithful departed is said. Whenever the *preces* are said on ferias at this season, or when the *Pater* is said without the *preces* as happens after the psalms for the dead and *Exultabunt* and *Dirige* [4]—when, that is, it is said before the final collects or after the *Verba mea* they are to bow over their desks. When the above-mentioned collect has been said he shall once more sit in his stall while another five psalms are said, each with a *Gloria* and the last with a *Pater*, and then again they shall bow over their desks while the collect is said by the priest. When that is said he shall sit in his stall while the final five psalms are said, each with a *Gloria* and the last with a *Pater*, and then as before he shall bow over his desk while the collect is said. When this has been said the *Deus in adjutorium* [5] shall straightway be said, and *Domine labia mea*, and immediately the *Domine quid multiplicati sunt* shall follow. When the *Gloria* is said all straightway shall bow over their desks, and this is done at each *Gloria*, that is, at the beginning of every Hour and at Lauds. That done, the invitatory and *Venite* shall follow. Here it is to be recalled that whenever the *Venite* is said they shall stand facing the altar, as also whenever they chant anything, and at all chapters and versicles and all suffrages and commemorations. During all psalmody and hymns all in both choirs shall stand facing each other. At every *Gloria* and the last verse of a hymn they shall sit and bow on their misericords ; they shall

et contra alium et hymnis. In omni gloria et ultimo
uersu ymni sedebunt super parua sedilia ; incuruati
intra formas iacebunt ut in feriis dum dicitur vii suffragia
ut ita dicetur et in collectis de suffragiis et memoriis.[1]
Item sciendum quod per psalmodiam trium psalmorum
in nocturnis unus sedebit et alius stabit et etiam hoc
generale per totum annum preterquam in tribus noctibus
ante pascha quando alia fit divisio ut tunc uidebatur *
F.377*b* quoniam tunc non / dicentur nisi ix psalmi ubi alio
tempore dicuntur xii^{cim}. Item Attendite [2] propter sui
magnitudinem equipollet tribus, et ideo illo loco dicto
qui sedebat surgit et stat cum dicitur psalmus sequens,
socio suo sedente. Dum dicitur Pater noster ante
lectionem sedebunt super parua sedilia et dum dicitur
oratio pro legente. Item fratri qui legerat eunti uersus
gradus inclinandum est semper.

De psalmodia psalmorum familiarium † [3]

Finitis matutinis similiter et omnibus horis dicantur
psalmi pro defunctis scilicet Deus in adiutorium cum
gloria et Ad te leuaui similiter cum gloria et De profundis
sine gloria et si fuerit aliquis frater mortuus per xxx dies
dicetur Voce mea et sicut in alia psalmodia obseruatur
statio et sessio quod invicem sedeant. Dictis hiis psalmis
cum collectis suis et dum dicitur collecta iacebunt super
formam dicentur laudes de omnibus sanctis cum suffragiis.
Quibus dictis dicetur Exultabunt [4] cum collectis suis.
Quibus finitis dicentur quinque psalmi scilicet Verba
mea, Domine ne in furore, Dilexi quoniam, Credidi
propter, De profundis. Item memorandum quod semper

---

* ? *pro* uidebitur   † familiorum MS
[1] This is apparently the meaning, but the Latin is difficult to grasp.
[2] Psalm lxxvii (A.V. lxviii) has 72 verses.
[3] For these see above, Introduction, p. xvii
[4] The first antiphon of Lauds of the Dead

bow profoundly between the desks as on ferias when the seven suffrages are said, so that they may be recited as is done with collects and suffrages and commemorations.[1] Also it should be known that during three psalms of the nocturns one brother shall sit and the next one stand, and this shall be the general practice throughout the year, save in the three nights before Easter when another division is made as shall be seen, since then only nine psalms are said, whereas at all other seasons twelve are said. Also, the psalm *Attendite*,[2] on account of its length, is the equal of three and so when that is said he who was seated rises and stands while the following psalm is said, his neighbour being seated. While the *Pater* is said before the lessons they shall sit on their misericords, as also while the prayer for the reader is said. Also all shall bow to the reader as he goes towards the steps.

Of the *psalmi familiares* [3]
At the end of Matins and all other Hours the psalms for the dead are said, that is *Deus in adjutorium* with a *Gloria* and *Ad te levavi* likewise with a *Gloria* and *De profundis* without a *Gloria*, and if a brother be recently dead the *Voce mea* shall be said for thirty days, and as during the other psalmody the alternate standing and sitting shall be observed. When these psalms and their collects are done—and during the collect they shall lie prostrate over their desks—Lauds of All Saints shall be said with the suffrages. After this the *Exultabunt* [4] shall be said with its collects. After this, five psalms shall be recited, that is, *Verba mea, Domine ne in furore, Dilexi quoniam, Credidi propter, De profundis*. Also it is to be noted that whenever the *Te Deum* is said, they are to bow towards the

cum dicitur Te Deum, in uersu illo Te eternum patrem
inclinandum est uersus alium chorum si prior uel archi-
episcopus inceperit Te Deum,[1] et similiter cum dicitur
Sanctus, sanctus, sanctus, illic semper inclinandum.
Hoc etiam memorandum quod hii quorum statio in
australi parte est, scilicet in parte archiepiscopi, quociens
transeunt per chorum suum semper ante altare sancti
F.378a Alphegi primo / inclinandum, secundo ante magnum
altare, tercio ante altare sancti Dunstani et intrandum
est in formas suas. Item sciendum est generaliter quod
quociens in feriis intrant chorum in horis statim dato
signo a priore incumbendum est super formas quamdiu
dicitur vel Miserere uel Pater noster secundum horam.

De modo habendi * *et de prioratu*

Si duo nouitii vel plures fuerint, semper prior illorum
medium locum teneat et secundus post illum a dextris
illius si fuerit de choro prioris a sinistris stabit.[2] Et sic
semper secundus post priorem in ordine suo stabit vel
incuruati iacebunt. Super formam iacere est genibus
flexis pectore super formam inposito incuruari. Que
quidem incuruatio per totam uigiliam primam id est
a festo sancti Ieronimi usque ad pascha nisi diebus
dominicis aut xii[cim] aut octabis aut cum agitur de beata
uirgine aut de reliquiis. Et hec etiam festa curtam
ueniam suspendunt ante altare. In omnibus prememo-
ratis † festis nouitius chorum ingressus erectus stabit ante
magnum altare quamdiu durauerit primus sonitus, quo
finito inclinabit se uersus altare et dicet Beati immaculati,
ut supra dictum est, et coram aliis altaribus alios psalmos
ut supra.

---

* *sic* MS   † premoratis MS
[1] Presumably because if they bowed towards the altar it would appear
as if they were saluting the superior who had just intoned the *Te Deum*

opposite side of the choir at the verse *Te eternum patrem*
if the prior or archbishop has begun the *Te Deum*,[1] and
likewise they are always to bow in this way when *Sanctus,
sanctus, sanctus* is said. It is also to be noted that those
on the south side—that is, the archbishop's side—as often
as they pass through the choir are to bow first before the
altar of St Alphege, next before the high altar, and
thirdly before the altar of St Dunstan, and so enter to
their desks. Also it should be known in general that on
ferial days, whenever they enter choir for an Hour, as
soon as the prior gives the sign they are to bow over
their desks while the *Miserere* or *Pater* is said according
to the particular Hour.

Of order and precedence
If two novices or more be together, the senior shall be
in the midst and the next in order shall be on his right,
but on his left if he be of the same side in choir as the
first.[2] And so the second shall always be in his order
after the first, whether standing or bowing. To lie upon
a desk is when one kneeling bows over the desk with his
breast upon it. Such a prostration is performed for the
whole of the first vigil, that is to say, from the feast
of St Jerome to Easter save on Sundays and feasts of
twelve lessons or during octaves or when a feast of the
Blessed Virgin or the Relics is being kept. And on these
feasts the low bow before the altar is omitted likewise.
On all the forementioned feasts the novice entering choir
shall stand upright before the high altar while the first
bell is ringing, and when it ceases shall bow towards the
altar and say *Beati immaculati* as aforesaid, and the other
psalms before the other altars as above.

---

[2] Presumably so as to ensure the due alternation of the members of the
two choirs in the order of precedence

De uenia tarde uenientis ad ecclesiam

Item notandum quod non licet ingredi chorum passim.
Qui uero aliquo casu ex neggligentia uel alia excusabili
uel inexcusabili casu extra chorum moram fecerit
F.378*b* quamdiu dicitur Venite et hymnus / ad primum psalmum
ueniens hoc modo intrabit : deposito caputio ingrediens
ad rubrum hostium, uel ad alium hostium iuxta priorem,
si ibi ingreditur procedet ante gradus ibique in medio
primo inclinabit se uersus altare, sumpta curta uenia,
iacebit quousque audierit signum datum ab illo qui
tunc prefuerit choro, et tunc surgens cum omni maturitate facto retro et ante ibit ad stallum suum, uel saltem
intra formas propinquius, et ibi iterum sumat curtam
ueniam et post surgens stans uel sedens secundum quod
socius suus uel propinquus suus se habuerit ; id est si
sederit stabit iste, si steterit sedebit iste. Et hoc festis
et feriis generaliter observandum est quoniam hoc est
de regula [1] et ideo deuotius tenendum.

Quando fit locus uenie

Si uero ante quintum psalmum non uenerit non intrabit
sed ante crucem cum aliis uel solus dicat matutinas, in
crastino responsurus sicut inferius dicetur quando de
capitulo agetur. Et hoc per omnes horas generaliter
obseruandum, quod si non uenerit in primo psalmo uel
saltem in gloria illius ad ueniam dicto modo uenient.
Similiter qui in laudibus non fuerit in psalmo Deus
misereatur non intrabit sine uenia. Et si non uenerit
ante Laudate Dominum de celis nullo modo intrabit.
Item prouideat sic tarde ueniens quod semper uersus
finem psalmi uel hymni ingrediatur chorum. Quoniam

---

[1] *Regula S. Benedicti*, ch. xliii

Of penance done by one coming late to the church

Also it is to be noted that the choir must not be entered in a casual way. He who for any reason of negligence or other excusable or inexcusable circumstance is out of choir when the *Venite* and hymn are sung, if he arrive during the first psalm he shall enter in this wise : lowering his hood and entering by the red door or the other door near the prior, he shall go to the steps and there bow to the altar, and bowing profoundly shall stay till he hear the signal given by whomsoever is presiding in choir, and then, rising swiftly and bowing all round he shall go to his stall, or at least to the desks, by the shortest way, and there again he shall bow profoundly, and then rising he shall stand or sit according to what his neighbour is doing ; that is, if he is sitting the late arrival shall stand ; if he is standing the other shall sit. And this is the normal observance on feasts and ferias, since this is in the Rule [1] and therefore devoutly to be observed.

When penance is to be done

If however he does not arrive before the fifth psalm he shall not enter, but shall say Matins alone or with others before the crucifix, and shall answer for it next day as shall be described below when we are dealing with the chapter. And this is to be observed generally at all the hours, namely, that if a brother does not arrive during the first psalm or at least during its *Gloria* he shall do penance as above. Similarly, he who is not at Lauds before the psalm *Deus misereatur* is done shall not enter without doing penance, and if he does not arrive before *Laudate Dominum de caelis* he shall in no wise enter. Also, such a late comer shall take care always to enter choir towards the end of a psalm or hymn, since if he were

si in principio uel ante medium transiret per chorum
F.379ᵃ omnes illi quasi in derisum/ut credo inclinabunt.   Si
uersus finem intrauerit, tunc propter gloria inclinabunt
se et non propter illum.   Hoc uero in uigilia prima habet
exceptionem ;   tunc enim passim ueniunt, quia de lectis
sine prouisione ueniunt.   Secus est in horis diei.

De Miserere dicendo

Item sciendum quod semper ante primam et ante
uesperas dicendum est Miserere dum fit genuflexio inter
formas, et audito signo a priore surgendum et faciendum
retro et ante ante Deus in adiutorium, et statim cum
dicitur gloria Patri iterum super formam genuflectendum
est.   Quod si non poterit tunc dicere Miserere quia tarde
uenit sed dicat quam cito poterit.   Item in principio
omnium horarum, et cantatis omnibus horis,* cum
dicitur Benedicamus faciendum est retro et ante ut
simul terminetur cum Deo gratias et similiter in fine
omnium missarum in choro.   Item memorandum quod
in vii suffragiis est genuflectendum intra formas, in
memoria scilicet sancte Trinitatis et sancte crucis et
beate Marie et sancti Thome et sancti Elphegi et sancti
Dunstani.   Et cum dicitur in extremis pro pace, nisi in
festis predictorum, quia tunc non est genuflectendum
sed incuruandum super paruum sedile dum dicitur
collecta de sancto.   In aliis suffragiis super parua sedilia
sedendum dum dicuntur collecte, et etiam antiphone,
sed dum dicuntur antiphone viiᵗᵉᵐ predicte standum est ;
et in collectis genuflectendum uel intra formas.   Diebus
dominicis uel festo xii leccionum, uel quando agitur de

* horas MS

to pass down the choir at the beginning or before the end all present would bow to him as it were in mockery, it seems to me. But if he enters towards the end, then they will bow on account of the *Gloria* and not because of him. An exception to this rule is in the first vigil : then they shall enter just as they come because they arrive from their beds at random as chance has it. But at the day Hours this is not so.

Of saying the Miserere

Also it is to be noted that before Prime and Vespers the *Miserere* is always to be said while a brother is kneeling at the desks, and when he hears the signal given by the prior he should rise and bow all round before the *Deus in adjutorium* and straightway when the Gloria is said he should again kneel at his desk. And if he cannot then say the Miserere because he comes late he shall say it as soon as may be. Also at the beginning of all the Hours and when each Hour has been sung, when the *Benedicamus Domino* is being said a bow all round is to be made, so as to end with the *Deo gratias*, and similarly at the end of all Masses in choir. Also note that in the seven suffrages a genuflexion is made at the desks—that is, at the commemoration of the Holy Trinity and the Holy Cross and the Blessed Virgin and St Thomas and St Alphege and St Dunstan and when finally the prayer for peace is said, unless it be a feast of one of the aforesaid, for then he does not genuflect, but bows upon the misericords while the collect of the saint is being said. During the other suffrages he sits on the misericords while the collects are said and the antiphons likewise, but while the seven foresaid antiphons are being said he stands, and genuflects at the collects or kneels at the desks. On Sundays and feasts of twelve lessons or when

beata uirgine uel reliquiis, nunquam in curta uenia uel
super formas est orandum.

F.379*b* *Quomodo pausandum post matutinas*

Hiis rite completis eundum in dormitorium ibique
pausandum cum summo silencio et tranquillitate, ita
quod nec sono uocis nec et motu alicuius rei strepitum
faciat, nec aliquid faciat quod audiri possit a proximo
fratre, nec aliquo modo tedium faciat fratribus suis.
Habitum suum ante lectum suum honeste collocet ut in
mane paratum inueniat, et similiter calciamenta sua
super pedale ponat. Si uero aliquid indecenter uel
incompetenter fieret uel moueretur uel poneretur, uigil
ipse, id est monachus qui in dormitorio semper uigilat
et sepius in nocte circuit scrutando siquid uideretur
correptioni dignum, mane illud in capitulo coram
omnibus illis recitabit et fiet emendatio. Ideo cauendum
ne quid fiat in noctibus quod pudeat mane audire. Et
si propter fratres cauendum, quid propter Deum quem
nichil latere potest, nec etiam cogitationes cordis latent
esset faciendum ? Et propter illum inimicum qui leo
rugiens circuit, querens quem devoret, non solum uerba
et actus sed etiam cogitationes uitande male et friuole
et uage, ad rem non pertinentes, fugiende sunt ; quoniam
quando minus uellemus inproperabit nobis hostis noster
peccatum etiam illud quod ipse suggessit, nisi bono
confessionis et satisfactionis a rotulo suo fuerit deletum.
Interius ergo et exterius fiant omnia honeste quoad nichil
appareat quod oculos iudicis possit offendere.

the office is of the Blessed Virgin or the Relics he never prays bowing or inclining over the desks.

How rest is taken after Matins

When the above offices are done he goes to the dormitory and there rests in absolute silence and quiet, so that neither by sound of voice nor by the movement of any object does anyone make a noise nor do anything that may be heard by his neighbour or may in any way be a nuisance to his brethren. Let him place his habit tidily before his bed so that he may find it to hand in the morning, and similarly let him put his footwear at the foot of his bed. If anything is done or shifted or placed untidily or awkwardly, the watchman, that is, the monk who remains awake in the dormitory and goes round often in the night to see if there be anything needing correction, shall tell of it in the morning at chapter in the presence of all, and satisfaction shall be made. Therefore we must take care that nothing be done at night that will be shameful to hear in the morning. And if one takes care because of the brethren, what should be done because of God, whom naught can escape and to whom not even the thoughts of the heart are hidden? And because of that enemy who goes about as a roaring lion, seeking whom he may devour, not only words and acts, but evil, frivolous, wandering and useless thoughts are to be shunned, since, when we least would wish it, our enemy will reproach us even with that sin which he himself suggested, unless it be blotted from his roll by the good action of confession and satisfaction. Let all therefore within and without be done fittingly so that nothing appear which could offend the eyes of our Judge.

F.380a *De prima hora diei*

Mane autem facto, statim cum auditus fuerit sonitus, surgendum est et sumende sunt botte nocturnales, et eundum ad ecclesiam ibique inter formas orandum cum Miserere quousque dicatur Deus in adiutorium. Post primam statim vii psalmi dicantur cum letania et prostratione, id est, post vii fiet prostratio. Post letaniam et collectas que secuntur statim eundum in dormitorium et post, assumptis libris, descendendum in claustrum ibique sedendum et studendum in libris, in loco sibi deputato, quousque audiatur sonitus qui dicitur ad calciamenta ; quo facto accepto cultello et pectine iterum descendendum in claustrum, et, positis libris super scampnum, eundum est ad aquam, et lotis manibus iterum iuxta libros stando pectendum capud, et sic sumpto libro honeste eundum est ad ecclesiam ad terciam.

De tercia et eius psalmis

Ecclesiam ingressi statim ante gradus in curta uenia orandum quousque pulsetur ad terciam. Audito sonitu mox incipiat Domine ne in furore ii,[1] et iterum audito signo a priore surgendum et procedendum ante altare beati Aelphegi ; in curta uenia dicatur Miserere. Quo dicto et audito signo, surgat et eat ante altare sancti Dunstani et ibidem iterum in curta uenia dicatur Domine exaudi i.[2] Quo dicto audito signo procedendum ad formas. In gloria post Deus in adiutorium flectendum super formas. Dicta tercia procedendum de anteriori F.380b forma / ad posteriorem. Quoniam semper in omni missa iuniores remotiores erunt ab altari et maiores proximiores.

---

[1] i.e. Ps. xxxvii (A.V. xxxviii), not Ps. vi
[2] i.e. Ps. ci (A.V. cii), not Ps. cxlii (A.V. xliii)

Of the first Hour of the day

When day has dawned he should rise straightway when the signal is heard and take his night shoes and go to the church, and there say the *Miserere* at the desks until *Deus in adjutorium* is said. After Prime the seven penitential psalms are straightway said with the litany and prostration—that is, we prostrate ourselves after the seven psalms. After the litany and the collects that follow he goes forthwith to the dormitory and then taking his book, descends into the cloister, and there sits and studies in his book, each in his appointed place, until the signal known as the 'shoe-signal' is heard. Then, shod and carrying knife and comb, he descends again to the cloister, and putting the books on the seat goes to the washing-place, and having washed his hands stands again by his book and combs his hair. Then, book in hand, he goes in order to church for Terce.

Of Terce and its psalms

Entering the church he straightway prays, bowing low before the step until the bell rings for Terce. When the bell is heard the brother shall straightway begin the psalm *Domine ne in furore* (ii),[1] and again when the prior's signal is heard he shall rise and go before the altar of blessed Alphege and say the *Miserere* bowing low. That done, when he hears the signal let him rise and go before the altar of St Dunstan and there again bow low and say the *Domine exaudi* (i).[2] That done, when he hears the signal he shall go to the desks, and at the *Gloria* after the *Deus in adjutorium* he shall bow over the desk. After Terce he should go from the front desk to the rear one, for always at all Masses the juniors shall be furthest from the altar and the seniors nearest.

De modo standi in missis ; quomodo eundum in capitulum

Post missam cito eundum in capitulum. In quo semper nouitius sedeat, et si plures fuerint secundum ordinem suum sedeant. Statim ingressi versus orientem inclinent se et sic procedant ad locum suum, et ibi antequam sedeant faciant ante et retro et sic sedeant et, habitu suo honeste circa pedes collocato, primo inclinet se versus fratrem qui in dextris sedet et post ad sinistram. Et sic sedeat quousque dicatur Preciosa, etcetera, et tunc surgat et stet usque dictum sit ter Deus in adiutorium, et tunc flectat genua uersus scamnum super quod sedet, et dicta collecta surgat, et iterum in loco suo sedeat quousque dicat prior Benedicite,[1] et tunc surgat et ante sedem suam inclinet se uersus orientem et, facto ante et retro, ualde composite capite discooperto procedat uersus hostium capituli, et tunc cum uenerit ad capud monumenti[2] et ibi iterum uertat se uersus orientem, inclinet et post sine mora exeat capitulum et eat ad capitulum suum, ibique sicut in alio capitulo ingressus, statim inclinet uersus orientem, et sic procedat ad locum suum et cum sederit inclinet uersus dextram et sinistram.

Quomodo eundum a capitulo

Et cum dixerit magister Benedicite, et si se reum in aliquo delicto quod pertineat ad obseruantiam regule senserit, F.381a surgat et capiat lon/gam ueniam et dicat extensus mea culpa gallice, et cum dixerit magister surge, surgat et eodem loco stet et dicat causam quare deliquerit, et in uoluntate magistri erit utrum uoluerit uel per uerbum uel per disciplinam delictum corrigi. Si dixerit corrigatur, statim si habuerit caputium deponat illud et ponat

---

[1] This was the signal for the business part of the seniors' chapter to begin.
[2] Presumably a monumental slab or effigy near the door of the chapter-house.

Of the manner of standing at Mass ; how they are to go into chapter

After Mass they go at once into chapter. There the novice shall always take his seat, and if there be many they shall sit in order. On entering they shall bow to the east and so proceed to their places, and there, before they sit down they shall bow all round and then sit, and having arranged his habit tidily about his feet he shall bow first to the brother on his right and then to the left, and shall sit until the *Pretiosa* etc. is said. Then he shall rise and stand until the *Deus in adjutorium* has been said thrice, and then he shall kneel facing the seat on which he sits, and when the collect has been said he shall rise and again sit in his place until the prior says *Benedicite*,[1] and then he shall rise and bow towards the east before his seat and bow all round with composure, his head being uncovered, and go to the door of the chapter-house, and then when he comes to the head of the monument [2] shall turn again and bow to the east and then without delay leave the chapter-house and go to his own chapter, and there, as in the other chapter, he shall on entry bow to the east and go to his place and when he sits he shall bow to right and left.

How he shall depart from chapter

And when his master says *Benedicite*, if he perceives that he is charged with any fault against the observance of the Rule he shall rise and prostrate himself, and lying at full length shall say in French *mea culpa*, and when his master says 'Rise' he shall rise and stand there and say why he committed the fault, and his master shall decide whether he wishes the fault to be corrected by word or by stripes. If he say 'Let him be punished,' straightway if the novice have a hood he shall put it

honeste iuxta se et zonam ; sedeat sicut illi fuerit dictum,
et exponat dorsum, et in omni ictu dicat gallice mea
culpa. Si dixerit sede et cave ne talia uel committas
similia, tunc inclinato capite eat ad locum suum. Si
contingat quod non gratis sumas ueniam, quia forte non
sentis te reum, uel quia non curas et alius super aliquo
te uelit impetere, sic dicet : Frater N. Statim surgat
nominatus et stet in loco medio et audiat quid sibi uelit
opponere. Quo audito, unum de tribus responsis
respondeat scilicet : non recolo, uel emendabo, uel
deciperis gallice ; si confitetur dicat causam quare
fecerit, et expectet iudicium magistri. Si dixerit corrigatur, fiet ut supra dictum est. Si dixerit sede, similiter
ut supra. Hoc bene prouideat quod siue iuste siue
iniuste dorsum exposuerit, non loquatur verbum nisi
uelit lucrum habere sed omnia in paciencia sustineat et
expecta * meritum a Deo.

De doctrina magistri in capitulo

Si contingat quod aliquid aduersus aliquem fratrem
[habeat †], dicat Frater N., et cum steterit coram magistro
dicat quod habeat uel sciat aduersus illum, loquens
F.381b magistro / sine omni rancore sed cum omni zelo Dei,
nec ad aliquod responsum moueatur. Hiis factis audiat
et discat obedienter que magister decreuerit de ordine
docenda, et dulutiones ‡ suas reuelet, et opponat de
ordine signa et articulos de ordine discat cum omni
humilitate.[1]

---

* *sic* MS ; *forsan locutio uiuida pro* exspectet
† habeat *suppleui* ‡ *sic* MS
[1] There would seem to be some corruption in the Latin of these last
two sentences, in which the phrase *de ordine* occurs thrice.

down and he shall put his girdle also tidily by him. He shall sit as bidden and bare his back, and at every stroke he shall say in French *mea culpa*. If the master say ' Be seated and take care not to do this or the like,' then he shall bow and go to his place. If it happen that you do not do penance gladly because haply you do not feel yourself guilty or because you do not care, and someone wishes to charge you on some point and says : 'Brother N.,' straightway let the one named rise and stand in the midst and hear what he wishes to say against him. Having heard it let him answer in French one of three things, that is, ' I have no recollection of this,' or ' I will mend my ways,' or ' You are mistaken,' or if he admits the charge he shall say why he did it. And he shall await the master's judgment ; if he say : ' Let him undergo correction,' all shall proceed as above. If he say ' Be seated,' the procedure likewise is as above. But let him see to it that whether he bare his back justly or unjustly he say no word if he wishes for a reward, but let him bear all in patience and expect to receive what he deserves from God.

Of the teaching of the master in chapter
If it happen that he have anything against any brother let him say : 'Brother N.,' and when the other stands before the master he shall say what he knows or has against him, speaking to the master without any rancour, but with all the zeal of God, and let him not be moved by any answer that he is given. When this is done, let him hear and learn obediently what the master decrees as regards regulations, and let him reveal his short-comings and set against them the teaching of the Rule. Let him learn the signs and details of the daily round with all humility.[1]

Quid faciendum post capitulum

Set cito cum exierit a capitulo intret claustrum et habeat colloquium sicut alii fratres, et nichil nisi de ordine et salute animarum est ibi loquendum, ibique sedeat quousque audiatur campana. Qua audita statim cum summa maturitate et silentio eundum ad ecclesiam ad horam. Ibique super formam oret et dicatur Pater noster quousque ui incipiatur, qua dicta iterum eundum in claustrum ad collocutionem, et statim audito pulsatu iterum eundum ad ecclesiam ad magnam missam. In missarum sollemniis ita obseruandus est ordo ut semper fronte apposita uersus alium chorum stet monachus dum cantatur uel officium uel kyrieleison uel Gloria in excelsis uel graduale uel alleluia uel prosa uel aliquis cantus. In evangelio semper uersus altare ; in canone uel super modicam sellam inter duas stantes sedeat uel stans uersus altare respiciat, uel orans uel ruminet leccionem suam. Post primum Agnus inter duas formas oret secrecius. In magna missa post primum Agnus super formam
F.382a inclinans dicetur / pro pace Deus misereatur et Deus uenerunt gentes et post inter formas orandum sicut supradictum est. Post missam statim ix^a dicetur. Qua dicta cum psalmis familiaribus statim post Deo gratias, facto retro et ante, eundum in dormitorium uel stati in claustrum et ad ablutorium et lotis manibus in refectorium.

De observanciis in refectorio

In refectorio talis ordo observandus. Statim ingressus ante locum sibi assignatum faciat retro et ante * mensam sedeat quousque ueniat prior qui illa die preerit mense, et cum audierit et viderit illum uenientem surgat et

---

* *sic* MS ; *forsan legendum* retro et ante, et ante mensam, etc.

What is to be done after chapter

But straightway when he departs from chapter he shall go into the cloister and hold speech as do the others ; and he is to speak nothing save of the daily round and the salvation of souls, and there he is to sit till he hear the bell ; when he hears this he is to go straightway to church with all speed and silence for the Hour. And there let him pray over his desk and say *Pater noster* until Sext begins ; when that is said he shall go into the cloister for speech and again when the bell is heard he shall go to church for the High Mass. At Mass this order is to be kept, viz. that each monk stands facing the opposite choir while the Office or *Kyrie* or *Gloria* or alleluia or prose or any other chant is being sung. At the gospel he always faces the altar ; during the Canon he either reclines on the misericord while one stands on each side of him or else he stands facing the altar or prays or cons his lesson. After the first *Agnus Dei* he shall pray in secret between the desks. At High Mass after the first *Agnus Dei* he shall bow over his desk and say the psalms for peace *Deus misereatur* and *Deus venerunt gentes*, and shall then pray between the desks as aforesaid. After the Mass None shall be said at once. That done, with the *psalmi familiares*, he shall, immediately after the *Deo gratias*, bow all round and go to the dormitory or straight into the cloister and to the washing-place, and having washed his hands, shall go into the refectory.

Of observances in the refectory

In the refectory the following order is to be kept. Going straight to the place assigned he shall bow all round and sit facing the table until the president of the day arrive, and when he hears and sees him coming he shall rise

inclinatus dicat cum aliis gratias que dicentur ante
mensam, et hiis dictis ascendat ad mensam. Ibique
oculos semper habeat in mensa et aurem in lectione.
Cum summo silentio comedat et bibat ; corpus cibo et
potu corporali et animam cibo spiritualis doctrine
studeat reficere. Si uero sonitum quod absit fecerit per
quem fratres in aliquo turbentur, uel sacra lectio impe-
diatur, uel minus audiatur, statim surgat qui deliquit
et ante mensam prioris in longa uenia prostratus iaceat
quousque a priore signum audierit. Quo audito surgat
et inclinato capite humiliter ad locum suum procedat.
Hoc idem faciat si potu suo et cibo mensam suam
F.382b fedauerit in tantum quod manu sua non / possit maculam
factam cooperire. Hoc ita ut predictum est faciat nisi
fratres alterius ordinis uel clerici uel layci in mensa
prioris uel in refectorio comedant ; tunc uero non
surget sed in crastino in capitulo suo sumpta uenia hoc
se fecisse confiteatur.

Quid faciendum post prandium [1]

Post mensam cum omni humilitate fit processio ad ecclesiam cum Miserere, et in ecclesia dicentur gratie
actionum ; quibus dictis eundum in dormitorium et
sumpto libro eundum in claustrum, ibique in loco suo
studendum quousque pulsetur ad uesperas. Audito
sonitu statim surgendum eundum ad ecclesiam et
orandum super formas et dicendum Miserere quousque
incipiatur Deus in adiutorium de beata uirgine, et quo *
audito statim surgendum et post uesperas de sancta
Maria et post uesperas diei in suffragiis genuflectendum
ut superius dictum est.

* *sic* MS
[1] This and the following sections are of interest as giving an account
of a period of the day ordinarily passed over in customaries. It will be
noted that the description is of a day on which the second meal is not
taken, i.e. a feria in winter, not a Sunday or feast.

and bow and say the grace before meals with the others, and when that is done shall go up to the table. There he shall always keep his eyes upon the table and his ears open to the reading. Let him eat and drink in absolute silence, and let him take care to refresh his body with bodily meat and drink, and his soul with the food of spiritual doctrine. If by mischance he make a sound which disturbs the brethren or hinders or drowns the reading, the offender shall rise forthwith and prostrate himself before the prior's table until he hear a signal from the prior ; then he shall rise and go humbly with bowed head to his place. He shall do likewise if he soil his table with liquid or meat to such an extent that he cannot cover the stain with his hand. He shall act as aforesaid unless brethren of another order or clerks or laymen are eating at the prior's table or in the refectory ; in that case he shall not rise, but next day in chapter he shall do penance and confess that he has so done.

What is to be done after dinner [1]

After the meal the monks go in procession with all humility to the church reciting the *Miserere*, and in the church grace shall be said : after this they go to the dormitory and taking each his book go to the cloister, where they study in their places till the bell rings for Vespers. When the bell is heard they are to rise straightway and go into church and pray over their desks and say the *Miserere* until the *Deus in adjutorium* of the office of the Blessed Virgin begins ; when this is heard they are to rise, and after Vespers of Our Lady and Vespers of the day they are to kneel as aforesaid during the suffrages.

Quid post uesperas

Post uesperas eundum in dormitorium et accepto libro eundum in claustrum ibique studendum quousque pulsetur ad Dirige ; et audito sonitu statim eundum ad ecclesiam, et post Dirige iterum eundum in claustrum ibi studendum quousque audiatur signum ad potandum, et tunc statim eundum ad abluendum manus et lotis manibus eundum in refectorium et potetur quantum F.383a satis est. Et post potionem iterum in claustrum eundum / et ibi sedendum quousque audiatur signum ad collationem quo audito statim eundum ad capitulum et ibi facto ante et retro ante sedem suam sedeat et audiat lectionem.

De completorio

Post lectionem eundum ad completorium. Quo dicto, procedendum a sede sua versus hostium chori, scilicet hostium prioris, et ibi in extremo loco post conuentum standum cum inclinatione et dicendus est psalmus Usquequo cum Pater.[1] Quo dicto, audito signo a priore a loco in quo stabat procedendum uersus altare sancti Elphegi, et ibi inclinatus dicat psalmum Iudica me Deus et discerne causam, etcetera, cum Pater. Quo dicto iterum audito signo procedat uersus altare sancti Dunstani, et semper coram magno altare inclinetur, et coram sancto Dunstano dicatur psalmus Nisi Deus cum Pater noster. Et post hoc eundum in dormitorium ad pausandum. Ibique honeste habitu collocato ante lectum quiescat in pace, et cum omni quiete sine fratrum aliqua molestia quousque pulsetur ad matutinas, et tunc ut supradictum est faciendum et orandum ante gradus.

---

[1] This psalm xii (A.V. xiii) and what follows make up the last *trina oratio* of the day.

What of the time after Vespers

After Vespers they are to go to the dormitory and taking their books go into the cloister and study till the bell rings for *Dirige*, and when this is heard forthwith they are to go into church and after the *Dirige* return to the cloister and there study till the signal for the drink, and then go at once to wash their hands and after this go into the refectory and drink to sufficiency. And after the drink they return to the cloister and there sit till the signal for the collation be heard, when straightway they are to go into chapter and there having bowed all round before their seats they are to sit down and hear the reading.

Of Compline

After the reading they shall go to Compline. When that is done the novice is to leave his stall and go to the door of the choir, that is, the prior's door, and there stand in the last place behind the community bowing, and the psalm *Usquequo* is said with *Pater noster*.[1] That done, when the prior's signal is heard, he shall go from the place where he stands to the altar of St Alphege and there bowing he shall say the psalm *Judica* with a *Pater*. That done, when a second signal is given, he shall go to the altar of St Dunstan (always bowing before the high altar) and there the psalm *Nisi Dominus* with a *Pater* shall be said. After this he is to go to the dormitory to sleep, and there, having put his habit tidily at the foot of his bed he shall sleep in peace and absolute silence, without causing any nuisance to his brethren till the bell ring for Matins, and then he shall do as said above and pray before the altar steps.

APPENDICES

A (page 19)

This follows fairly closely Bernard of Cluny II xiii 304, where the *Armarius* is responsible for the books. The passage has been cited (e.g. by C. H. Haskins in his chapter on Libraries in *The Renaissance of the Twelfth Century*) to prove the narrow compass of a library of which the contents could be accommodated on a piece of carpet. But it is clear from Bernard of Cluny that a previous selection had been made, and that the number of books on the carpet corresponded to the number of the community. There is an interesting list of 64 books and their recipients in Albers I 185-6 (Farfa). The selection is a formidable one, and most of the books are long treatises or commentaries, e.g. Gualo receives Augustine *de Trinitate*, Brother Stephen the *Etymologiae* of Isidore, Umbert the *Historia Ecclesiastica* of Eusebius, Peter the *Moralia* of Gregory the Great, Girbert the *Historia Anglorum*, presumably of Bede. Brother Henry, however, receives the Book of Kings, Atto the Pauline Epistles, and Stephen, no scholar, his own psalter (*psalterium suum*). Of the more unusual numbers, the *Life* of St Mary of Egypt, which fell to John, and the *Historia Titi Livii*, drawn by Peter, may be mentioned.

B (page 23)

Cf. Porée, *Bec* II 595. For this procession *v.* E. Bishop, *Liturgica Historica*, 276–300, and Knowles, *Monastic Order*, 545. The order of the procession at Canterbury, which was a dramatic representation of Our Lord's entry into Jerusalem (Matt. xxi.1–17 ; Jo. xii.12), and which the text tends to confuse, was as follows. (1) The whole community walks in procession,

with chant, to a chosen spot outside the walls of the city, where a halt is made. (2) Two priests then take up a portable shrine, containing the Blessed Sacrament, previously brought thither. The others surround the shrine—the children representing the Hebrew children, and the monks the crowd. (3) All then move in procession back to the gate of the city (representing the gates of Jerusalem), where a second halt is made and the hymn *Gloria, laus* is sung by the children and monks ; this part of the ceremony, now performed outside the church door, still figures in the Roman missal. (4) All then move to the main door of the church, where a third halt is made, and anthems are chanted recalling the conduct of Caiaphas and the Pharisees. (5) All then enter the church, and a fourth halt is made before the crucifix at the entry to the choir.

At Cluny (Bernard II xiv 307) the procession went to the church of St Mayeul, where a sermon was preached to the people, but there is no mention of the elaborate halts or of the Blessed Sacrament. At Bec there were four halts (Porée, *Bec* II 595), and the Blessed Sacrament was carried. Martène, *De antiquis mon. ritibus* III xii 363, notes the presence of the Blessed Sacrament only there and at Lire. This feature of the procession probably originated in Normandy, and may possibly, as Mr C. N. L. Brooke has suggested to me, have some connection with the Eucharistic controversy in which Lanfranc took part. The custom became common in England, and the Palm Sunday procession to the churchyard cross or elsewhere served as a model for the later procession on Corpus Christi day.

C (page 93)

Bernard of Cluny I xxix 212–14. It is uncertain when regular bleeding was introduced into monastic regulations : there is no hint of it in the Rule. Strangely enough, neither medieval writers nor modern antiquaries and physicians are in agreement

as to the precise purpose of the practice ; probably the feeling of physical malaise brought about by an unbalanced diet and a sedentary life demanded some kind of violent relief, though whatever relief, real or imaginary, was temporarily obtained must soon have been offset by the fortifying regime of richer and more plentiful food allowed as compensation to those recently bled.

Monastic constitutions attempted to prevent the occasion becoming purely recreative, but this inevitably occurred, and the periodical bloodletting became a time of holiday ; Jocelin's reference to the season ' when monks of the cloister are wont to reveal each to the other the secrets of the heart ' (*Jocelin of Brakelond*, Nelson's Medieval Classics, p. 14) is familiar. For a detailed account of the whole matter, *v.* L. Gougaud, *Anciennes Coutumes Claustrales*, 49–68. Lanfranc nowhere states the annual number of these *minutiones* ; practice varied greatly : sometimes the individual was allowed to choose, elsewhere seyneys occurred at intervals of six or seven weeks, or as seldom as five times a year.

INDEX